MznLnx

Missing Links Exam Preps

Exam Prep for

Accounting: What the Numbers Mean

Marshall, McManus, & Viele, 7th Edition

The MznLnx Exam Prep is your link from the texbook and lecture to your exams.
The MznLnx Exam Preps are unauthorized and comprehensive reviews of your textbooks.

All material provided by MznLnx and Rico Publications (c) 2010
Textbook publishers and textbook authors do not particpate in or contribute to these reviews.

MznLnx

Rico Publications

Exam Prep for Accounting: What the Numbers Mean
7th Edition
Marshall, McManus, & Viele

Publisher: Raymond Houge	*Product Manager:* Dave Mason
Assistant Editor: Michael Rouger	*Editorial Assitant:* Rachel Guzmanji
Text and Cover Designer: Lisa Buckner	*Pedagogy:* Debra Long
Marketing Manager: Sara Swagger	*Cover Image:* Jim Reed/Getty Images
Project Manager, Editorial Production: Jerry Emerson	*Text and Cover Printer:* City Printing, Inc.
Art Director: Vernon Lowerui	*Compositor:* Media Mix, Inc.

(c) 2010 Rico Publications

ALL RIGHTS RESERVED. No part of this work covered by the copyright may be reproduced or used in any form or by an means--graphic, electronic, or mechanical, including photocopying, recording, taping, Web distribution, information storage, and retrieval systems, or in any other manner--without the written permission of the publisher.

Printed in the United States
ISBN:

For more information about our products, contact us at:
Dave.Mason@RicoPublications.com

For permission to use material from this text or product, submit a request online to:
Dave.Mason@RicoPublications.com

Contents

CHAPTER 1
Accounting—Present and Past — 1

CHAPTER 2
Financial Statements and Accounting Concepts/Principles — 16

CHAPTER 3
Fundamental Interpretations Made from Financial Statement Data — 34

CHAPTER 4
The Bookkeeping Process and Transaction Analysis — 42

CHAPTER 5
Accounting for and Presentation of Current Assets — 49

CHAPTER 6
Accounting for and Presentation of Property, and Other Noncurrent Assets — 65

CHAPTER 7
Accounting for and Presentation of Liabilities — 77

CHAPTER 8
Accounting for and Presentation of Owners' Equity — 95

CHAPTER 9
The Income Statement and the Statement of Cash Flows — 108

CHAPTER 10
Corporate Governance, Explanatory Notes, and Other Disclosures — 121

CHAPTER 11
Financial Statement Analysis — 137

CHAPTER 12
Managerial Accounting and Cost-Volume-Profit Relationships — 150

CHAPTER 13
Cost Accounting and Reporting Systems — 155

CHAPTER 14
Cost Analysis for Planning — 161

CHAPTER 15
Cost Analysis for Control — 167

CHAPTER 16
Cost Analysis for Decision Making — 174

ANSWER KEY — 190

TO THE STUDENT

COMPREHENSIVE

The *MznLnx* Exam Prep series is designed to help you pass your exams. Editors at MznLnx review your textbooks and then prepare these practice exams to help you master the textbook material. Unlike study guides, workbooks, and practice tests provided by the texbook publisher and textbook authors, *MznLnx* gives you **all** of the material in each chapter in exam form, not just samples, so you can be sure to nail your exam.

MECHANICAL

The MznLnx Exam Prep series creates exams that will help you learn the subject matter as well as test you on your understanding. Each question is designed to help you master the concept. Just working through the exams, you gain an understanding of the subject--its a simple mechanical process that produces success.

INTEGRATED STUDY GUIDE AND REVIEW

MznLnx is not just a set of exams designed to test you, its also a comprehensive review of the subject content. Each exam question is also a review of the concept, making sure that you will get the answer correct without having to go to other sources of material. You learn as you go! Its the easiest way to pass an exam.

HUMOR

Studying can be tedious and dry. MznLnx's instructional design includes moderate humor within the exam questions on occassion, to break the tedium and revitalize the brain

Chapter 1. Accounting—Present and Past

1. _____ is a legally declared inability or impairment of ability of an individual or organization to pay its creditors. Creditors may file a _____ petition against a debtor ('involuntary _____') in an effort to recoup a portion of what they are owed or initiate a restructuring. In the majority of cases, however, _____ is initiated by the debtor (a 'voluntary _____' that is filed by the bankrupt individual or organization.)
   a. Bankruptcy protection
   b. 3M Company
   c. BMC Software, Inc.
   d. Bankruptcy

2. The term _____ usually refers to a company that is permitted to offer its registered securities (stock, bonds, etc.) for sale to the general public, typically through a stock exchange, or occasionally a company whose stock is traded over the counter (OTC) via market makers who use non-exchange quotation services.

   The term '_____' may also refer to a company owned by the government.

   a. Public Company
   b. Governmental Accounting Standards Board
   c. Professional association
   d. MicroStrategy

3. The _____ (sometimes called 'Peekaboo') is a private-sector, non-profit corporation created by the Sarbanes-Oxley Act, a 2002 United States federal law, to oversee the auditors of public companies. Its stated purpose is to 'protect the interests of investors and further the public interest in the preparation of informative, fair, and independent audit reports'. Although a private entity, the _____ has many government-like regulatory functions, making it in some ways similar to the private Self Regulatory Organizations (SROs) that regulate stock markets and other aspects of the financial markets in the United States.
   a. Pension Benefit Guaranty Corporation
   b. Financial Crimes Enforcement Network
   c. 3M Company
   d. Public Company Accounting Oversight Board

4. The _____ of 2002 (Pub.L. 107-204, 116 Stat. 745, enacted July 30, 2002), also known as the Public Company Accounting Reform and Investor Protection Act of 2002, is a United States federal law enacted on July 30, 2002 in response to a number of major corporate and accounting scandals including those affecting Enron, Tyco International, Adelphia, Peregrine Systems and WorldCom. The legislation establishes new or enhanced standards for all U.S. public company boards, management, and public accounting firms. It does not apply to privately held companies.
   a. Lease
   b. FCPA
   c. Fair Labor Standards Act
   d. Sarbanes-Oxley Act

5. A _____ is a fungible, negotiable instrument representing financial value. they are broadly categorized into debt securities (such as banknotes, bonds and debentures), and equity securities; e.g., common stocks. The company or other entity issuing the _____ is called the issuer.
   a. BMC Software, Inc.
   b. Security
   c. Tracking stock
   d. 3M Company

6. The U.S. _____ is an independent agency of the United States government which holds primary responsibility for enforcing the federal securities laws and regulating the securities industry, the nation's stock and options exchanges, and other electronic securities markets. The SEC was created by section 4 of the Securities Exchange Act of 1934 (now codified as 15 U.S.C. § 78d and commonly referred to as the 1934 Act.)
   a. BNSF Railway
   b. BMC Software, Inc.
   c. Securities and Exchange Commission
   d. 3M Company

7. _____ of something is, in finance, the adding together of interest or different investments over a period of time such as atoms (1 - the act or process of accruing; 2 - the amount that accrues.) It holds specific meanings in accounting and payroll.

_____, in accounting, describes the accounting method known as _____ basis, whereby revenues and expenses are recognized when they are accrued, i.e. accumulated (earned or incurred), regardless when the actual cash is received or paid out.

a. Earnings before interest, taxes, depreciation and amortization
b. Accounts receivable
c. Assets
d. Accrual

8. A _____ is a party (e.g. person, organization, company, or government) that has a claim to the services of a second party. It is a person or institution to whom money is owed. The first party, in general, has provided some property or service to the second party under the assumption (usually enforced by contract) that the second party will return an equivalent property or service.
a. Payback period
b. Treasury company
c. Par value
d. Creditor

9. Employment is a contract between two parties, one being the employer and the other being the _____. An _____ may be defined as: 'A person in the service of another under any contract of hire, express or implied, oral or written, where the employer has the power or right to control and direct the _____ in the material details of how the work is to be performed.' Black's Law Dictionary page 471 (5th ed. 1979.)
a. AIG
b. AMEX
c. ABC Television Network
d. Employee

10. A _____ is an annual report required by the U.S. Securities and Exchange Commission (SEC), that gives a comprehensive summary of a public company's performance. Although similarly named, the annual report on _____ is distinct from the often glossy 'annual report to shareholders', which a company must send to its shareholders when it holds an annual meeting to elect directors (though some companies combine the annual report and the 10-K into one document.) The 10-K includes information such as company history, organizational structure, executive compensation, equity, subsidiaries, and audited financial statements, among other information.
a. Form 10-Q
b. Form 8-K
c. 3M Company
d. Form 10-K

11. An _____ is a practitioner of accountancy, which is the measurement, disclosure or provision of assurance about financial information that helps managers, investors, tax authorities and other decision makers make resource allocation decisions.

The word '_____' is derived from the French 'Compter' which took its origin from the Latin 'Computare'. The word was formerly written in English as 'Accomptant', but in process of time the word, which was always pronounced by dropping the 'p', became gradually changed both in pronunciation and in orthography to its present form.

Chapter 1. Accounting—Present and Past

a. AMEX
b. AIG
c. ABC Television Network
d. Accountant

12. _____ is the statutory title of qualified accountants in the United States who have passed the Uniform _____ Examination and have met additional state education and experience requirements for certification as a _____. Individuals who have passed the Exam but have not either accomplished the required on-the-job experience or have previously met it but in the meantime have lapsed their continuing professional education are, in many states, permitted the designation '_____ Inactive' or an equivalent phrase. In most U.S. states, only _____s who are licensed are able to provide to the public attestation (including auditing) opinions on financial statements.

a. Chartered Certified Accountant
b. Certified General Accountant
c. Chartered Accountant
d. Certified public accountant

13. _____ is one of the largest professional services organizations in the world and one of the Big Four auditors, along with PricewaterhouseCoopers, Ernst ' Young, and KPMG.

According to the organization's website as of 2008, Deloitte has approximately 165,000 professionals at work in 140 countries, delivering audit, tax, consulting and financial advisory services through its member firms.

a. Deloitte Touche Tohmatsu
b. BNSF Railway
c. 3M Company
d. BMC Software, Inc.

14. _____ is an umbrella term which refers to the various accounting systems used by various public sector entities. In the United States, for instance, there are two levels of government which follow different accounting standards set forth by independent, private sector boards. At the federal level, the Federal Accounting Standards Advisory Board (FASAB) sets forth the accounting standards to follow.

a. Management accounting
b. Governmental accounting
c. Product control
d. Nonassurance services

15. _____ is an international group of non-governmental organization for the protection and conservation of the environment. _____ uses direct action, lobbying and research to achieve its goals. _____ has a worldwide presence with national and regional offices in 46 countries, which are affiliated to the Amsterdam-based _____ International.

a. BMC Software, Inc.
b. 3M Company
c. Greenpeace
d. BNSF Railway

16. _____ is the world's largest professional services firm. It was formed in 1998 from a merger between Price Waterhouse and Coopers ' Lybrand, both formed in London.

_____ earned aggregated worldwide revenues of $28 billion for fiscal 2008, and employed over 146,000 people in 150 countries.

a. Serial bonds
b. Daybook
c. PricewaterhouseCoopers
d. Total-factor productivity

17. _____ is the recording of the value of assets, liabilities, income, and expenses in the daybooks, journals, and ledgers, in which debit and credit entries are chronologically posted to record changes in value. _____ is often mistaken for accounting, which is the system of recording, verifying, and reporting such information. Practitioners of accounting are called accountants.

    a. Controlling account
    b. Double-entry bookkeeping
    c. Bookkeeping
    d. Debit and credit

18. _____ is the balance of the amounts of cash being received and paid by a business during a defined period of time, sometimes tied to a specific project. Measurement of _____ can be used

- to evaluate the state or performance of a business or project.
- to determine problems with liquidity. Being profitable does not necessarily mean being liquid. A company can fail because of a shortage of cash, even while profitable.
- to project rate of returns. The time of _____s into and out of projects are used as inputs to financial models such as internal rate of return, and net present value.
- to examine income or growth of a business when it is believed that accrual accounting concepts do not represent economic realities. Alternately, _____ can be used to 'validate' the net income generated by accrual accounting.

_____ as a generic term may be used differently depending on context, and certain _____ definitions may be adapted by analysts and users for their own uses. Common terms include operating _____ and free _____.

    a. Cash flow
    b. Commercial paper
    c. Controlling interest
    d. Flow-through entity

19. _____ is the term used to refer to the standard framework of guidelines for financial accounting used in any given jurisdiction. _____ includes the standards, conventions, and rules accountants follow in recording and summarizing transactions, and in the preparation of financial statements.

Financial accounting information must be assembled and reported objectively.

    a. Generally accepted accounting principles
    b. General ledger
    c. Current asset
    d. Long-term liabilities

20. The _____ is the national, professional association of CPAs in the United States, with more than 330,000 members, including CPAs in business and industry, public practice, government, and education; student affiliates; and international associates. It sets ethical standards for the profession and U.S. auditing standards for audits of private companies; federal, state and local governments; and non-profit organizations.

Approximately 40% of its members are engaged in the practice of public accounting, in areas such as auditing, accounting, taxation, general business consulting, business valuation, personal financial planning and business technology.

    a. American Institute of Certified Public Accountants
    b. ABC Television Network
    c. Other postemployment benefits
    d. AIG

Chapter 1. Accounting—Present and Past

21. The title _____ is a professional designation awarded by various professional bodies around the world.

The _____ designation is a post-nominal award issued to individuals who have achieved a peer-based criteria of professional competency in the field of Management Accounting. Management accounting qualifications differ from those such as the ACA or CPA 'Chartered' or 'Public' accounting qualifications in a number of ways.

a. Convey Compliance Systems
b. Certified Management Accountant
c. BMC Software, Inc.
d. 3M Company

22. In economics, business, retail, and accounting, a _____ is the value of money that has been used up to produce something, and hence is not available for use anymore. In economics, a _____ is an alternative that is given up as a result of a decision. In business, the _____ may be one of acquisition, in which case the amount of money expended to acquire it is counted as _____.

a. Cost of quality
b. Prime cost
c. Cost allocation
d. Cost

23. In management accounting, _____ establishes budget and actual cost of operations, processes, departments or product and the analysis of variances, profitability or social use of funds. Managers use _____ to support decision-making to cut a company's costs and improve profitability. As a form of management accounting, _____ need not follow standards such as GAAP, because its primary use is for internal managers, rather than outside users, and what to compute is instead decided pragmatically.

a. Cost-volume-profit analysis
b. Prime cost
c. Marginal cost
d. Cost accounting

24. _____ is concerned with the provisions and use of accounting information to managers within organizations, to provide them with the basis to make informed business decisions that will allow them to be better equipped in their management and control functions.

In contrast to financial accountancy information, _____ information is:

- usually confidential and used by management, instead of publicly reported;
- forward-looking, instead of historical;
- pragmatically computed using extensive management information systems and internal controls, instead of complying with accounting standards.

This is because of the different emphasis: _____ information is used within an organization, typically for decision-making.

a. Governmental accounting
b. Grenzplankostenrechnung
c. Nonassurance services
d. Management accounting

25. _____ are liabilities which have occurred, but have not been paid or logged under accounts payable during an accounting period; in other words, obligations for goods and services provided to a company for which invoices have not yet been received. Examples would include accrued wages payable, accrued sales tax payable, and accrued rent payable.

There are two general types of _____:

- Routine and recurring
- Infrequent or non-routine

Most companies pay their employees on a predetermined schedule. Let's say that the 'Imaginary company Ltd.' pays its employees each Friday for the hours worked that week.

a. AIG
b. Accrued liabilities
c. AMEX
d. ABC Television Network

26. _____ are formal records of a business' financial activities.

In British English, including United Kingdom company law, _____ are often referred to as accounts, although the term _____ is also used, particularly by accountants.

_____ provide an overview of a business' financial condition in both short and long term.

a. Notes to the financial statements
b. Statement of retained earnings
c. 3M Company
d. Financial statements

27. In financial accounting, a _____ is defined as an obligation of an entity arising from past transactions or events, the settlement of which may result in the transfer or use of assets, provision of services or other yielding of economic benefits in the future.

a. Vested
b. Liability
c. Corporate governance
d. False Claims Act

28. _____ are additional notes and information added to the end of the financial statements to supplement the reader with more information. Notes to Financial Statements help explain the computation of specific items in the financial statements as well as provide a more comprehensive assessment of a company's financial condition. Notes to Financial Statements can include information on debt, going concern, accounts, contingent liabilities, or contextual information explaining the financial numbers (e.g. to indicate a lawsuit.)

a. 3M Company
b. Statement of retained earnings
c. Notes to the financial statements
d. Financial statements

29. An _____ is a comprehensive report on a company's activities throughout the preceding year. _____s are intended to give shareholders and other interested persons information about the company's activities and financial performance. Most jurisdictions require companies to prepare and disclose _____s, and many require the _____ to be filed at the company's registry.

a. AIG
b. AMEX
c. ABC Television Network
d. Annual report

30. The general definition of an _____ is an evaluation of a person, organization, system, process, project or product. _____s are performed to ascertain the validity and reliability of information; also to provide an assessment of a system's internal control. The goal of an _____ is to express an opinion on the person/organization/system (etc) in question, under evaluation based on work done on a test basis.

   a. Assurance service   b. Audit
   c. Institute of Chartered Accountants of India   d. Audit regime

31. _____ are ten auditing standards, developed by the AICPA, consisting of general standards, standards of field work, and standards of reporting, along with interpretations. They were developed by the AICPA in 1947 and have undergone minor changes since then.

The _____ are as follows:

1. The auditor must have adequate technical training and proficiency to perform the audit
2. The auditor must maintain independence in mental attitude in all matters related to the audit.
3. The auditor must use due professional care during the performance of the audit and the preparation of the report.

1. The auditor must adequately plan the work and must properly supervise any assistants.
2. The auditor must obtain a sufficient understanding of the entity and its environment, including its internal control, to assess the risk of material misstatement of the financial statements whether due to error or fraud, and to design the nature, timing, and extent of further audit procedures.
3. The auditor must obtain sufficient appropriate audit evidence by performing audit procedures to afford a reasonable basis for an opinion regarding the financial statements under audit.

The new standards are in effect for audits of financial statements for periods beginning on or after December 15, 2006.

1. The auditor must state in the auditor's report whether the financial statements are in accordance with generally accepted accounting principles (GAAP.)
2. The auditor must identify in the auditor's report those circumstances in which such principles have not been consistently observed in the current period in relation to the preceding period.
3. When the auditor determines that informative disclosures are not reasonably adequate, the auditor must so state in the auditor's report.
4. The auditor must either express an opinion regarding the financial statements, taken as a whole the auditor should state the reasons therefore in the auditor's report. In all cases where the auditor's name is associated with the financial statements, the auditor should clearly indicate the character of the auditor's work, if any, and the degree of responsibility the auditor is taking, in the auditor's report.

   a. Generally accepted auditing standards   b. Continuous auditing
   c. Joint audit   d. Negative assurance

32. An _____ is a term used in behavioral economics to describe those types of behaviors that impose costs on a person in the long-run that are not taken into account when making decisions in the present. Classical Economics discourages government from creating legislation that targets internalities, because it is assumed that the consumer takes these personal costs into account when paying for the good that causes the _____. For example, cigarettes should be taxed because of the negative consumption externalities that they impose, such as second-hand smoke, not because the smoker harms him or herself by smoking.
   a. Operating budget
   b. Authorised capital
   c. Inventory turnover ratio
   d. Internality

33. Internal auditing is a profession and activity involved in helping organisations achieve their stated objectives. It does this by utilizing a systematic methodology for analyzing business processes, procedures and activities with the goal of highlighting organizational problems and recommending solutions. Professionals called _____ are employed by organizations to perform the internal auditing activity.
   a. Auditor independence
   b. Auditing Standards Board
   c. Internal auditors
   d. Internal Auditing

34. _____ is a profession and activity involved in helping organisations achieve their stated objectives. It does this by using a systematic methodology for analyzing business processes, procedures and activities with the goal of highlighting organizational problems and recommending solutions. Professionals called internal auditors are employed by organizations to perform the _____ activity.
   a. Assurance service
   b. ITGCs
   c. Information audit
   d. Internal auditing

35. _____ is a system of financial accounting where each transaction is recorded in at least two accounts: at least one account is debited and at least one account is credited, so that the total debits of the transaction equal to the total credits. For example, if Company A sells an item to Company B, and Company B pays by cheque, then the bookkeeper of Company A credits the account 'Sales' and debits the account 'Bank'. Conversely, the bookkeeper of Company B debits the account 'Purchases' and credits the account 'Bank'.
   a. Bookkeeping
   b. Cookie jar accounting
   c. Debit and credit
   d. Double-entry bookkeeping

36. An _____ is a tax levied on the financial income of people, corporations, or other legal entities. Various _____ systems exist, with varying degrees of tax incidence. Income taxation can be progressive, proportional, or regressive.
   a. Individual Retirement Arrangement
   b. Income tax
   c. Ordinary income
   d. Implied level of government service

37. The _____ is the former authoritative body of the American Institute of Certified Public Accountants (AICPA.) It was created by the American Institute of Certified Public Accountants in 1959 and issued pronouncements on accounting principles until 1973, when it was replaced by the Financial Accounting Standards Board (FASB.)

The _____ was disbanded in the hopes that the smaller, fully-independent FASB could more effectively create accounting standards.

a. American Payroll Association
b. International Federation of Accountants
c. Institute of Management Accountants
d. Accounting Principles Board

38. _____ were published by Accounting Principles Board (APB.) The board was created by American Institute of Certified Public Accountants (AICPA) in 1959 and was replaced by Financial Accounting Standards Board (FASB) in 1973. Its mission was to develop an overall conceptual framework of US generally accepted accounting principles (US GAAP.)
a. Accounting Principles Board Opinions
b. AIG
c. ABC Television Network
d. AMEX

39. _____ were documents issued by the Committee on Accounting Procedure between 1938 and 1959 on various accounting problems. They were discontinued with the dissolution of the Committee in 1959 under a recommendation from the Special Committee on Research Program. In all, 51 bulletins were issued, however, the lack of binding authority over AICPA's membership reduced the influence of, and compliance with the content of the bulletins.
a. AIG
b. Accounting Research Bulletins
c. Other postemployment benefits
d. ABC Television Network

40. The _____ was a predecessor of the Accounting Principles Board, itself a predecessor to the Financial Accounting Standards Board in the United States. Its formation and activities were early efforts to rationalize and legitimize the reporting of business performance. However, it is widely regarded as having failed.
a. Consolidated financial statements
b. Price variance
c. Lump sum
d. Committee on Accounting Procedure

41. A _____ is used in research to outline possible courses of action or to present a preferred approach to an idea or thought. For example, the philosopher Isaiah Berlin used the 'hedgehogs' versus 'foxes' approach; a 'hedgehog' might approach the world in terms of a single organizing principle; a 'fox' might pursue multiple conflicting goals simultaneously. Alternatively, an empiricist might approach a subject by direct examination, whereas an intuitionist might simply intuit what's next.
a. BMC Software, Inc.
b. BNSF Railway
c. 3M Company
d. Conceptual Framework

42. The _____ is located in Norwalk, Connecticut. It is an independent, organization in the private sector that is responsible for oversight of the Financial Accounting Standards Board (FASB), the Governmental Accounting Standards Board (GASB), and their respective advisory councils.
a. Financial Accounting Foundation
b. BNSF Railway
c. BMC Software, Inc.
d. 3M Company

43. The _____ is a private, not-for-profit organization whose primary purpose is to develop generally accepted accounting principles (GAAP) within the United States in the public's interest. The Securities and Exchange Commission (SEC) designated the _____ as the organization responsible for setting accounting standards for public companies in the U.S. It was created in 1973, replacing the Accounting Principles Board and the Committee on Accounting Procedure of the American Institute of Certified Public Accountants. The _____'s mission is 'to establish and improve standards of financial accounting and reporting for the guidance and education of the public, including issuers, auditors, and users of financial information.'

The _____ is not a governmental body.

a. Governmental Accounting Standards Board
b. Public company
c. Fannie Mae
d. Financial Accounting Standards Board

44. _____ is a company's financial statement that indicates how the revenue is transformed into the net income The purpose of the _____ is to show managers and investors whether the company made or lost money during the period being reported.

The important thing to remember about an _____ is that it represents a period of time.

a. ABC Television Network
b. AMEX
c. AIG
d. Income statement

45. _____ is an equity (stock) exchange located at 11 Wall Street in lower Manhattan, New York, USA.) It is the largest stock exchange in the world by dollar value of its listed companies' securities. As of October 2008, the combined capitalization of all domestic _____ listed companies was US$10.1 trillion.

a. New York Stock Exchange
b. BMC Software, Inc.
c. 3M Company
d. BNSF Railway

46. Congress enacted the _____, in the aftermath of the stock market crash of 1929 and during the ensuing Great Depression.

a. Bookkeeping
b. Sustainability measurement
c. Securities Act of 1933
d. Monte Carlo methods

47. The _____ of 1934 is a law governing the secondary trading of securities (stocks, bonds, and debentures) in the United States of America. The Act, 48 Stat. 881 (enacted June 6, 1934), codified at 15 U.S.C.

a. BMC Software, Inc.
b. 3M Company
c. BNSF Railway
d. Securities Exchange Act

48. The _____ is a law governing the secondary trading of securities (stocks, bonds, and debentures) in the United States of America. The Act, 48 Stat. 881 (enacted June 6, 1934), codified at 15 U.S.C.

a. BMC Software, Inc.
b. 3M Company
c. BNSF Railway
d. Securities Exchange Act of 1934

49. A _____, (formerly a securities exchange) is a corporation or mutual organization which provides 'trading' facilities for stock brokers and traders, to trade stocks and other securities. _____s also provide facilities for the issue and redemption of securities as well as other financial instruments and capital events including the payment of income and dividends. The securities traded on a _____ include: shares issued by companies, unit trusts, derivatives, pooled investment products and bonds.

a. 3M Company
b. Stock Exchange
c. BMC Software, Inc.
d. BNSF Railway

50. The _____ is a 'voluntary organization of persons interested in accounting education and research'. It was formed in 1916. Its main publication, the The Accounting Review, was first published in 1926.

a. Australian Accounting Standards Board
b. International Accounting Standards Board
c. American Accounting Association
d. Institute of Management Accountants

Chapter 1. Accounting—Present and Past

51. The _____ is a professional organization headquartered in Montvale, New Jersey consisting of over 70,000 members worldwide. The IMA is dedicated to advancing the role of the management accountant and financial manager within the business organization, and provides relevant professional certification.

The IMA awards the Certified Management Accountant (CMA) designation in the United States.

- a. Institute of Management Accountants
- b. International Accounting Standards Committee
- c. Emerging technologies
- d. American Accounting Association

52. _____ is the acquisition of goods and/or services at the best possible total cost of ownership, in the right quantity and quality, at the right time, in the right place and from the right source for the direct benefit or use of corporations or individuals, generally via a contract. Simple _____ may involve nothing more than repeat purchasing. Complex _____ could involve finding long term partners - or even 'co-destiny' suppliers that might fundamentally commit one organization to another.
- a. Customer satisfaction
- b. Free cash flow
- c. Time to market
- d. Procurement

53. _____ LLP, based in Chicago, was once one of the 'Big Five' accounting firms among PricewaterhouseCoopers, Deloitte Touche Tohmatsu, Ernst ' Young and KPMG, providing auditing, tax, and consulting services to large corporations. In 2002, the firm voluntarily surrendered its licenses to practice as Certified Public Accountants in the United States after being found guilty of criminal charges relating to the firm's handling of the auditing of Enron, the energy corporation, resulting in the loss of 85,000 jobs. Although the verdict was subsequently overturned by the Supreme Court of the United States, it has not returned as a viable business.
- a. AIG
- b. Arthur Andersen
- c. ABC Television Network
- d. AMEX

54. In the United States, the _____ is the senior technical committee designated by the American Institute of Certified Public Accountants (AICPA) to issue auditing, attestation, and quality control statements, standards and guidance to certified public accountants (CPAs) for non-public company audits. Created in October 1978, it is composed of 19 members representing various industries and sectors, including public accountants and private, educational, and governmental entities. It issues pronouncements in the form of statements, interpretations, and guidelines, which all CPAs must adhere to when performing audits and attestations.
- a. Auditing Standards Board
- b. Assurance service
- c. Information audit
- d. Engagement Letter

55. _____ refers to the independence of the auditor from parties, that have an interest in the financial statements of an entity. It is essentially an attitude of mind characterized by integrity and an objective approach to the audit process. The concept requires the auditor to carry out his work freely and in an objective manner.
- a. Auditor independence
- b. Information audit
- c. Internal Auditing
- d. Audit

56. A _____ occurs when an individual or organization (such as a policeman, lawyer, insurance adjuster, politician, engineer, executive, director of a corporation, medical research scientist, physician, writer, editor, or an individual or organization cited as a source) has an interest that might compromise their reliability. A _____ exists even if no improper act results from it, and can create an appearance of impropriety that can undermine confidence in the conflicted individual or organization. A conflict can be mitigated by third party verification or third party evaluation noted below - but it still exists.
   a. Conflict of interest
   b. 3M Company
   c. BNSF Railway
   d. BMC Software, Inc.

57. The _____ is currently the source of generally accepted accounting principles (GAAP) used by State and Local governments in the [[United States of America]]. As with most of the entities involved in creating GAAP in the United States, it is a private, non-governmental organization.

The _____ is subject to oversight by the Financial Accounting Foundation (FAF), which selects the members of the _____ and the Financial Accounting Standards Board, and funds both organizations.

   a. Fannie Mae
   b. National Conference of Commissioners on Uniform State Laws
   c. Multinational corporation
   d. Governmental Accounting Standards Board

58. _____ is a political and social term from the Latin verb conservare meaning to save or preserve. As the name suggests it usually indicates support for tradition and traditional values though the meaning has changed in different countries and time periods. The modern political term conservative was used by French politician Chateaubriand in 1819.
   a. 3M Company
   b. BMC Software, Inc.
   c. Politicized issue
   d. Conservatism

59. _____ is a fee paid on borrowed assets. It is the price paid for the use of borrowed money , or, money earned by deposited funds .Assets that are sometimes lent with _____ include money, shares, consumer goods through hire purchase, major assets such as aircraft, and even entire factories in finance lease arrangements. The _____ is calculated upon the value of the assets in the same manner as upon money.
   a. Insolvency
   b. Interest
   c. AIG
   d. ABC Television Network

60. The _____ is the main body of domestic statutory tax law of the United States organized topically, including laws covering the income tax , payroll taxes, gift taxes, estate taxes and statutory excise taxes. The _____ is published as Title 26 of the United States Code (USC), and is also known as the internal revenue title.
   a. Ordinary income
   b. Income tax
   c. Equity of condition
   d. Internal Revenue Code

61. The _____ founded on April 1, 2001 is the successor of the International Accounting Standards Committee (IASC) founded in June 1973 in London. It is responsible for developing the International Financial Reporting Standards (new name for the International Accounting Standards issued after 2001), and promoting the use and application of these standards.

The _____ is an independent, privately-funded accounting standard-setter based in London, UK.

a. Institute of Management Accountants
b. Emerging technologies
c. International Accounting Standards Board
d. Information Systems Audit and Control Association

62. _____ was founded in June 1973 in London and replaced by the International Accounting Standards Board on April 1, 2001. It was responsible for developing the International Accounting Standards and promoting the use and application of these standards.

The _____ was founded as a result of an agreement between accountancy bodies in the following countries:

- Australia (Institute of Chartered Accountants in Australia (ICAA) and the CPA Australia (formerly known as Australian Society of Certified Practising Accountants (ASCPA))

- Canada (Canadian Institute of Chartered Accountants (CICA))

- France (Ordre des Experts Comptable et des Comptables Agrees (Order of Accounting Experts and Qualified Accountants))

- Germany and the Wirtschaftsprüferkammer (WPK) (Chamber of Auditors))

- Japan Nihon Kouninkaikeishi Kyoukai)

- Mexico (Instituto Mexicano de Contadores Publicos (IMCP) (Mexican Institute of Public Accountants)) (removed from the board in 1987 due to non-payment of dues; resumed in 1995.)

- the Netherlands (Nederlands Instituut van Registeraccountants (NIVRA)

(Netherlands Institute of Registered Auditors))

- the United Kingdom and Ireland (counted as one) (Institute of Chartered Accountants in England and Wales (ICAEW), Institute of Chartered Accountants of Scotland (ICAS), Institute of Chartered Accountants in Ireland (ICAI), Association of Certified Accountants, Institute of Cost and Management Accountants, and the Institute of Municipal Treasurers and Accountants)

- the United States of America (American Institute of Certified Public Accountants (AICPA))

The Institute of Chartered Accountants of Nigeria became an associate member in 1976 and a member of the board from 1978 to 1987.

The National Council of Chartered Accountants (South Africa) became an associate member in 1974 and joined the board in 1978.

a. American Payroll Association
b. International Accounting Standards Committee
c. American Accounting Association
d. International Accounting Standards Board

63. Established in 1941, The _____ is internationally recognized as a trustworthy guidance-setting body. Serving members in 165 countries, The IIA is the internal audit profession's global voice, chief advocate, recognized authority, acknowledged leader, and principal educator, with global headquarters in Altamonte Springs, Fla., United States.

The stated mission of The _____ is to provide dynamic leadership for the global profession of internal auditing.

- a. Auditor independence
- b. Event data
- c. Audit regime
- d. Institute of Internal Auditors

64. _____ is a form of applied ethics that examines ethical principles and moral or ethical problems that arise in a business environment. It applies to all aspects of business conduct and is relevant to the conduct of individuals and business organizations as a whole. Applied ethics is a field of ethics that deals with ethical questions in many fields such as medical, technical, legal and _____.

- a. BMC Software, Inc.
- b. BNSF Railway
- c. 3M Company
- d. Business ethics

65. The _____ are rules that set out a uniform sentencing policy for convicted felons in the United States federal courts system.

The Guidelines are the product of the United States Sentencing Commission and are part of an overall federal sentencing reform package that took effect in the mid-1960s. The implementation of this reform package was the result of bipartisan cooperation, led chiefly by Senator Edward Kennedy, as Chair of the Senate Judiciary Committee, and Attorney General Edwin Meese.

- a. Hospital Survey and Construction Act
- b. Letter of credit
- c. Primary authority
- d. Federal Sentencing Guidelines

66. The _____ of 1977 (15 U.S.C. ÂÂ§ÂÂ§ 78dd-1, et seq.) is a United States federal law known primarily for two of its main provisions, one that addresses accounting transparency requirements under the Securities Exchange Act of 1934 and another concerning bribery of foreign officials.

- a. Pre-emption right
- b. Lease
- c. Competition law
- d. Foreign Corrupt Practices Act

67. In accounting and organizational theory, _____ is defined as a process effected by an organization's structure, work and authority flows, people and management information systems, designed to help the organization accomplish specific goals or objectives. It is a means by which an organization's resources are directed, monitored, and measured. It plays an important role in preventing and detecting fraud and protecting the organization's resources, both physical (e.g., machinery and property) and intangible (e.g., reputation or intellectual property such as trademarks.)

- a. Audit risk
- b. Auditor independence
- c. Audit committee
- d. Internal control

Chapter 1. Accounting—Present and Past

68. Procter is a surname, and may also refer to:

- Bryan Waller Procter (pseud. Barry Cornwall), English poet
- Goodwin Procter, American law firm
- _____, consumer products multinational

a. Procter ' Gamble
b. Markup
c. Welfare
d. Screening

69. _____ is a method of accounting whereby economic activities (rather than cash flow) of financial events are considered, because of two complementary principles, which (together) determine the point, at which expenses and revenues are recognized. According to revenue recognition principle, revenues are realized when earned, whether or not they are received in cash.

a. Accrual
b. Accrued revenue
c. Earnings before interest, taxes, depreciation and amortization
d. Accrual basis accounting

70. _____ is a specific term used in companies' financial reporting from the company-whole point of view. Because that use excludes the effects of changing ownership interest, an economic measure of _____ is necessary for financial analysis from the shareholders' point of view

_____ is defined by the Financial Accounting Standards Board, or FASB, as 'the change in equity [net assets] of a business enterprise during a period from transactions and other events and circumstances from nonowner sources. It includes all changes in equity during a period except those resulting from investments by owners and distributions to owners.'

_____ is the sum of net income and other items that must bypass the income statement because they have not been realized, including items like an unrealized holding gain or loss from available for sale securities and foreign currency translation gains or losses.

a. BMC Software, Inc.
b. BNSF Railway
c. 3M Company
d. Comprehensive income

Chapter 2. Financial Statements and Accounting Concepts/ Principles

1. _____ is the term used to refer to the standard framework of guidelines for financial accounting used in any given jurisdiction. _____ includes the standards, conventions, and rules accountants follow in recording and summarizing transactions, and in the preparation of financial statements.

Financial accounting information must be assembled and reported objectively.

a. General ledger	b. Long-term liabilities
c. Current asset	d. Generally accepted accounting principles

2. An _____ is a comprehensive report on a company's activities throughout the preceding year. _____s are intended to give shareholders and other interested persons information about the company's activities and financial performance. Most jurisdictions require companies to prepare and disclose _____s, and many require the _____ to be filed at the company's registry.

a. ABC Television Network	b. AIG
c. Annual report	d. AMEX

3. _____ are ten auditing standards, developed by the AICPA, consisting of general standards, standards of field work, and standards of reporting, along with interpretations. They were developed by the AICPA in 1947 and have undergone minor changes since then.

The _____ are as follows:

1. The auditor must have adequate technical training and proficiency to perform the audit
2. The auditor must maintain independence in mental attitude in all matters related to the audit.
3. The auditor must use due professional care during the performance of the audit and the preparation of the report.

1. The auditor must adequately plan the work and must properly supervise any assistants.
2. The auditor must obtain a sufficient understanding of the entity and its environment, including its internal control, to assess the risk of material misstatement of the financial statements whether due to error or fraud, and to design the nature, timing, and extent of further audit procedures.
3. The auditor must obtain sufficient appropriate audit evidence by performing audit procedures to afford a reasonable basis for an opinion regarding the financial statements under audit.

Chapter 2. Financial Statements and Accounting Concepts/ Principles 17

The new standards are in effect for audits of financial statements for periods beginning on or after December 15, 2006.

1. The auditor must state in the auditor's report whether the financial statements are in accordance with generally accepted accounting principles (GAAP.)
2. The auditor must identify in the auditor's report those circumstances in which such principles have not been consistently observed in the current period in relation to the preceding period.
3. When the auditor determines that informative disclosures are not reasonably adequate, the auditor must so state in the auditor's report.
4. The auditor must either express an opinion regarding the financial statements, taken as a whole the auditor should state the reasons therefore in the auditor's report. In all cases where the auditor's name is associated with the financial statements, the auditor should clearly indicate the character of the auditor's work, if any, and the degree of responsibility the auditor is taking, in the auditor's report.

a. Negative assurance
b. Continuous auditing
c. Joint audit
d. Generally accepted auditing standards

4. In economics, the _____, (or _____) measures the payments that flow between any individual country and all other countries. It is used to summarize all international economic transactions for that country during a specific time period, usually a year. The _____ is determined by the country's exports and imports of goods, services, and financial capital, as well as financial transfers.

a. Moving average
b. Stock split
c. Yield to maturity
d. Balance of payments

5. _____ are formal records of a business' financial activities.

In British English, including United Kingdom company law, _____ are often referred to as accounts, although the term _____ is also used, particularly by accountants.

_____ provide an overview of a business' financial condition in both short and long term.

a. Notes to the financial statements
b. 3M Company
c. Statement of retained earnings
d. Financial statements

6. _____ are additional notes and information added to the end of the financial statements to supplement the reader with more information. Notes to Financial Statements help explain the computation of specific items in the financial statements as well as provide a more comprehensive assessment of a company's financial condition. Notes to Financial Statements can include information on debt, going concern, accounts, contingent liabilities, or contextual information explaining the financial numbers (e.g. to indicate a lawsuit.)

a. 3M Company
b. Statement of retained earnings
c. Financial statements
d. Notes to the financial statements

Chapter 2. Financial Statements and Accounting Concepts/ Principles

7. _____ is a concept whereby a person's financial liability is limited to a fixed sum, most commonly the value of a person's investment in a company or partnership with _____. A shareholder in a limited company is not personally liable for any of the debts of the company, other than for the value of his investment in that company. The same is true for the members of a _____ partnership and the limited partners in a limited partnership.
   a. Limited liability
   b. Joint venture
   c. Burden of proof
   d. Due diligence

8. A _____ in the law of the vast majority of United States jurisdictions is a legal form of business company that provides limited liability to its owners. Often incorrectly called a 'limited liability corporation' (instead of company), it is a hybrid business entity having certain characteristics of both a corporation and a partnership. The primary characteristic an _____ shares with a corporation is limited liability, and the primary characteristic it shares with a partnership is the availability of pass-through income taxation.
   a. Consumer protection laws
   b. Data protection
   c. Bond market
   d. Limited liability company

9. A _____ is a partnership in which some or all partners (depending on the jurisdiction) have limited liability. It therefore exhibits elements of partnerships and corporations. In an _____ one partner is not responsible or liable for another partner's misconduct or negligence.
   a. Dow Jones ' Company
   b. Privately held
   c. Financial Accounting Standards Board
   d. Limited liability partnership

10. A _____ is a type of business entity in which partners (owners) share with each other the profits or losses of the business undertaking in which all have invested. _____s are often favored over corporations for taxation purposes, as the _____ structure does not generally incur a tax on profits before it is distributed to the partners (i.e. there is no dividend tax levied.) However, depending on the _____ structure and the jurisdiction in which it operates, owners of a _____ may be exposed to greater personal liability than they would as shareholders of a corporation.
    a. Resource Conservation and Recovery Act
    b. Corporate governance
    c. Partnership
    d. National Information Infrastructure Protection Act

11. A sole _____, or simply _____ is a type of business entity which legally has no separate existence from its owner. Hence, the limitations of liability enjoyed by a corporation and limited liability partnerships do not apply to sole proprietors. All debts of the business are debts of the owner.
    a. Safety stock
    b. Free cash flow
    c. Pre-determined overhead rate
    d. Proprietorship

12. A mutual shareholder or _____ is an individual or company (including a corporation) that legally owns one or more shares of stock in a joint stock company. A company's shareholders collectively own that company. Thus, the typical goal of such companies is to enhance shareholder value.
    a. Growth investing
    b. Stockholder
    c. 3M Company
    d. Stock split

13. In financial accounting, a _____ is defined as an obligation of an entity arising from past transactions or events, the settlement of which may result in the transfer or use of assets, provision of services or other yielding of economic benefits in the future.

Chapter 2. Financial Statements and Accounting Concepts/ Principles

a. False Claims Act
b. Vested
c. Corporate governance
d. Liability

14. The basic _____ is the foundation for the double-entry bookkeeping system. It shows how assets were financed: either by borrowing money from someone (liability) or by paying your own money (shareholders' equity.)

Assets = Liabilities + (Shareholders or Owners equity)

For example: A student buys a computer for $945.

a. AIG
b. AMEX
c. ABC Television Network
d. Accounting equation

15. In business and accounting, _____ are everything of value that is owned by a person or company. It is a claim on the property your income of a borrower. The balance sheet of a firm records the monetary value of the _____ owned by the firm.

a. Assets
b. Accrual basis accounting
c. Accounts receivable
d. Earnings before interest, taxes, depreciation and amortization

16. In financial accounting, a _____ or statement of financial position is a summary of a person's or organization's balances. Assets, liabilities and ownership equity are listed as of a specific date, such as the end of its financial year. A _____ is often described as a snapshot of a company's financial condition.

a. Statement of retained earnings
b. 3M Company
c. Financial statements
d. Balance sheet

17. The term _____ refers to government debt, expenditures and revenues, or to finance (particularly financial revenue) in general.

- _____ deficit is the budget deficit of federal or local government
- _____ policy is the discretionary spending of governments. Contrasts with monetary policy.
- _____ year and _____ quarter are reporting periods for firms and other agencies.

See also

- Procurator _____ and Crown Office and Procurator _____ Service

a. Comparable
b. Scientific Research and Experimental Development Tax Incentive Program
c. Swap
d. Fiscal

18. A _____ is a period used for calculating annual financial statements in businesses and other organizations. In many jurisdictions, regulatory laws regarding accounting and taxation require such reports once per twelve months, but do not require that the period reported on constitutes a calendar year (i.e., January through December.) _____s vary between businesses and countries.

a. 3M Company
b. BMC Software, Inc.
c. Fiscal year
d. BNSF Railway

19. _____ is a company's financial statement that indicates how the revenue is transformed into the net income The purpose of the _____ is to show managers and investors whether the company made or lost money during the period being reported.

The important thing to remember about an _____ is that it represents a period of time.

a. Income statement
b. ABC Television Network
c. AMEX
d. AIG

20. _____ is a political and social term from the Latin verb conservare meaning to save or preserve. As the name suggests it usually indicates support for tradition and traditional values though the meaning has changed in different countries and time periods. The modern political term conservative was used by French politician Chateaubriand in 1819.

a. Politicized issue
b. 3M Company
c. BMC Software, Inc.
d. Conservatism

21. _____ are sometimes the same as net worth, or shareholders' equity - assets minus liabilities. The term _____ is commonly used with charities or not for profit entities. Although these entities don't make money, it is important to maintain reasonable reserves to help future growth.

a. Net assets
b. Debtor days
c. Sortino ratio
d. Net interest spread

22. In business, _____ is the total assets minus total outside liabilities of an individual or a company. For a company, this is called shareholders' equity and may be referred to as book value. _____ is stated as at a particular point in time.

a. Debtor
b. Net worth
c. Creditor
d. Restructuring

23. _____ is a file or account that contains money that a person or company owes to suppliers, but has not paid yet (a form of debt.) When you receive an invoice you add it to the file, and then you remove it when you pay. Thus, the A/P is a form of credit that suppliers offer to their purchasers by allowing them to pay for a product or service after it has already been received.

a. Accounts payable
b. Accounts receivable
c. Earnings before interest, taxes, depreciation and amortization
d. Accrual

24. _____ is one of a series of accounting transactions dealing with the billing of customers who owe money to a person, company or organization for goods and services that have been provided to the customer. In most business entities this is typically done by generating an invoice and mailing or electronically delivering it to the customer, who in turn must pay it within an established timeframe called credit or payment terms.

An example of a common payment term is Net 30, meaning payment is due in the amount of the invoice 30 days from the date of invoice.

Chapter 2. Financial Statements and Accounting Concepts/ Principles

a. Accrual
c. Accounts receivable
b. Accrued revenue
d. Adjusting entries

25. _____ are liabilities which have occurred, but have not been paid or logged under accounts payable during an accounting period; in other words, obligations for goods and services provided to a company for which invoices have not yet been received. Examples would include accrued wages payable, accrued sales tax payable, and accrued rent payable.

There are two general types of _____:

- Routine and recurring
- Infrequent or non-routine

Most companies pay their employees on a predetermined schedule. Let's say that the 'Imaginary company Ltd.' pays its employees each Friday for the hours worked that week.

a. ABC Television Network
c. AMEX
b. Accrued liabilities
d. AIG

26. Book Value = Original Cost - _____

Book value at the end of year becomes book value at the beginning of next year. The asset is depreciated until the book value equals scrap value.

If the vehicle were to be sold and the sales price exceeded the depreciated value (net book value) then the excess would be considered a gain and subject to depreciation recapture.

a. ABC Television Network
c. AMEX
b. AIG
d. Accumulated depreciation

27. In accounting, a _____ is an asset on the balance sheet which is expected to be sold or otherwise used up in the near future, usually within one year, or one business cycle - whichever is longer. Typical _____s include cash, cash equivalents, accounts receivable, inventory, the portion of prepaid accounts which will be used within a year, and short-term investments.

On the balance sheet, assets will typically be classified into _____s and long-term assets.

a. Pro forma
c. Deferred
b. General ledger
d. Current asset

28. In accounting, _____ are considered liabilities of the business that are to be settled in cash within the fiscal year or the operating cycle, whichever period is longer.

For example accounts payable for goods, services or supplies that were purchased for use in the operation of the business and payable within a normal period of time would be _____.

Bonds, mortgages and loans that are payable over a term exceeding one year would be fixed liabilities.

a. Payroll
b. Current liabilities
c. Closing entries
d. Treasury stock

29. _____ is a term used in accounting, economics and finance to spread the cost of an asset over the span of several years.

In simple words we can say that _____ is the reduction in the value of an asset due to usage, passage of time, wear and tear, technological outdating or obsolescence, depletion, inadequacy, rot, rust, decay or other such factors.

In accounting, _____ is a term used to describe any method of attributing the historical or purchase cost of an asset across its useful life, roughly corresponding to normal wear and tear.

a. General ledger
b. Depreciation
c. Current asset
d. Net profit

30. In economic models, the _____ time frame assumes no fixed factors of production. Firms can enter or leave the marketplace, and the cost (and availability) of land, labor, raw materials, and capital goods can be assumed to vary. In contrast, in the short-run time frame, certain factors are assumed to be fixed, because there is not sufficient time for them to change.

a. 3M Company
b. Short-run
c. BMC Software, Inc.
d. Long-run

31. In economics, the concept of the _____ refers to the decision-making time frame of a firm in which at least one factor of production is fixed. Costs which are fixed in the _____ have no impact on a firms decisions. For example a firm can raise output by increasing the amount of labour through overtime.

a. BMC Software, Inc.
b. Long-run
c. 3M Company
d. Short-run

32. In physics, and more specifically kinematics, _____ is the change in velocity over time. Because velocity is a vector, it can change in two ways: a change in magnitude and/or a change in direction. In one dimension, _____ is the rate at which something speeds up or slows down.

a. Acceleration
b. AMEX
c. ABC Television Network
d. AIG

33. In economics, business, retail, and accounting, a _____ is the value of money that has been used up to produce something, and hence is not available for use anymore. In economics, a _____ is an alternative that is given up as a result of a decision. In business, the _____ may be one of acquisition, in which case the amount of money expended to acquire it is counted as _____.

a. Cost of quality
b. Cost allocation
c. Prime cost
d. Cost

Chapter 2. Financial Statements and Accounting Concepts/ Principles 23

34. _____ is that which is owed; usually referencing assets owed, but the term can also cover moral obligations and other interactions not requiring money. In the case of assets, _____ is a means of using future purchasing power in the present before a summation has been earned. Some companies and corporations use _____ as a part of their overall corporate finance strategy.

a. Debenture
b. Loan
c. Debt
d. Lender

35. _____ is a specific term used in companies' financial reporting from the company-whole point of view. Because that use excludes the effects of changing ownership interest, an economic measure of _____ is necessary for financial analysis from the shareholders' point of view

_____ is defined by the Financial Accounting Standards Board, or FASB, as 'the change in equity [net assets] of a business enterprise during a period from transactions and other events and circumstances from nonowner sources. It includes all changes in equity during a period except those resulting from investments by owners and distributions to owners.'

_____ is the sum of net income and other items that must bypass the income statement because they have not been realized, including items like an unrealized holding gain or loss from available for sale securities and foreign currency translation gains or losses.

a. 3M Company
b. BMC Software, Inc.
c. Comprehensive income
d. BNSF Railway

36. In accounting, _____ has a very specific meaning. It is an outflow of cash or other valuable assets from a person or company to another person or company. This outflow of cash is generally one side of a trade for products or services that have equal or better current or future value to the buyer than to the seller.

a. Expense
b. AMEX
c. ABC Television Network
d. AIG

37. _____ is equal to the income that a firm has after subtracting costs and expenses from the total revenue. _____ can be distributed among holders of common stock as a dividend or held by the firm as retained earnings.

The items deducted will typically include tax expense, financing expense (interest expense), and minority interest. Likewise, preferred stock dividends will be subtracted too, though they are not an expense.

a. Matching principle
b. Long-term liabilities
c. Generally accepted accounting principles
d. Net income

38. In bookkeeping, accounting, and finance, _____ are operating revenues earned by a company when it sells its products. Revenue (_____) are reported directly on the income statement as Sales or _____.

In financial ratios that use income statement sales values, 'sales' refers to _____, not gross sales.

a. Deferred
b. Historical cost
c. Net sales
d. Matching principle

24 *Chapter 2. Financial Statements and Accounting Concepts/ Principles*

39. A _____ is the pinnacle activity involved in selling products or services in return for money or other compensation. It is an act of completion of a commercial activity.

A _____ is completed by the seller, the owner of the goods.

a. Tertiary sector of economy
b. Sale
c. Maturity
d. High yield stock

40. In financial accounting, _____ or cost of sales includes the direct costs attributable to the production of the goods sold by a company. This amount includes the materials cost used in creating the goods along with the direct labor costs used to produce the good. It excludes indirect expenses such as distribution costs and sales force costs.

a. Reorder point
b. 3M Company
c. Cost of goods sold
d. FIFO and LIFO accounting

41. _____ are the earnings returned on the initial investment amount.

In the US, the Financial Accounting Standards Board (FASB) requires companies' income statements to report _____ for each of the major categories of the income statement: continuing operations, discontinued operations, extraordinary items, and net income.

The _____ formula does not include preferred dividends for categories outside of continued operations and net income.

a. Average accounting return
b. Earnings yield
c. Invested capital
d. Earnings per share

42. In accounting, _____ or sales profit is the difference between revenue and the cost of making a product or providing a service, before deducting overhead, payroll, taxation, and interest payments. Note that this is different from operating profit (earnings before interest and taxes.)

Net sales are calculated:

Net sales = Sales - Sales returns and allowances.

a. Gross profit
b. Commercial paper
c. Capital structure
d. Participating preferred stock

43. An _____ is a tax levied on the financial income of people, corporations, or other legal entities. Various _____ systems exist, with varying degrees of tax incidence. Income taxation can be progressive, proportional, or regressive.

a. Individual Retirement Arrangement
b. Ordinary income
c. Implied level of government service
d. Income tax

Chapter 2. Financial Statements and Accounting Concepts/ Principles

44. _____ is a fee paid on borrowed assets. It is the price paid for the use of borrowed money , or, money earned by deposited funds .Assets that are sometimes lent with _____ include money, shares, consumer goods through hire purchase, major assets such as aircraft, and even entire factories in finance lease arrangements. The _____ is calculated upon the value of the assets in the same manner as upon money.

a. AIG
b. Interest
c. ABC Television Network
d. Insolvency

45. _____ relates to the cost of borrowing money. It is the price that a lender charges a borrower for the use of the lender's money. _____ is different from OPEX and CAPEX, for it relates to the capital structure of a company.

a. Interest
b. ABC Television Network
c. AIG
d. Interest expense

46. _____ is a form of corporation equity ownership represented in the securities. It is a stock whose dividends are based on market fluctuations. It is dangerous in comparison to preferred shares and some other investment options, in that in the event of bankruptcy, _____ investors receive their funds after preferred stock holders, bondholders, creditors, etc. On the other hand, common shares on average perform better than preferred shares or bonds over time.

a. 3M Company
b. Growth investing
c. Stock split
d. Common stock

47. _____, Gross profit margin or Gross Profit Rate can be defined as the amount of contribution to the business enterprise, after paying for direct-fixed and direct-variable unit costs, required to cover overheads (fixed commitments) and provide a buffer for unknown items. It expresses the relationship between gross profit and sales revenue.

It can be expressed in absolute terms:

Gross Profit = Revenue − Cost of Goods Sold

or as the ratio of gross profit to sales revenue, usually in the form of a percentage:

_____ Percentage = (Revenue-Cost of Goods Sold)/Revenue

Cost of goods sold includes variable costs and fixed costs directly linked to the product, such as material and labor.

a. 3M Company
b. BMC Software, Inc.
c. BNSF Railway
d. Gross margin

48. At its simplest, a company's _____ as it sometimes called, is computed in by multiplying the income before tax number, as reported to shareholders, by the appropriate tax rate. In reality, the computation is typically considerably more complex due to things such as expenses considered not deductible by taxing authorities ('add backs'), the range of tax rates applicable to various levels of income, different tax rates in different jurisdictions, multiple layers of tax on income, and other issues.

Historically, in many places, a revenue-expense method was used, in which the income statement was seen as primary, and the balance sheet as secondary.

a. Payroll
b. Total Expense Ratio
c. 3M Company
d. Tax expense

49. _____ are payments made by a corporation to its shareholder members. It is the portion of corporate profits paid out to stockholders. When a corporation earns a profit or surplus, that money can be put to two uses: it can either be re-invested in the business (called retained earnings), or it can be paid to the shareholders as a dividend.
   a. Dividend stripping
   b. Dividend yield
   c. Dividend payout ratio
   d. Dividends

50. _____, in finance and accounting, means stated value or face value. From this comes the expressions at par (at the _____), over par (over _____) and under par (under _____).

_____ is a nominal value of a security which is determined by an issuer company at a minimum price. _____ of an equity (a stock) is a somewhat archaic concept. The _____ of a stock was the share price upon initial offering; the issuing company promised not to issue further shares below _____, so investors could be confident that no one else was receiving a more favorable issue price. This was far more important in unregulated equity markets than in the regulated markets that exist today.

   a. Par value
   b. Creditor
   c. Restructuring
   d. Net worth

51. In economics, _____ or _____ goods or real _____ refers to factors of production used to create goods or services that are not themselves significantly consumed (though they may depreciate) in the production process. _____ goods may be acquired with money or financial _____. In finance and accounting, _____ generally refers to financial wealth, especially that used to start or maintain a business.
   a. Disclosure
   b. Screening
   c. Vyborg Appeal
   d. Capital

52. A budget _____ occurs when an entity spends more money than it takes in. The opposite of a budget _____ is a budget surplus. Debt is essentially an accumulated flow of _____s.
   a. Progressive tax
   b. Windfall profits tax
   c. Land value taxation
   d. Deficit

53. _____ is the balance of the amounts of cash being received and paid by a business during a defined period of time, sometimes tied to a specific project. Measurement of _____ can be used

- to evaluate the state or performance of a business or project.
- to determine problems with liquidity. Being profitable does not necessarily mean being liquid. A company can fail because of a shortage of cash, even while profitable.
- to project rate of returns. The time of _____s into and out of projects are used as inputs to financial models such as internal rate of return, and net present value.
- to examine income or growth of a business when it is believed that accrual accounting concepts do not represent economic realities. Alternately, _____ can be used to 'validate' the net income generated by accrual accounting.

Chapter 2. Financial Statements and Accounting Concepts/ Principles 27

_____ as a generic term may be used differently depending on context, and certain _____ definitions may be adapted by analysts and users for their own uses. Common terms include operating _____ and free _____.

a. Cash flow
b. Controlling interest
c. Flow-through entity
d. Commercial paper

54. In financial accounting, a _____ or Statement of cash flows is a financial statement that shows a company's flow of cash. The money coming into the business is called cash inflow, and money going out from the business is called cash outflow. The statement shows how changes in balance sheet and income accounts affect cash and cash equivalents, and breaks the analysis down to operating, investing, and financing activities.

a. 3M Company
b. BNSF Railway
c. BMC Software, Inc.
d. Cash flow statement

55. _____ are financial statements that factor the holding company's subsidiaries into its aggregated accounting figure. It is a representation of how the holding company is doing as a group. The consolidated accounts should provide a true and fair view of the financial and operating conditions of the group.

a. Replacement cost
b. Redemption value
c. Committee on Accounting Procedure
d. Consolidated financial statements

56. A _____ is a business that functions without the intention or threat of liquidation for the foreseeable future, usually regarded as at least within 12 months.

In accounting, '_____' refers to a company's ability to continue functioning as a business entity. It is the responsibility of the directors to assess whether the _____ assumption is appropriate when preparing the financial statements.

a. BMC Software, Inc.
b. 3M Company
c. Payment
d. Going concern

57. A _____, in business matters, is an entity that is controlled by a bigger and more powerful entity. The controlled entity is called a company, corporation, or limited liability company, and the controlling entity is called its parent (or the parent company.) The reason for this distinction is that a lone company cannot be a _____ of any organization; only an entity representing a legal fiction as a separate entity can be a _____.

a. Subsidiary
b. 3M Company
c. BMC Software, Inc.
d. Parent company

58. An _____ is a period with reference to which United Kingdom corporation tax is charged. It helps dictate when tax is paid on income and gains. An _____ begins whenever a company comes within the corporation tax charge, and whenever an _____ ends without the company ceasing to be within the charge.

a. AMEX
b. Accounting period
c. ABC Television Network
d. AIG

Chapter 2. Financial Statements and Accounting Concepts/ Principles

59. _____ of something is, in finance, the adding together of interest or different investments over a period of time such as atoms (1 - the act or process of accruing; 2 - the amount that accrues.) It holds specific meanings in accounting and payroll.

_____, in accounting, describes the accounting method known as _____ basis, whereby revenues and expenses are recognized when they are accrued, i.e. accumulated (earned or incurred), regardless when the actual cash is received or paid out.

   a. Earnings before interest, taxes, depreciation and amortization
   b. Accounts receivable
   c. Assets
   d. Accrual

60. _____ is the recording of the value of assets, liabilities, income, and expenses in the daybooks, journals, and ledgers, in which debit and credit entries are chronologically posted to record changes in value. _____ is often mistaken for accounting, which is the system of recording, verifying, and reporting such information. Practitioners of accounting are called accountants.
   a. Controlling account
   b. Debit and credit
   c. Double-entry bookkeeping
   d. Bookkeeping

61. _____ was a maxim coined by Josiah Warren, indicating a (prescriptive) version of the labor theory of value. Warren maintained that the just compensation for labor (or for its product) could only be an equivalent amount of labor (or a product embodying an equivalent amount.) Thus, profit, rent, and interest were considered unjust economic arrangements.
   a. Cost the limit of price
   b. 3M Company
   c. BMC Software, Inc.
   d. Politicized issue

62. _____ is a cornerstone of accrual accounting together with the revenue recognition principle. They both determine the accounting period, in which revenues and expenses are recognized. According to the principle, expenses are recognized when obligations are (1) incurred (usually when goods are transferred or services rendered, e.g. sold), and (2) offset against recognized revenues, which were generated from those expenses (related on the cause-and-effect basis), no matter when cash is paid out.
   a. Current liabilities
   b. Payroll
   c. Net sales
   d. Matching principle

63. An _____, operating expenditure, operational expense, operational expenditure or OPEX is an on-going cost for running a product, business, or system. Its counterpart, a capital expenditure (CAPEX), is the cost of developing or providing non-consumable parts for the product or system. For example, the purchase of a photocopier is the CAPEX, and the annual paper and toner cost is the OPEX.
   a. AIG
   b. Operating expense
   c. ABC Television Network
   d. AMEX

64. _____ principle is a cornerstone of accrual accounting together with matching principle. They both determine the accounting period, in which revenues and expenses are recognized. According to the principle, revenues are recognized when they are (1) realized or realizable, and are (2) earned (usually when goods are transferred or services rendered), no matter when cash is received.

Chapter 2. Financial Statements and Accounting Concepts/ Principles

a. Net realizable value
b. 3M Company
c. BMC Software, Inc.
d. Revenue recognition

65. _____ is a method of accounting whereby economic activities (rather than cash flow) of financial events are considered, because of two complementary principles, which (together) determine the point, at which expenses and revenues are recognized. According to revenue recognition principle, revenues are realized when earned, whether or not they are received in cash.
   a. Accrual basis accounting
   b. Accrual
   c. Accrued revenue
   d. Earnings before interest, taxes, depreciation and amortization

66. A _____ proof is a mathematical proof that a particular theory is consistent. The early development of mathematical proof theory was driven by the desire to provide finitary _____ proofs for all of mathematics as part of Hilbert's program. Hilbert's program was strongly impacted by incompleteness theorems, which showed that sufficiently strong proof theories cannot prove their own _____
   a. Monte Carlo methods
   b. Consumption
   c. Daybook
   d. Consistency

67. In computer security, _____ means to disclose all the details of a security problem which are known. It is a philosophy of security management completely opposed to the idea of security through obscurity. The concept of _____ is controversial, but not new; it has been an issue for locksmiths since the 19th century.
   a. 3M Company
   b. BMC Software, Inc.
   c. BNSF Railway
   d. Full disclosure

Chapter 2. Financial Statements and Accounting Concepts/ Principles

68. _____ means the giving out of information, either voluntarily or to be in compliance with legal regulations or workplace rules.

- In Computer security, full _____ means disclosing full information about vulnerabilities.
- In computing, _____ widget
- Journalism, full _____ refers to disclosing the interests of the writer which may bear on the subject being written about, for example, if the writer has worked with an interview subject in the past.

- In law:
  - The law of England and Wales, _____ refers to a process that may form part of legal proceedings, whereby parties inform to other parties the existence of any relevant documents that are, or have been, in their control. This compares with the process known as discovery in the course of legal proceedings in the United States.
  - In U.S. civil procedure (litigation rules for civil cases), _____ is a stage prior to trial. In civil cases, each party must disclose to the opposing party the following: names of witnesses which it may use to support its side, copies of documents (or mere description of these documents) in its control which it may use to support its side, computation of damages claimed, and certain insurance information. _____ is related to, but technically prior to, the discovery stage.
  - In Company law (known as 'corporate law' in the United States), _____ refers to giving out information about public or limited companies or their officers, which might be kept secret if the company was a private company or a partnership.

- In real property transactions, _____ refers to providing to a buyer information known to the seller or broker/agent concerning the condition or other aspects of real property that would affect the property's value or desirability. These rules regarding what information must be disclosed, and whether the information must be disclosed even if a buyer does not ask, vary from one jurisdiction to the next.

a. Disclosure
b. Trailing
c. Controlled Foreign Corporations
d. Tax harmonisation

69. _____ is a term that refers both to:

- a formal discipline used to help appraise, or assess, the case for a project or proposal, which itself is a process known as project appraisal; and
- an informal approach to making decisions of any kind.

Under both definitions the process involves, whether explicitly or implicitly, weighing the total expected costs against the total expected benefits of one or more actions in order to choose the best or most profitable option. The formal process is often referred to as either CBA (_____) or BCost-benefit analysis

Chapter 2. Financial Statements and Accounting Concepts/ Principles 31

A hallmark of CBA is that all benefits and all costs are expressed in money terms, and are adjusted for the time value of money, so that all flows of benefits and flows of project costs over time (which tend to occur at different points in time) are expressed on a common basis in terms of their 'e;present value.'e; Closely related, but slightly different, formal techniques include Cost-effectiveness analysis, Economic impact analysis, Fiscal impact analysis and Social Return on Investment(SROI) analysis. The latter builds upon the logic of _____, but differs in that it is explicitly designed to inform the practical decision-making of enterprise managers and investors focused on optimising their social and environmental impacts.

a. BNSF Railway
b. Cost-benefit analysis
c. 3M Company
d. BMC Software, Inc.

70. _____ are defined as identifiable non-monetary assets that cannot be seen, touched or physically measured, which are created through time and/or effort and that are identifiable as a separate asset. There are two primary forms of intangibles - legal intangibles (such as trade secrets (e.g., customer lists), copyrights, patents, trademarks, and goodwill) and competitive intangibles (such as knowledge activities (know-how, knowledge), collaboration activities, leverage activities, and structural activities.) Legal intangibles are known under the generic term intellectual property and generate legal property rights defensible in a court of law.

a. ABC Television Network
b. AIG
c. Overhead
d. Intangible assets

71. _____ is an approach to valuing and reporting inventory. Normally ending inventory is stated at historical cost (what was paid to obtain it) but there are times when the original cost of the ending inventory is greater than the cost of replacement thus the inventory has lost value. If the inventory has decreased in value below historical cost then its carrying value is reduced and reported on the balance sheet.

a. Certified Practising Accountant
b. Lower of cost or market
c. Remittance advice
d. Bankruptcy prediction

72. A _____ is a fungible, negotiable instrument representing financial value. they are broadly categorized into debt securities (such as banknotes, bonds and debentures), and equity securities; e.g., common stocks. The company or other entity issuing the _____ is called the issuer.

a. Security
b. Tracking stock
c. 3M Company
d. BMC Software, Inc.

73. The U.S. _____ is an independent agency of the United States government which holds primary responsibility for enforcing the federal securities laws and regulating the securities industry, the nation's stock and options exchanges, and other electronic securities markets. The SEC was created by section 4 of the Securities Exchange Act of 1934 (now codified as 15 U.S.C. ÂÂ§ 78d and commonly referred to as the 1934 Act.)

a. BNSF Railway
b. 3M Company
c. BMC Software, Inc.
d. Securities and Exchange Commission

Chapter 2. Financial Statements and Accounting Concepts/ Principles

74. A _____ or trade mark, identified by the symbols â"¢ (not yet registered) and Â® (registered), is a distinctive sign or indicator used by an individual, business organization or other legal entity to identify that the products and/or services to consumers with which the _____ appears originate from a unique source, and to distinguish its products or services from those of other entities. A _____ is a type of intellectual property, and typically a name, word, phrase, logo, symbol, design, image, or a combination of these elements. There is also a range of non-conventional _____s comprising marks which do not fall into these standard categories.

  a. FIFO
  b. Trademark
  c. Risk management
  d. Kanban

75. _____ can be considered the quality control standards applicable for real property, personal property, intangibles, and business valuation appraisal analysis and reports in the United States and its territories. USPAP, as it is commonly known, was first developed in the 1980s by a joint committee representing the major U.S. and Canadian appraisal organizations. As a result of the Savings and Loan Crisis, the Appraisal Foundation (TAF) was formed by these same groups, along with support and input from major industry and educational groups, and TAF took over administration of USPAP.

  a. Uniform Standards of Professional Appraisal Practice
  b. AMEX
  c. ABC Television Network
  d. AIG

76. Most patent law systems require that a patent application disclose a claimed invention in sufficient detail for the notional person skilled in the art to carry out that claimed invention. This requirement is often known as sufficiency of disclosure or enablement, depending on the jurisdiction.

The _____ lies at the heart and origin of patent law. A state or government grants an inventor, or the inventor's assignee, a monopoly for a given period of time in exchange for the inventor disclosing to the public how to make or practice his or her invention. If a patent fails to contain such information, then the bargain is violated, and the patent is unenforceable.

  a. Tax patent
  b. Disclosure requirement
  c. False Claims Act
  d. Pre-emption right

77. A _____ is any one of a variety of different systems, institutions, procedures, social relations and infrastructures whereby persons trade, and goods and services are exchanged, forming part of the economy. It is an arrangement that allows buyers and sellers to exchange things. _____s vary in size, range, geographic scale, location, types and variety of human communities, as well as the types of goods and services traded.

  a. Market Failure
  b. Recession
  c. Perfect competition
  d. Market

78. _____ is the price at which an asset would trade in a competitive Walrasian auction setting. _____ is often used interchangeably with open _____, fair value or fair _____, although these terms have distinct definitions in different standards, and may differ in some circumstances.

International Valuation Standards defines _____ as 'the estimated amount for which a property should exchange on the date of valuation between a willing buyer and a willing seller in an arme;s-length transaction after proper marketing wherein the parties had each acted knowledgeably, prudently, and without compulsion.'

Chapter 2. Financial Statements and Accounting Concepts/ Principles   33

_____ is a concept distinct from market price, which is e;the price at which one can transacte;, while _____ is e;the true underlying valuee; according to theoretical standards.

a. Market value
c. Sinking fund

b. Debtor
d. Segregated portfolio company

79. In mathematics, two elements x and y of a set partially ordered by a relation ≤ are said to be _____ if and only if x ≤ y or y ≤ x if and only if x < y or y < x or y = x. For example, two sets are _____ with respect to inclusion if and only if one is a subset of the other.

In a classification of mathematical objects such as topological spaces, two criteria are said to be _____ when the objects that obey one criterion constitute a subset of the objects that obey the other one .

a. Database auditing
c. Consumption

b. Scientific Research and Experimental Development Tax Incentive Program
d. Comparable

80. _____ or economic opportunity loss is the value of the next best alternative foregone as the result of making a decision. _____ analysis is an important part of a company's decision-making processes but is not treated as an actual cost in any financial statement. The next best thing that a person can engage in is referred to as the _____ of doing the best thing and ignoring the next best thing to be done.

a. Inflation
c. AIG

b. ABC Television Network
d. Opportunity cost

81. In economics, _____ is a rise in the general level of prices of goods and services in an economy over a period of time. When the general price level rises, each unit of currency buys fewer goods and services; consequently, _____ is also a decline in the real value of money--a loss of purchasing power in the medium of exchange which is also the monetary unit of account in the economy. A chief measure of general price-level _____ is the general _____ rate, which is the percentage change in a general price index (normally the Consumer Price Index) over time.

a. Opportunity cost
c. AIG

b. Inflation
d. ABC Television Network

82. Straight-line depreciation is the simplest and most often used technique, in which the company estimates the _____ of the asset at the end of the period during which it will be used to generate revenues (useful life), and will expense a portion of original cost in equal increments over that period. The _____ is an estimate of the value of the asset at the time it will be sold or disposed of; it may be zero. _____ is scrap value, by another name.

a. Closing entries
c. Generally accepted accounting principles

b. Net profit
d. Salvage value

Chapter 3. Fundamental Interpretations Made from Financial Statement Data

1. A _____ is a party (e.g. person, organization, company, or government) that has a claim to the services of a second party. It is a person or institution to whom money is owed. The first party, in general, has provided some property or service to the second party under the assumption (usually enforced by contract) that the second party will return an equivalent property or service.
    a. Payback period
    b. Par value
    c. Treasury company
    d. Creditor

2. _____ is the term used to refer to the standard framework of guidelines for financial accounting used in any given jurisdiction. _____ includes the standards, conventions, and rules accountants follow in recording and summarizing transactions, and in the preparation of financial statements.

    Financial accounting information must be assembled and reported objectively.
    a. Generally accepted accounting principles
    b. Long-term liabilities
    c. General ledger
    d. Current asset

3. In finance, a _____ or accounting ratio is a ratio of two selected numerical values taken from an enterprise's financial statements. There are many standard ratios used to try to evaluate the overall financial condition of a corporation or other organization. _____s may be used by managers within a firm, by current and potential shareholders (owners) of a firm, and by a firm's creditors.
    a. Current ratio
    b. Financial ratio
    c. Price/cash flow ratio
    d. Return of capital

4. _____ is a business, economics or investment term that refers to an asset's ability to be easily converted through an act of buying or selling without causing a significant movement in the price and with minimum loss of value. Money, or cash on hand, is the most liquid asset. An act of exchange of a less liquid asset with a more liquid asset is called liquidation.
    a. Market liquidity
    b. Spot rate
    c. Transfer agent
    d. Financial instruments

5. _____ measures the rate of return on the ownership interest (shareholders' equity) of the common stock owners. It measures a firm's efficiency at generating profits from every dollar of shareholders' equity (also known as net assets or assets minus liabilities.) It shows how well a company uses investment dollars to generate earnings growth.
    a. Return on capital employed
    b. Like for like
    c. Sortino ratio
    d. Return on equity

6. In finance, _____ also known as return on investment, rate of profit or sometimes just return, is the ratio of money gained or lost on an investment relative to the amount of money invested. The amount of money gained or lost may be referred to as interest, profit/loss, gain/loss, or net income/loss. The money invested may be referred to as the asset, capital, principal, or the cost basis of the investment.
    a. Theoretical ex-rights price
    b. Rate of return
    c. Debt to capital ratio
    d. Capital employed

7. The term '_____' refers to the concept of collecting information and attempting to spot a pattern in the information. In some fields of study, the term '_____' has more formally-defined meanings.

    In project management _____ is a mathematical technique that uses historical results to predict future outcome.

Chapter 3. Fundamental Interpretations Made from Financial Statement Data

a. 3M Company
c. Multicollinearity
b. Regression analysis
d. Trend analysis

8. _____ is systematic determination of merit, worth, and significance of something or someone using criteria against a set of standards. _____ often is used to characterize and appraise subjects of interest in a wide range of human enterprises, including the arts, criminal justice, foundations and non-profit organizations, government, health care, and other human services.

Depending on the topic of interest, there are professional groups which look to the quality and rigor of the _____ process.

a. Evaluation
c. ABC Television Network
b. AMEX
d. AIG

9. In financial accounting, a _____ or statement of financial position is a summary of a person's or organization's balances. Assets, liabilities and ownership equity are listed as of a specific date, such as the end of its financial year. A _____ is often described as a snapshot of a company's financial condition.

a. Balance sheet
c. 3M Company
b. Statement of retained earnings
d. Financial statements

10. _____ is a form of corporation equity ownership represented in the securities. It is a stock whose dividends are based on market fluctuations. It is dangerous in comparison to preferred shares and some other investment options, in that in the event of bankruptcy, _____ investors receive their funds after preferred stock holders, bondholders, creditors, etc. On the other hand, common shares on average perform better than preferred shares or bonds over time.

a. Growth investing
c. Stock split
b. 3M Company
d. Common stock

11. _____ is a fee paid on borrowed assets. It is the price paid for the use of borrowed money , or, money earned by deposited funds .Assets that are sometimes lent with _____ include money, shares, consumer goods through hire purchase, major assets such as aircraft, and even entire factories in finance lease arrangements. The _____ is calculated upon the value of the assets in the same manner as upon money.

a. ABC Television Network
c. Insolvency
b. AIG
d. Interest

12. An _____ is the price a borrower pays for the use of money they do not own, for instance a small company might borrow from a bank to kick start their business, and the return a lender receives for deferring the use of funds, by lending it to the borrower. _____s are normally expressed as a percentage rate over the period of one year.

_____s targets are also a vital tool of monetary policy and are used to control variables like investment, inflation, and unemployment.

a. AIG
c. Interest rate
b. ABC Television Network
d. AMEX

13. Depending on the nature of the investment, the type of _____ will vary.

A common concern with any investment is that you may lose the money you invest - your capital. This risk is therefore often referred to as 'capital risk.'

If the assets you invest in are held in another currency there is a risk that currency movements alone may affect the value.

a. AIG
b. AMEX
c. ABC Television Network
d. Investment risk

14. A _____ is any one of a variety of different systems, institutions, procedures, social relations and infrastructures whereby persons trade, and goods and services are exchanged, forming part of the economy. It is an arrangement that allows buyers and sellers to exchange things. _____s vary in size, range, geographic scale, location, types and variety of human communities, as well as the types of goods and services traded.

a. Perfect competition
b. Market Failure
c. Recession
d. Market

15. _____ is the price at which an asset would trade in a competitive Walrasian auction setting. _____ is often used interchangeably with open _____, fair value or fair _____, although these terms have distinct definitions in different standards, and may differ in some circumstances.

International Valuation Standards defines _____ as 'the estimated amount for which a property should exchange on the date of valuation between a willing buyer and a willing seller in an arme;s-length transaction after proper marketing wherein the parties had each acted knowledgeably, prudently, and without compulsion.'

_____ is a concept distinct from market price, which is e;the price at which one can transacte;, while _____ is e;the true underlying valuee; according to theoretical standards.

a. Debtor
b. Sinking fund
c. Market value
d. Segregated portfolio company

16. _____ is equal to the income that a firm has after subtracting costs and expenses from the total revenue. _____ can be distributed among holders of common stock as a dividend or held by the firm as retained earnings.

The items deducted will typically include tax expense, financing expense (interest expense), and minority interest. Likewise, preferred stock dividends will be subtracted too, though they are not an expense.

a. Matching principle
b. Net income
c. Generally accepted accounting principles
d. Long-term liabilities

17. _____ is typically a 'higher ranking' stock than voting shares, and its terms are negotiated between the corporation and the investor.

_____ usually carries no voting rights, but may carry superior priority over common stock in the payment of dividends and upon liquidation. _____ may carry a dividend that is paid out prior to any dividends being paid to common stock holders.

a. Gross income
b. Cash flow
c. Preferred stock
d. Restricted stock

18. The _____ percentage shows how profitable a company's assets are in generating revenue.

_____ can be computed as:

$$ROA = \frac{\text{Net Income - Interest Expense - Interest Tax savings}}{\text{Average Total Assets}}$$

This number tells you what the company can do with what it has, i.e. how many dollars of earnings they derive from each dollar of assets they control. Its a useful number for comparing competing companies in the same industry.

a. Capital employed
b. Statutory Liquidity Ratio
c. Return on sales
d. Return on assets

19. _____ is a concept that denotes the precise probability of specific eventualities. Technically, the notion of _____ is independent from the notion of value and, as such, eventualities may have both beneficial and adverse consequences. However, in general usage the convention is to focus only on potential negative impact to some characteristic of value that may arise from a future event.

a. Discount factor
b. Discounting
c. Risk adjusted return on capital
d. Risk

20. In business and accounting, _____ are everything of value that is owned by a person or company. It is a claim on the property your income of a borrower. The balance sheet of a firm records the monetary value of the _____ owned by the firm.

a. Earnings before interest, taxes, depreciation and amortization
b. Accrual basis accounting
c. Accounts receivable
d. Assets

21. In finance, a _____ is a debt security, in which the authorized issuer owes the holders a debt and, depending on the terms of the _____, is obliged to pay interest (the coupon) and/or to repay the principal at a later date, termed maturity. It is a formal contract to repay borrowed money with interest at fixed intervals.

Thus a _____ is like a loan: the issuer is the borrower, the _____ holder is the lender, and the coupon is the interest.

a. Bond
b. Coupon rate
c. Revenue bonds
d. Zero-coupon bond

Chapter 3. Fundamental Interpretations Made from Financial Statement Data

22. In finance, a _____ is a type of bond that can be converted into shares of stock in the issuing company, usually at some pre-announced ratio. It is a hybrid security with debt- and equity-like features. Although it typically has a low coupon rate, the holder is compensated with the ability to convert the bond to common stock, usually at a substantial discount to the stock's market value.
    a. Coupon rate
    b. Zero-coupon bond
    c. Zero-coupon
    d. Convertible bond

23. _____ is a specific term used in companies' financial reporting from the company-whole point of view. Because that use excludes the effects of changing ownership interest, an economic measure of _____ is necessary for financial analysis from the shareholders' point of view

_____ is defined by the Financial Accounting Standards Board, or FASB, as 'the change in equity [net assets] of a business enterprise during a period from transactions and other events and circumstances from nonowner sources. It includes all changes in equity during a period except those resulting from investments by owners and distributions to owners.'

_____ is the sum of net income and other items that must bypass the income statement because they have not been realized, including items like an unrealized holding gain or loss from available for sale securities and foreign currency translation gains or losses.

   a. BMC Software, Inc.
   b. BNSF Railway
   c. 3M Company
   d. Comprehensive income

24. In financial and business accounting, _____ is a measure of a firm's profitability that excludes interest and income tax expenses.

EBIT = Operating Revenue - Operating Expenses (OPEX) + Non-operating Income

Operating Income = Operating Revenue - Operating Expenses

Operating income is the difference between operating revenues and operating expenses, but it is also sometimes used as a synonym for EBIT and operating profit. This is true if the firm has no non-operating income.

   a. ABC Television Network
   b. AIG
   c. AMEX
   d. Earnings before interest and taxes

25. _____ is a financial ratio that measures the efficiency of a company's use of its assets in generating sales revenue or sales income to the company.

$$Asset\ Turnover = \frac{Sales}{Average\ Total\ Assets}$$

- 'Sales' is the value of 'Net Sales' or 'Sales' from the company's income statement
- 'Average Total Assets' is the value of 'Total assets' from the company's balance sheet in the beginning and the end of the fiscal period divided by 2.

a. Enterprise Value/Sales
b. Asset turnover
c. Information ratio
d. Average propensity to consume

26. In accounting, a _____ is an asset on the balance sheet which is expected to be sold or otherwise used up in the near future, usually within one year, or one business cycle - whichever is longer. Typical _____s include cash, cash equivalents, accounts receivable, inventory, the portion of prepaid accounts which will be used within a year, and short-term investments.

On the balance sheet, assets will typically be classified into _____s and long-term assets.

a. Pro forma
b. General ledger
c. Deferred
d. Current asset

27. In accounting, _____ are considered liabilities of the business that are to be settled in cash within the fiscal year or the operating cycle, whichever period is longer.

For example accounts payable for goods, services or supplies that were purchased for use in the operation of the business and payable within a normal period of time would be _____.

Bonds, mortgages and loans that are payable over a term exceeding one year would be fixed liabilities.

a. Payroll
b. Treasury stock
c. Closing entries
d. Current liabilities

28. _____ is a financial metric which represents operating liquidity available to a business. Along with fixed assets such as plant and equipment, _____ is considered a part of operating capital. It is calculated as current assets minus current liabilities.

a. Working capital management
b. BMC Software, Inc.
c. Working capital
d. 3M Company

29. In economics, _____ or _____ goods or real _____ refers to factors of production used to create goods or services that are not themselves significantly consumed (though they may depreciate) in the production process. _____ goods may be acquired with money or financial _____. In finance and accounting, _____ generally refers to financial wealth, especially that used to start or maintain a business.

a. Screening
b. Disclosure
c. Capital
d. Vyborg Appeal

30. In financial accounting, a _____ is defined as an obligation of an entity arising from past transactions or events, the settlement of which may result in the transfer or use of assets, provision of services or other yielding of economic benefits in the future.

   a. Vested
   b. False Claims Act
   c. Liability
   d. Corporate governance

31. In finance, the _____ or quick ratio or liquid ratio measures the ability of a company to use its near cash or quick assets to immediately extinguish or retire its current liabilities. Quick assets include those current assets that presumably can be quickly converted to cash at close to their book values.

$$\text{Quick (Acid Test) Ratio} = \frac{\text{Cash} + \text{Marketable Securities} + \text{Accounts Receivables}}{\text{Current Liabilities}}$$

Generally, the acid test ratio should be 1:1 or better, however this varies widely by industry.

   a. Invested capital
   b. Earnings per share
   c. Acid-test
   d. Inventory turnover

32. The _____ is a financial ratio that measures whether or not a firm has enough resources to pay its debts over the next 12 months. It compares a firm's current assets to its current liabilities. It is expressed as follows:

$$\text{Current ratio} = \frac{\text{Current Assets}}{\text{Current Liabilities}}$$

For example, if WXY Company's current assets are $50,000,000 and its current liabilities are $40,000,000, then its _____ would be $50,000,000 divided by $40,000,000, which equals 1.25.

   a. Current ratio
   b. Return on capital
   c. Net Interest Income
   d. Times interest earned

33. _____ is the risk of loss due to a debtor's non-payment of a loan or other line of credit (either the principal or interest (coupon) or both)

Most lenders employ their own models (credit scorecards) to rank potential and existing customers according to risk, and then apply appropriate strategies. With products such as unsecured personal loans or mortgages, lenders charge a higher price for higher risk customers and vice versa. With revolving products such as credit cards and overdrafts, risk is controlled through the setting of credit limits.

   a. Credit risk
   b. 3M Company
   c. Market risk
   d. Currency risk

34. In economics, the _____, (or _____) measures the payments that flow between any individual country and all other countries. It is used to summarize all international economic transactions for that country during a specific time period, usually a year. The _____ is determined by the country's exports and imports of goods, services, and financial capital, as well as financial transfers.

a. Moving average
c. Yield to maturity
b. Stock split
d. Balance of payments

35. A _____ has several related meanings:

- a daily record of events or business; a private _____ is usually referred to as a diary.
- a newspaper or other periodical, in the literal sense of one published each day;
- many publications issued at stated intervals, such as magazines, or scholarly academic _____s, or the record of the transactions of a society, are often called _____s. Although _____ is sometimes used, erroneously, as a synonym for 'magazine,' in academic use, a _____ refers to a serious, scholarly publication, most often peer-reviewed. A non-scholarly magazine written for an educated audience about an industry or an area of professional activity is usually called a professional magazine.

The word 'journalist' for one whose business is writing for the public press has been in use since the end of the 17th century.

Open access _____s are scholarly _____s that are available to the reader without financial or other barrier other than access to the internet itself. Some are subsidized, and some require payment on behalf of the author. Subsidized _____s are financed by an academic institution or a government information center.

a. 3M Company
c. BNSF Railway
b. Journal
d. BMC Software, Inc.

Chapter 4. The Bookkeeping Process and Transaction Analysis

1. In financial accounting, a _____ or statement of financial position is a summary of a person's or organization's balances. Assets, liabilities and ownership equity are listed as of a specific date, such as the end of its financial year. A _____ is often described as a snapshot of a company's financial condition.
   - a. Statement of retained earnings
   - b. 3M Company
   - c. Financial statements
   - d. Balance sheet

2. _____ is the recording of the value of assets, liabilities, income, and expenses in the daybooks, journals, and ledgers, in which debit and credit entries are chronologically posted to record changes in value. _____ is often mistaken for accounting, which is the system of recording, verifying, and reporting such information. Practitioners of accounting are called accountants.
   - a. Bookkeeping
   - b. Debit and credit
   - c. Double-entry bookkeeping
   - d. Controlling account

3. _____ is equal to the income that a firm has after subtracting costs and expenses from the total revenue. _____ can be distributed among holders of common stock as a dividend or held by the firm as retained earnings.

   The items deducted will typically include tax expense, financing expense (interest expense), and minority interest. Likewise, preferred stock dividends will be subtracted too, though they are not an expense.

   - a. Matching principle
   - b. Long-term liabilities
   - c. Net income
   - d. Generally accepted accounting principles

4. The term _____, derived from the distinctive T shape, is frequently used when discussing or analyzing accounting or business transactions. _____s are used to represent general ledger accounts.

   Typically one or more Ts are drawn on a white board or blank piece of paper. A general ledger account name or number is then written above each T. Debit entries are recorded on the left side of the 'T' and credit entries are recorded on the right side of the 'T'.

   - a. BNSF Railway
   - b. T account
   - c. BMC Software, Inc.
   - d. 3M Company

5. In economics, the _____, (or _____) measures the payments that flow between any individual country and all other countries. It is used to summarize all international economic transactions for that country during a specific time period, usually a year. The _____ is determined by the country's exports and imports of goods, services, and financial capital, as well as financial transfers.
   - a. Yield to maturity
   - b. Stock split
   - c. Moving average
   - d. Balance of payments

6. _____ is a form of corporation equity ownership represented in the securities. It is a stock whose dividends are based on market fluctuations. It is dangerous in comparison to preferred shares and some other investment options, in that in the event of bankruptcy, _____ investors receive their funds after preferred stock holders, bondholders, creditors, etc. On the other hand, common shares on average perform better than preferred shares or bonds over time.
   - a. Common stock
   - b. Stock split
   - c. 3M Company
   - d. Growth investing

Chapter 4. The Bookkeeping Process and Transaction Analysis 43

7. In economics, _____ or _____ goods or real _____ refers to factors of production used to create goods or services that are not themselves significantly consumed (though they may depreciate) in the production process. _____ goods may be acquired with money or financial _____. In finance and accounting, _____ generally refers to financial wealth, especially that used to start or maintain a business.

    a. Screening   b. Capital

    c. Vyborg Appeal   d. Disclosure

8. _____ are payments made by a corporation to its shareholder members. It is the portion of corporate profits paid out to stockholders. When a corporation earns a profit or surplus, that money can be put to two uses: it can either be re-invested in the business (called retained earnings), or it can be paid to the shareholders as a dividend.

    a. Dividend yield   b. Dividend stripping

    c. Dividend payout ratio   d. Dividends

9. A _____ has several related meanings:

- a daily record of events or business; a private _____ is usually referred to as a diary.
- a newspaper or other periodical, in the literal sense of one published each day;
- many publications issued at stated intervals, such as magazines, or scholarly academic _____s, or the record of the transactions of a society, are often called _____s. Although _____ is sometimes used, erroneously, as a synonym for 'magazine,' in academic use, a _____ refers to a serious, scholarly publication, most often peer-reviewed. A non-scholarly magazine written for an educated audience about an industry or an area of professional activity is usually called a professional magazine.

The word 'journalist' for one whose business is writing for the public press has been in use since the end of the 17th century.

Open access _____s are scholarly _____s that are available to the reader without financial or other barrier other than access to the internet itself. Some are subsidized, and some require payment on behalf of the author. Subsidized _____s are financed by an academic institution or a government information center.

    a. BMC Software, Inc.   b. BNSF Railway

    c. Journal   d. 3M Company

10. _____ of something is, in finance, the adding together of interest or different investments over a period of time such as atoms (1 - the act or process of accruing; 2 - the amount that accrues.) It holds specific meanings in accounting and payroll.

_____, in accounting, describes the accounting method known as _____ basis, whereby revenues and expenses are recognized when they are accrued, i.e. accumulated (earned or incurred), regardless when the actual cash is received or paid out.

    a. Assets   b. Earnings before interest, taxes, depreciation and amortization

    c. Accounts receivable   d. Accrual

11. _____ is a specific term used in companies' financial reporting from the company-whole point of view. Because that use excludes the effects of changing ownership interest, an economic measure of _____ is necessary for financial analysis from the shareholders' point of view

_____ is defined by the Financial Accounting Standards Board, or FASB, as 'the change in equity [net assets] of a business enterprise during a period from transactions and other events and circumstances from nonowner sources. It includes all changes in equity during a period except those resulting from investments by owners and distributions to owners.'

_____ is the sum of net income and other items that must bypass the income statement because they have not been realized, including items like an unrealized holding gain or loss from available for sale securities and foreign currency translation gains or losses.

a. BNSF Railway
b. Comprehensive income
c. 3M Company
d. BMC Software, Inc.

12. _____ is a list of the accounts including a unique number of each allowing to locate it in each ledger. The list is typically arranged in the order of the customary appearance of accounts in the financial statements. A _____ can track a specific financial information.

a. General journal
b. Journal entry
c. General ledger
d. Chart of accounts

13. _____ and credit are formal bookkeeping and accounting terms. They are the most fundamental concepts in accounting, representing the two records that one party in a transaction makes on its records, transferring a money balance from one account to another, one representing a reduction of liability or increase in asset, and the other representing a balancing increase in liability or reduction of asset.

Introduction

_____s and credits are a system of notation used in accounting to keep track of money movements (transactions) into and out of an account.

a. Debit and credit
b. Cookie jar accounting
c. Debit
d. Bookkeeping

14. A _____, in accounting, is a logging of transcriptions into items accounting journal. The _____ can consist of several items, each of which is either a debit or a credit. The total of the debits must equal the total of the credits, or the _____ is said to be 'unbalanced.' Journal entries can record unique items or recurring items such as depreciation or bond amortization.

a. Sales journal
b. General journal
c. General ledger
d. Journal entry

15. A _____ is a common type of chart, that represents an algorithm or process, showing the steps as boxes of various kinds, and their order by connecting these with arrows. _____s are used in analyzing, designing, documenting or managing a process or program in various fields.

Chapter 4. The Bookkeeping Process and Transaction Analysis 45

The first structured method for documenting process flow, the 'flow process chart', was introduced by Frank Gilbreth to members of ASME in 1921 as the presentation e;Process Charts--First Steps in Finding the One Best Waye;.

a. BMC Software, Inc.
b. BNSF Railway
c. 3M Company
d. Flowchart

16. _____ are formal records of a business' financial activities.

In British English, including United Kingdom company law, _____ are often referred to as accounts, although the term _____ is also used, particularly by accountants.

_____ provide an overview of a business' financial condition in both short and long term.

a. Statement of retained earnings
b. 3M Company
c. Notes to the financial statements
d. Financial statements

17. An _____ invented by esteemed professor Karen Osterheld is the system of records a business keeps to maintain its accounting system. This includes the purchase, sales, and other financial processes of the business. The purpose of an _____ is to accumulate data and provide decision makers (investors, creditors, and managers) with information to make decision While this was previously a paper-based process, most modern businesses now use accounting software such as UBS, MYOB etc.

a. AIG
b. ABC Television Network
c. AMEX
d. Accounting information system

18. _____ is application software that records and processes accounting transactions within functional modules such as accounts payable, accounts receivable, payroll, and trial balance. It functions as an accounting information system. It may be developed in-house by the company or organization using it, may be purchased from a third party, or may be a combination of a third-party application software package with local modifications.

a. AIG
b. Economic value added
c. Amgen
d. Accounting software

19. _____ describes commerce transactions between businesses, such as between a manufacturer and a wholesaler, or between a wholesaler and a retailer. Contrasting terms are business-to-consumer (B2C) and business-to-government (B2G.)

The volume of B2B transactions is much higher than the volume of B2C transactions.

a. Market share
b. Value chain
c. Market segment
d. Business-to-business

20. The US Department of Commerce created the Safe Harbor certification program in response to the 1995 Directive on _____ of the European Commission Historically, establishing adequacy required the creation of national laws broadly equivalent to those implemented by Directive 95/46/EU.

a. Laffer curve
b. Data protection
c. North American Free Trade Agreement
d. Return on assets

21. _____ is a term used in accounting, economics and finance to spread the cost of an asset over the span of several years.

In simple words we can say that _____ is the reduction in the value of an asset due to usage, passage of time, wear and tear, technological outdating or obsolescence, depletion, inadequacy, rot, rust, decay or other such factors.

In accounting, _____ is a term used to describe any method of attributing the historical or purchase cost of an asset across its useful life, roughly corresponding to normal wear and tear.

a. Current asset
b. Depreciation
c. General ledger
d. Net profit

22. _____, commonly known as e-commerce or eCommerce, consists of the buying and selling of products or services over electronic systems such as the Internet and other computer networks. The amount of trade conducted electronically has grown extraordinarily since the spread of the Internet. A wide variety of commerce is conducted in this way, spurring and drawing on innovations in electronic funds transfer, supply chain management, Internet marketing, online transaction processing, electronic data interchange (EDI), inventory management systems, and automated data collection systems.

a. ABC Television Network
b. AIG
c. Electronic data interchange
d. Electronic commerce

23. In physics, and more specifically kinematics, _____ is the change in velocity over time. Because velocity is a vector, it can change in two ways: a change in magnitude and/or a change in direction. In one dimension, _____ is the rate at which something speeds up or slows down.

a. AIG
b. AMEX
c. Acceleration
d. ABC Television Network

24. _____ is a method of accounting whereby economic activities (rather than cash flow) of financial events are considered, because of two complementary principles, which (together) determine the point, at which expenses and revenues are recognized. According to revenue recognition principle, revenues are realized when earned, whether or not they are received in cash.

a. Accrual basis accounting
b. Earnings before interest, taxes, depreciation and amortization
c. Accrual
d. Accrued revenue

25. In accounting, _____ has a very specific meaning. It is an outflow of cash or other valuable assets from a person or company to another person or company. This outflow of cash is generally one side of a trade for products or services that have equal or better current or future value to the buyer than to the seller.

a. Expense
b. AMEX
c. ABC Television Network
d. AIG

Chapter 4. The Bookkeeping Process and Transaction Analysis

26. _____ is a company's financial statement that indicates how the revenue is transformed into the net income The purpose of the _____ is to show managers and investors whether the company made or lost money during the period being reported.

The important thing to remember about an _____ is that it represents a period of time.

a. ABC Television Network
b. Income statement
c. AMEX
d. AIG

27. _____ principle is a cornerstone of accrual accounting together with matching principle. They both determine the accounting period, in which revenues and expenses are recognized. According to the principle, revenues are recognized when they are (1) realized or realizable, and are (2) earned (usually when goods are transferred or services rendered), no matter when cash is received.

a. Net realizable value
b. 3M Company
c. BMC Software, Inc.
d. Revenue recognition

28. _____ are liabilities which have occurred, but have not been paid or logged under accounts payable during an accounting period; in other words, obligations for goods and services provided to a company for which invoices have not yet been received. Examples would include accrued wages payable, accrued sales tax payable, and accrued rent payable.

There are two general types of _____:

- Routine and recurring
- Infrequent or non-routine

Most companies pay their employees on a predetermined schedule. Let's say that the 'Imaginary company Ltd.' pays its employees each Friday for the hours worked that week.

a. AMEX
b. AIG
c. Accrued liabilities
d. ABC Television Network

29. In financial accounting, a _____ is defined as an obligation of an entity arising from past transactions or events, the settlement of which may result in the transfer or use of assets, provision of services or other yielding of economic benefits in the future.

a. Vested
b. Corporate governance
c. False Claims Act
d. Liability

30. _____ are additional notes and information added to the end of the financial statements to supplement the reader with more information. Notes to Financial Statements help explain the computation of specific items in the financial statements as well as provide a more comprehensive assessment of a company's financial condition. Notes to Financial Statements can include information on debt, going concern, accounts, contingent liabilities, or contextual information explaining the financial numbers (e.g. to indicate a lawsuit.)

a. Financial statements
b. 3M Company
c. Notes to the financial statements
d. Statement of retained earnings

31. A _____ is a compensation, usually financial, received by a worker in exchange for their labor.

Compensation in terms of _____s is given to worker and compensation in terms of salary is given to employees. Compensation is a monetary benefits given to employees in returns of the services provided by them.

   a. Retirement plan   b. BMC Software, Inc.
   c. Wage   d. 3M Company

32. _____ refers to services paid for in advance. Examples include tolls, pay as you go cell phones, and stored-value cards such as gift cards and preloaded credit cards. _____ accounts are assets, and they are increased by debiting the account(s.)
   a. Prepaid   b. 3M Company
   c. BMC Software, Inc.   d. BNSF Railway

33. _____, in law and economics, is a form of risk management primarily used to hedge against the risk of a contingent loss. _____ is defined as the equitable transfer of the risk of a loss, from one entity to another, in exchange for a premium, and can be thought of as a guaranteed small loss to prevent a large, possibly devastating loss. An insurer is a company selling the _____; an insured is the person or entity buying the _____.
   a. AIG   b. AMEX
   c. ABC Television Network   d. Insurance

34. _____ is a business, economics or investment term that refers to an asset's ability to be easily converted through an act of buying or selling without causing a significant movement in the price and with minimum loss of value. Money, or cash on hand, is the most liquid asset. An act of exchange of a less liquid asset with a more liquid asset is called liquidation.
   a. Spot rate   b. Financial instruments
   c. Transfer agent   d. Market liquidity

Chapter 5. Accounting for and Presentation of Current Assets

1. _____ is one of a series of accounting transactions dealing with the billing of customers who owe money to a person, company or organization for goods and services that have been provided to the customer. In most business entities this is typically done by generating an invoice and mailing or electronically delivering it to the customer, who in turn must pay it within an established timeframe called credit or payment terms.

An example of a common payment term is Net 30, meaning payment is due in the amount of the invoice 30 days from the date of invoice.

   a. Accrued revenue
   b. Adjusting entries
   c. Accounts receivable
   d. Accrual

2. In business and accounting, _____ are everything of value that is owned by a person or company. It is a claim on the property your income of a borrower. The balance sheet of a firm records the monetary value of the _____ owned by the firm.

   a. Accrual basis accounting
   b. Earnings before interest, taxes, depreciation and amortization
   c. Accounts receivable
   d. Assets

3. In financial accounting, a _____ or statement of financial position is a summary of a person's or organization's balances. Assets, liabilities and ownership equity are listed as of a specific date, such as the end of its financial year. A _____ is often described as a snapshot of a company's financial condition.

   a. Financial statements
   b. 3M Company
   c. Statement of retained earnings
   d. Balance sheet

4. _____ is a company's financial statement that indicates how the revenue is transformed into the net income The purpose of the _____ is to show managers and investors whether the company made or lost money during the period being reported.

The important thing to remember about an _____ is that it represents a period of time.

   a. ABC Television Network
   b. AIG
   c. AMEX
   d. Income statement

5. _____ is the process of matching and comparing figures from accounting records against those presented on a bank statement. Less any items which have no relation to the bank statement, the balance of the accounting ledger should reconcile (match) to the balance of the bank statement.

_____ allows companies or individuals to compare their account records to the bank's records of their account balance in order to uncover any possible discrepancies.

   a. Bankruptcy prediction
   b. Lower of Cost or Market
   c. Credit memo
   d. Bank reconciliation

6. In finance, a _____ is a debt security, in which the authorized issuer owes the holders a debt and, depending on the terms of the _____, is obliged to pay interest (the coupon) and/or to repay the principal at a later date, termed maturity. It is a formal contract to repay borrowed money with interest at fixed intervals.

Chapter 5. Accounting for and Presentation of Current Assets

Thus a _____ is like a loan: the issuer is the borrower, the _____ holder is the lender, and the coupon is the interest.

a. Zero-coupon bond
b. Revenue bonds
c. Coupon rate
d. Bond

7. _____ are the most liquid assets found within the asset portion of a company's balance sheet. Cash equivalents are assets that are readily convertible into cash, such as money market holdings, short-term government bonds or Treasury bills, marketable securities and commercial paper. _____ are distinguished from other investments through their short-term existence; they mature within 3 months whereas short-term investments are 12 months or less, and long-term investments are any investments that mature in excess of 12 months.

a. Cash and cash equivalents
b. Par value
c. Debtor
d. Payback period

8. In United States banking, _____ is a marketing term for certain services offered primarily to larger business customers. It may be used to describe all bank accounts (such as checking accounts) provided to businesses of a certain size, but it is more often used to describe specific services such as cash concentration, zero balance accounting, and automated clearing house facilities. Sometimes, private banking customers are given _____ services.

a. Profitability index
b. 3M Company
c. Finance lease
d. Cash management

9. An _____ is a term used in behavioral economics to describe those types of behaviors that impose costs on a person in the long-run that are not taken into account when making decisions in the present. Classical Economics discourages government from creating legislation that targets internalities, because it is assumed that the consumer takes these personal costs into account when paying for the good that causes the _____. For example, cigarettes should be taxed because of the negative consumption externalities that they impose, such as second-hand smoke, not because the smoker harms him or herself by smoking.

a. Inventory turnover ratio
b. Operating budget
c. Authorised capital
d. Internality

10. In accounting and organizational theory, _____ is defined as a process effected by an organization's structure, work and authority flows, people and management information systems, designed to help the organization accomplish specific goals or objectives. It is a means by which an organization's resources are directed, monitored, and measured. It plays an important role in preventing and detecting fraud and protecting the organization's resources, both physical (e.g., machinery and property) and intangible (e.g., reputation or intellectual property such as trademarks.)

a. Audit risk
b. Auditor independence
c. Audit committee
d. Internal control

11. _____ is often a small amount of discretionary funds in the form of cash used for expenditures where it is not sensible to make the disbursement by check, because of the inconvenience and costs of writing, signing and then cashing the check.

The most common way of accounting expenditures is to use the imprest system. The initial fund would be created by issuing a check for the desired amount.

Chapter 5. Accounting for and Presentation of Current Assets

a. Minority interest
c. Fixed asset
b. Remittance advice
d. Petty cash

12. In finance, _____ also known as return on investment, rate of profit or sometimes just return, is the ratio of money gained or lost on an investment relative to the amount of money invested. The amount of money gained or lost may be referred to as interest, profit/loss, gain/loss, or net income/loss. The money invested may be referred to as the asset, capital, principal, or the cost basis of the investment.

a. Debt to capital ratio
c. Theoretical ex-rights price
b. Capital employed
d. Rate of return

13. A _____ is a fungible, negotiable instrument representing financial value. they are broadly categorized into debt securities (such as banknotes, bonds and debentures), and equity securities; e.g., common stocks. The company or other entity issuing the _____ is called the issuer.

a. Tracking stock
c. BMC Software, Inc.
b. 3M Company
d. Security

14. The term _____ is used in finance theory to refer to any terminating stream of fixed payments over a specified period of time. This usage is most commonly seen in academic discussions of finance, usually in connection with the valuation of the stream of payments, taking into account time value of money concepts such as interest rate and future value.

Examples of these are regular deposits to a savings account, monthly home mortgage payments and monthly insurance payments.

a. Appropriation
c. Improvement
b. Intangible
d. Annuity

15. In the global money market, _____ is an unsecured promissory note with a fixed maturity of one to 270 days. _____ is a money-market security issued (sold) by large banks and corporations to get money to meet short term debt obligations (for example, payroll), and is only backed by an issuing bank or corporation's promise to pay the face amount on the maturity date specified on the note. Since it is not backed by collateral, only firms with excellent credit ratings from a recognized rating agency will be able to sell their _____ at a reasonable price.

a. Gross profit margin
c. Controlling interest
b. Commercial paper
d. Flow-through entity

16. In accounting, a _____ is an asset on the balance sheet which is expected to be sold or otherwise used up in the near future, usually within one year, or one business cycle - whichever is longer. Typical _____s include cash, cash equivalents, accounts receivable, inventory, the portion of prepaid accounts which will be used within a year, and short-term investments.

On the balance sheet, assets will typically be classified into _____s and long-term assets.

a. Pro forma
c. Deferred
b. Current asset
d. General ledger

Chapter 5. Accounting for and Presentation of Current Assets

17. A _____ is a bond which is worth a certain monetary value and which may only be spent for specific reasons or on specific goods. Examples include -- but are not limited to -- housing, travel and food _____s. The term _____ is also a synonym for receipt, and is often used to refer to receipts used as evidence of, for example, the declaration that a service has been performed or that an expenditure has been made.
- a. Source document
- b. Voucher
- c. BMC Software, Inc.
- d. 3M Company

18. _____ is the concept of having more than one person required to complete a task. It is alternatively called segregation of duties or, in the political realm, separation of powers.

_____ is one of the key concepts of internal control and is the most difficult and sometimes the most costly one to achieve. The term _____ is already well-known in financial accounting systems. Companies in all sizes understand not to combine roles such as receiving checks (payment on account) and approving write-offs, depositing cash and reconciling bank statements, approving time cards and have custody of pay checks, etc.

- a. BMC Software, Inc.
- b. Salary
- c. 3M Company
- d. Separation of duties

19. In economics, the _____, (or _____) measures the payments that flow between any individual country and all other countries. It is used to summarize all international economic transactions for that country during a specific time period, usually a year. The _____ is determined by the country's exports and imports of goods, services, and financial capital, as well as financial transfers.
- a. Yield to maturity
- b. Balance of payments
- c. Moving average
- d. Stock split

20. _____ is the balance of the amounts of cash being received and paid by a business during a defined period of time, sometimes tied to a specific project. Measurement of _____ can be used

- to evaluate the state or performance of a business or project.
- to determine problems with liquidity. Being profitable does not necessarily mean being liquid. A company can fail because of a shortage of cash, even while profitable.
- to project rate of returns. The time of _____s into and out of projects are used as inputs to financial models such as internal rate of return, and net present value.
- to examine income or growth of a business when it is believed that accrual accounting concepts do not represent economic realities. Alternately, _____ can be used to 'validate' the net income generated by accrual accounting.

_____ as a generic term may be used differently depending on context, and certain _____ definitions may be adapted by analysts and users for their own uses. Common terms include operating _____ and free _____.

- a. Controlling interest
- b. Cash flow
- c. Flow-through entity
- d. Commercial paper

Chapter 5. Accounting for and Presentation of Current Assets

21. A _____ is any one of a variety of different systems, institutions, procedures, social relations and infrastructures whereby persons trade, and goods and services are exchanged, forming part of the economy. It is an arrangement that allows buyers and sellers to exchange things. _____s vary in size, range, geographic scale, location, types and variety of human communities, as well as the types of goods and services traded.
- a. Market Failure
- b. Recession
- c. Perfect competition
- d. Market

22. _____ is the price at which an asset would trade in a competitive Walrasian auction setting. _____ is often used interchangeably with open _____, fair value or fair _____, although these terms have distinct definitions in different standards, and may differ in some circumstances.

International Valuation Standards defines _____ as 'the estimated amount for which a property should exchange on the date of valuation between a willing buyer and a willing seller in an arme;s-length transaction after proper marketing wherein the parties had each acted knowledgeably, prudently, and without compulsion.'

_____ is a concept distinct from market price, which is e;the price at which one can transacte;, while _____ is e;the true underlying valuee; according to theoretical standards.

- a. Segregated portfolio company
- b. Debtor
- c. Market value
- d. Sinking fund

23. In economics, the concept of the _____ refers to the decision-making time frame of a firm in which at least one factor of production is fixed. Costs which are fixed in the _____ have no impact on a firms decisions. For example a firm can raise output by increasing the amount of labour through overtime.
- a. BMC Software, Inc.
- b. 3M Company
- c. Long-run
- d. Short-run

24. The term _____, derived from the distinctive T shape, is frequently used when discussing or analyzing accounting or business transactions. _____s are used to represent general ledger accounts.

Typically one or more Ts are drawn on a white board or blank piece of paper. A general ledger account name or number is then written above each T. Debit entries are recorded on the left side of the 'T' and credit entries are recorded on the right side of the 'T'.

- a. BMC Software, Inc.
- b. 3M Company
- c. BNSF Railway
- d. T account

25. _____ are securities that can be easily converted into cash. Such securities will generally have highly liquid markets allowing the security to be sold at a reasonable price very quickly. This is a usual feature in real estate .
- a. Marketable
- b. 3M Company
- c. BMC Software, Inc.
- d. Tracking stock

Chapter 5. Accounting for and Presentation of Current Assets

26. In finance, _____ is the process of estimating the potential market value of a financial asset or liability. They can be done on assets (for example, investments in marketable securities such as stocks, options, business enterprises, or intangible assets such as patents and trademarks) or on liabilities (e.g., Bonds issued by a company.) A _____ is required in many contexts including investment analysis, capital budgeting, merger and acquisition transactions, financial reporting, taxable events to determine the proper tax liability, and in litigation.
   a. Vyborg Appeal
   b. Daybook
   c. Disclosure
   d. Valuation

27. _____ is a fee paid on borrowed assets. It is the price paid for the use of borrowed money, or, money earned by deposited funds. Assets that are sometimes lent with _____ include money, shares, consumer goods through hire purchase, major assets such as aircraft, and even entire factories in finance lease arrangements. The _____ is calculated upon the value of the assets in the same manner as upon money.
   a. ABC Television Network
   b. Insolvency
   c. AIG
   d. Interest

28. _____ is a cornerstone of accrual accounting together with the revenue recognition principle. They both determine the accounting period, in which revenues and expenses are recognized. According to the principle, expenses are recognized when obligations are (1) incurred (usually when goods are transferred or services rendered, e.g. sold), and (2) offset against recognized revenues, which were generated from those expenses (related on the cause-and-effect basis), no matter when cash is paid out.
   a. Net sales
   b. Current liabilities
   c. Matching principle
   d. Payroll

29. _____ of something is, in finance, the adding together of interest or different investments over a period of time such as atoms (1 - the act or process of accruing; 2 - the amount that accrues.) It holds specific meanings in accounting and payroll.

   _____, in accounting, describes the accounting method known as _____ basis, whereby revenues and expenses are recognized when they are accrued, i.e. accumulated (earned or incurred), regardless when the actual cash is received or paid out.

   a. Earnings before interest, taxes, depreciation and amortization
   b. Assets
   c. Accounts receivable
   d. Accrual

30. In finance, _____ is the interest that has accumulated since the principal investment, or since the previous interest payment if there has been one already. For a financial instrument such as a bond, interest is calculated and paid in set intervals.

The primary formula for calculating the interest accrued in a given period is:

$$I_A = T \times P \times R$$

where I_A is the _____, T is the fraction of the year, P is the principal, and R is the annualized interest rate.

Chapter 5. Accounting for and Presentation of Current Assets 55

a. Interest
b. AIG
c. ABC Television Network
d. Accrued interest

31. In financial accounting and finance, _____ is the portion of receivables that can no longer be collected, typically from accounts receivable or loans. _____ in accounting is considered an expense.

There are two methods to account for _____:

1. Direct write off method (Non - GAAP)

A receivable which is not considered collectible is charged directly to the income statement.

1. Allowance method (GAAP)

An estimate is made at the end of each fiscal year of the amount of _____. This is then accumulated in a provision which is then used to reduce specific receivable accounts as and when necessary.

a. 3M Company
b. Total Expense Ratio
c. Tax expense
d. Bad debt

32. In accounting, _____ or carrying value is the value of an asset according to its balance sheet account balance. For assets, the value is based on the original cost of the asset less any depreciation, amortization or impairment costs made against the asset. Traditionally, a company's _____ is its total assets minus intangible assets and liabilities.
a. Generally accepted accounting principles
b. Matching principle
c. Depreciation
d. Book value

33. _____ is the risk of loss due to a debtor's non-payment of a loan or other line of credit (either the principal or interest (coupon) or both)

Most lenders employ their own models (credit scorecards) to rank potential and existing customers according to risk, and then apply appropriate strategies. With products such as unsecured personal loans or mortgages, lenders charge a higher price for higher risk customers and vice versa. With revolving products such as credit cards and overdrafts, risk is controlled through the setting of credit limits.

a. Credit risk
b. Market risk
c. Currency risk
d. 3M Company

34. _____ is the term used to refer to the standard framework of guidelines for financial accounting used in any given jurisdiction. _____ includes the standards, conventions, and rules accountants follow in recording and summarizing transactions, and in the preparation of financial statements.

Financial accounting information must be assembled and reported objectively.

a. Long-term liabilities
b. General ledger
c. Current asset
d. Generally accepted accounting principles

35. _____ is a method of evaluating an asset's worth when held in inventory, in the field of accounting. _____ is part of the Generally Accepted Accounting Principles that apply to valuing inventory, so as to not overstate or understate the value of inventory goods. Net realisable value is generally equal to the selling price of the inventory goods less the selling costs (completion and disposal).
a. Net realizable value
b. BMC Software, Inc.
c. Revenue recognition
d. 3M Company

36. _____ is that which is owed; usually referencing assets owed, but the term can also cover moral obligations and other interactions not requiring money. In the case of assets, _____ is a means of using future purchasing power in the present before a summation has been earned. Some companies and corporations use _____ as a part of their overall corporate finance strategy.
a. Lender
b. Debt
c. Loan
d. Debenture

37. In accounting, _____ has a very specific meaning. It is an outflow of cash or other valuable assets from a person or company to another person or company. This outflow of cash is generally one side of a trade for products or services that have equal or better current or future value to the buyer than to the seller.
a. AMEX
b. AIG
c. Expense
d. ABC Television Network

38. _____ is a concept that denotes the precise probability of specific eventualities. Technically, the notion of _____ is independent from the notion of value and, as such, eventualities may have both beneficial and adverse consequences. However, in general usage the convention is to focus only on potential negative impact to some characteristic of value that may arise from a future event.
a. Risk
b. Discounting
c. Discount factor
d. Risk adjusted return on capital

39. A _____ is the pinnacle activity involved in selling products or services in return for money or other compensation. It is an act of completion of a commercial activity.

A _____ is completed by the seller, the owner of the goods.

a. High yield stock
b. Sale
c. Tertiary sector of economy
d. Maturity

40. The term _____ describes a reduction in recognized value. In accounting terminology, it refers to recognition of the reduced or zero value of an asset. In income tax statements, it refers to a reduction of taxable income as recognition of certain expenses required to produce the income.
a. Current asset
b. Payroll
c. Write-off
d. Salvage value

Chapter 5. Accounting for and Presentation of Current Assets

41. _____ are reductions to a basic price of goods or services. They can occur anywhere in the distribution channel, modifying either the manufacturer's list price (determined by the manufacturer and often printed on the package), the retail price (set by the retailer and often attached to the product with a sticker), or the list price (which is quoted to a potential buyer, usually in written form.) The market price (also called effective price) is the amount actually paid.
   a. Target costing
   b. Pricing
   c. Resale price maintenance
   d. Discounts and allowances

42. An _____ or bill is a commercial document issued by a seller to the buyer, indicating the products, quantities, and agreed prices for products or services the seller has provided the buyer. An _____ indicates the buyer must pay the seller, according to the payment terms.

In the rental industry, an _____ must include a specific reference to the duration of the time being billed, so rather than quantity, price and discount the invoicing amount is based on quantity, price, discount and duration.

   a. ABC Television Network
   b. AMEX
   c. AIG
   d. Invoice

43. Discounting is a financial mechanism in which a debtor obtains the right to delay payments to a creditor, for a defined period of time, in exchange for a charge or fee. Essentially, the party that owes money in the present purchases the right to delay the payment until some future date. The _____, or charge, is simply the difference between the original amount owed in the present and the amount that has to be paid in the future to settle the debt.
   a. Risk aversion
   b. Discount
   c. Discounting
   d. Discount factor

44. Title _____s serve as guarantees to the recipient of property, ensuring that the recipient receives what he or she bargained for. The English _____s of title, sometimes included in deeds to real property, are that the grantor is lawfully seized (in fee simple) of the property, (2) that the grantor has the right to convey the property to the grantee, (3) that the property is conveyed without encumbrances (this _____ is frequently modified to allow for certain encumbrances), (4) that the grantor has done no act to encumber the property, (5) that the grantee shall have quiet possession of the property, and (6) that the grantor will execute such further assurances of the land as may be requisite (Nos. 3 and 4, which overlap significantly, are sometimes treated as one item.)
   a. Patent
   b. Liability
   c. Tax patent
   d. Covenant

45. _____ represents claims for which formal instruments of credit are issued as evidence of debt, such as a promissory note. The credit instrument normally requires the debtor to pay interest and extends for time periods of 60-90 days or longer.
   a. Notes receivable
   b. Restricted stock
   c. Moving average
   d. Public offering

46. An _____ is a loan that is repaid over time with a set number of scheduled payments. The term of loan may be as little as a few months and as long as 30 years. A mortgage, for example, may be considered a type of _____.
   a. AIG
   b. ABC Television Network
   c. AMEX
   d. Installment loan

Chapter 5. Accounting for and Presentation of Current Assets

47. A _____ is a type of debt Like all debt instruments, a _____ entails the redistribution of financial assets over time, between the lender and the borrower.
   a. Debenture
   b. Loan to value
   c. Lender
   d. Loan

48. In economics, business, retail, and accounting, a _____ is the value of money that has been used up to produce something, and hence is not available for use anymore. In economics, a _____ is an alternative that is given up as a result of a decision. In business, the _____ may be one of acquisition, in which case the amount of money expended to acquire it is counted as _____.
   a. Cost allocation
   b. Prime cost
   c. Cost
   d. Cost of quality

49. In financial accounting, _____ or cost of sales includes the direct costs attributable to the production of the goods sold by a company. This amount includes the materials cost used in creating the goods along with the direct labor costs used to produce the good. It excludes indirect expenses such as distribution costs and sales force costs.
   a. Reorder point
   b. FIFO and LIFO accounting
   c. 3M Company
   d. Cost of goods sold

50. Procter is a surname, and may also refer to:

   - Bryan Waller Procter (pseud. Barry Cornwall), English poet
   - Goodwin Procter, American law firm
   - _____, consumer products multinational

   a. Markup
   b. Procter ' Gamble
   c. Welfare
   d. Screening

51. _____ methods are means of managing inventory and financial matters involving the money a company ties up within inventory of produced goods, raw materials, parts, components, or feed stocks. FIFO stands for first-in, first-out, meaning that the oldest inventory items are recorded as sold first. LIFO stands for last-in, first-out, meaning that the most recently purchased items are recorded as sold first.
   a. Reorder point
   b. 3M Company
   c. Finished good
   d. FIFO and LIFO accounting

52. _____ principle is a cornerstone of accrual accounting together with matching principle. They both determine the accounting period, in which revenues and expenses are recognized. According to the principle, revenues are recognized when they are (1) realized or realizable, and are (2) earned (usually when goods are transferred or services rendered), no matter when cash is received.
   a. Net realizable value
   b. BMC Software, Inc.
   c. Revenue recognition
   d. 3M Company

Chapter 5. Accounting for and Presentation of Current Assets 59

53. In law, _____ refers to the process by which a company (or part of a company) is brought to an end, and the assets and property of the company redistributed. _____ can also be referred to as winding-up or dissolution, although dissolution technically refers to the last stage of _____. The process of _____ also arises when customs, an authority or agency in a country responsible for collecting and safeguarding customs duties, determines the final computation or ascertainment of the duties or drawback accruing on an entry.

    a. Liquidation   b. Bankruptcy protection
    c. 3M Company   d. BMC Software, Inc.

54. In economics, _____ is a sustained decrease in the general price level of goods and services. _____ occurs when the annual inflation rate falls below zero percent, resulting in an increase in the real value of money -- a negative inflation rate. This should not be confused with disinflation, a slow-down in the inflation rate (i.e. when the inflation decreases, but still remains positive.)

    a. Nominal value   b. Market Failure
    c. Recession   d. Deflation

55. In economics, _____ is a rise in the general level of prices of goods and services in an economy over a period of time. When the general price level rises, each unit of currency buys fewer goods and services; consequently, _____ is also a decline in the real value of money--a loss of purchasing power in the medium of exchange which is also the monetary unit of account in the economy. A chief measure of general price-level _____ is the general _____ rate, which is the percentage change in a general price index (normally the Consumer Price Index) over time.

    a. Opportunity cost   b. AIG
    c. Inflation   d. ABC Television Network

56. In mathematics _____s are numbers or other things that get multiplied. In particular, see:

- Factorization, the decomposition of an object into a product of other objects
- Integer factorization, the process of breaking down a composite number into smaller non-trivial divisors
- A coefficient
- A divisor of a particular number, or of an element of a monoid
- A von Neumann algebra with a trivial center

In statistics

- _____ analysis is the study of how _____s or certain variables affect variables.

In technology:

- Human _____s, a profession that focuses on how people interact with products, tools, or procedures
- 'Functionality, Application domain, Conditions, Technology, Objects and Responsibility;', In object-oriented programming

60 *Chapter 5. Accounting for and Presentation of Current Assets*

In computer science and information technology:

- Authentication _____, a piece of information used to verify a person's identity for security purposes
- _____, a Unix command for numbers factorization
- _____ (programming language), an experimental Forth-like programming language

In television:

- The O'Reilly _____, an American talk show hosted by Bill O'Reilly on Fox News.
- The Krypton _____, a British game show hosted by Gordon Burns, formally on ITV. Also had an American version.

a. Valuation
b. The Goodyear Tire ' Rubber Company
c. Merck ' Co., Inc.
d. Factor

57. An _____ is a tax levied on the financial income of people, corporations, or other legal entities. Various _____ systems exist, with varying degrees of tax incidence. Income taxation can be progressive, proportional, or regressive.

a. Individual Retirement Arrangement
b. Ordinary income
c. Implied level of government service
d. Income tax

58. The _____ is the United States federal government agency that collects taxes and enforces the internal revenue laws. It is an agency within the U.S. Dept of the treasury responsible for interpretation and application of Federal tax law. The official U.S. Treasury regulations provide (in part):

The _____ is a bureau of the Department of the Treasury under the immediate direction of the Commissioner of Internal Revenue.

a. Use tax
b. Income tax
c. Indirect tax
d. Internal Revenue Service

59. _____, in accrual accounting, is any account where the asset or liability is not realized until a future date (accounting period), e.g. annuities, charges, taxes, income, etc. The _____ item may be carried, dependent on type of deferral, as either an asset or liability.

a. Pro forma
b. Payroll
c. Deferred
d. Cash basis accounting

60. _____s are goods that have completed the manufacturing process but have not yet been sold or distributed to the end user.

Chapter 5. Accounting for and Presentation of Current Assets

Manufacturing has three classes of inventory:

1. Raw material
2. Work in process
3. _____s

A good purchased as a 'raw material' goes into the manufacture of a product. A good only partially completed during the manufacturing process is called 'work in process'. When the good is completed as to manufacturing but not yet sold or distributed to the end-user is called a '_____'.

a. 3M Company
c. Reorder point
b. FIFO and LIFO accounting
d. Finished good

61. _____ is a process where a business physically counts its entire inventory. A _____ may be mandated by financial accounting rules or the tax regulations to place an accurate value on the inventory, or the business may need to count inventory so component parts or raw materials can be restocked. Businesses may use several different tactics to minimize the disruption caused by _____.

a. BMC Software, Inc.
c. 3M Company
b. BNSF Railway
d. Physical inventory

62. A _____ is something that is acted upon or used by or by human labour or industry, for use as a building material to create some product or structure. Often the term is used to denote material that came from nature and is in an unprocessed or minimally processed state. Iron ore, logs, and crude oil, would be examples.

a. 3M Company
c. BMC Software, Inc.
b. BNSF Railway
d. Raw material

63. _____ or in-process inventory includes the set at large of unfinished items for products in a production process. These items are not yet completed but either just being fabricated or waiting in a queue for further processing or in a buffer storage. The term is used in production and supply chain management.

a. Work in process
c. 3M Company
b. BNSF Railway
d. BMC Software, Inc.

64. _____ is equal to the income that a firm has after subtracting costs and expenses from the total revenue. _____ can be distributed among holders of common stock as a dividend or held by the firm as retained earnings.

The items deducted will typically include tax expense, financing expense (interest expense), and minority interest. Likewise, preferred stock dividends will be subtracted too, though they are not an expense.

a. Generally accepted accounting principles
c. Net income
b. Long-term liabilities
d. Matching principle

65. _____ and credit are formal bookkeeping and accounting terms. They are the most fundamental concepts in accounting, representing the two records that one party in a transaction makes on its records, transferring a money balance from one account to another, one representing a reduction of liability or increase in asset, and the other representing a balancing increase in liability or reduction of asset.

Chapter 5. Accounting for and Presentation of Current Assets

Introduction

_____s and credits are a system of notation used in accounting to keep track of money movements (transactions) into and out of an account.

a. Debit and credit
b. Cookie jar accounting
c. Bookkeeping
d. Debit

66. In accounting, _____ or sales profit is the difference between revenue and the cost of making a product or providing a service, before deducting overhead, payroll, taxation, and interest payments. Note that this is different from operating profit (earnings before interest and taxes.)

Net sales are calculated:

    Net sales = Sales - Sales returns and allowances.

a. Gross profit
b. Participating preferred stock
c. Commercial paper
d. Capital structure

67. _____ is an approach to valuing and reporting inventory. Normally ending inventory is stated at historical cost (what was paid to obtain it) but there are times when the original cost of the ending inventory is greater than the cost of replacement thus the inventory has lost value. If the inventory has decreased in value below historical cost then its carrying value is reduced and reported on the balance sheet.

a. Certified Practising Accountant
b. Lower of cost or market
c. Bankruptcy prediction
d. Remittance advice

68. _____ refers to services paid for in advance. Examples include tolls, pay as you go cell phones, and stored-value cards such as gift cards and preloaded credit cards. _____ accounts are assets, and they are increased by debiting the account(s.)

a. 3M Company
b. BNSF Railway
c. BMC Software, Inc.
d. Prepaid

69. An _____, operating expenditure, operational expense, operational expenditure or OPEX is an on-going cost for running a product, business, or system. Its counterpart, a capital expenditure (CAPEX), is the cost of developing or providing non-consumable parts for the product or system. For example, the purchase of a photocopier is the CAPEX, and the annual paper and toner cost is the OPEX.

a. Operating expense
b. AIG
c. AMEX
d. ABC Television Network

70. _____, in law and economics, is a form of risk management primarily used to hedge against the risk of a contingent loss. _____ is defined as the equitable transfer of the risk of a loss, from one entity to another, in exchange for a premium, and can be thought of as a guaranteed small loss to prevent a large, possibly devastating loss. An insurer is a company selling the _____; an insured is the person or entity buying the _____.

Chapter 5. Accounting for and Presentation of Current Assets

   a. AMEX
   c. ABC Television Network
   b. AIG
   d. Insurance

71. _____ is an accounting concept, meaning a future tax liability or asset, resulting from temporary differences between book (accounting) value of assets and liabilities and their tax value, or timing differences between the recognition of gains and losses in financial statements and their recognition in a tax computation.

Temporary differences are differences between the carrying amount of an asset or liability recognised in the balance sheet and the amount attributed to that asset or liability for tax purposes (the tax base.)

   a. Tax refund
   c. Federal tax revenue by state
   b. Deficit
   d. Deferred tax

72. The term _____ refers to government debt, expenditures and revenues, or to finance (particularly financial revenue) in general.

- _____ deficit is the budget deficit of federal or local government
- _____ policy is the discretionary spending of governments. Contrasts with monetary policy.
- _____ year and _____ quarter are reporting periods for firms and other agencies.

See also

- Procurator _____ and Crown Office and Procurator _____ Service

   a. Comparable
   c. Swap
   b. Scientific Research and Experimental Development Tax Incentive Program
   d. Fiscal

73. A _____ is a period used for calculating annual financial statements in businesses and other organizations. In many jurisdictions, regulatory laws regarding accounting and taxation require such reports once per twelve months, but do not require that the period reported on constitutes a calendar year (i.e., January through December.) _____s vary between businesses and countries.

   a. BMC Software, Inc.
   c. BNSF Railway
   b. 3M Company
   d. Fiscal year

74. In financial accounting, a _____ is defined as an obligation of an entity arising from past transactions or events, the settlement of which may result in the transfer or use of assets, provision of services or other yielding of economic benefits in the future.

   a. False Claims Act
   c. Vested
   b. Corporate governance
   d. Liability

75. _____ is an American publishing and financial information firm.

The company was founded in 1882 by three reporters: Charles Dow, Edward Jones, and Charles Bergstresser. Like The New York Times and the Washington Post, the company was in recent years publicly traded but privately controlled.

a. Professional association

b. MicroStrategy

c. Multinational corporation

d. Dow Jones ' Company

Chapter 6. Accounting for and Presentation of Property, and Other Noncurrent Assets   **65**

1. In business and accounting, _____ are everything of value that is owned by a person or company. It is a claim on the property your income of a borrower. The balance sheet of a firm records the monetary value of the _____ owned by the firm.

   a. Earnings before interest, taxes, depreciation and amortization
   b. Accrual basis accounting
   c. Assets
   d. Accounts receivable

2. In economics, _____ or _____ goods or real _____ refers to factors of production used to create goods or services that are not themselves significantly consumed (though they may depreciate) in the production process. _____ goods may be acquired with money or financial _____. In finance and accounting, _____ generally refers to financial wealth, especially that used to start or maintain a business.

   a. Screening
   b. Capital
   c. Vyborg Appeal
   d. Disclosure

3. _____ is a type of lease - the other being an operating lease. A _____ effectively allows a firm to finance the purchase of an asset, even if, strictly speaking, the firm never acquires the asset. Typically, a _____ will give the lessee control over an asset for a large proportion of the asset's useful life, providing them the benefits and risks of ownership.

   a. 3M Company
   b. Debt ratio
   c. Profitability index
   d. Finance lease

4. A _____ is a contract conferring a right on one person to possess property belonging to another person (called a landlord or lessor) to the exclusion of the owner landlord. It is a rental agreement between landlord and tenant. The relationship between the tenant and the landlord is called a tenancy, and the right to possession by the tenant is sometimes called a leasehold interest.

   a. Robinson-Patman Act
   b. Model Code of Professional Responsibility
   c. Federal Sentencing Guidelines
   d. Lease

5. In financial accounting, a _____ or statement of financial position is a summary of a person's or organization's balances. Assets, liabilities and ownership equity are listed as of a specific date, such as the end of its financial year. A _____ is often described as a snapshot of a company's financial condition.

   a. 3M Company
   b. Financial statements
   c. Balance sheet
   d. Statement of retained earnings

6. _____ is a company's financial statement that indicates how the revenue is transformed into the net income The purpose of the _____ is to show managers and investors whether the company made or lost money during the period being reported.

The important thing to remember about an _____ is that it represents a period of time.

   a. ABC Television Network
   b. AIG
   c. AMEX
   d. Income statement

7. In finance, _____ also known as return on investment, rate of profit or sometimes just return, is the ratio of money gained or lost on an investment relative to the amount of money invested. The amount of money gained or lost may be referred to as interest, profit/loss, gain/loss, or net income/loss. The money invested may be referred to as the asset, capital, principal, or the cost basis of the investment.

a. Rate of return
c. Debt to capital ratio
b. Theoretical ex-rights price
d. Capital employed

8. The term _____ is used in finance theory to refer to any terminating stream of fixed payments over a specified period of time. This usage is most commonly seen in academic discussions of finance, usually in connection with the valuation of the stream of payments, taking into account time value of money concepts such as interest rate and future value.

Examples of these are regular deposits to a savings account, monthly home mortgage payments and monthly insurance payments.

a. Intangible
c. Improvement
b. Appropriation
d. Annuity

9. In economics, business, retail, and accounting, a _____ is the value of money that has been used up to produce something, and hence is not available for use anymore. In economics, a _____ is an alternative that is given up as a result of a decision. In business, the _____ may be one of acquisition, in which case the amount of money expended to acquire it is counted as _____.

a. Cost allocation
c. Cost
b. Prime cost
d. Cost of quality

10. A _____ is the pinnacle activity involved in selling products or services in return for money or other compensation. It is an act of completion of a commercial activity.

A _____ is completed by the seller, the owner of the goods.

a. Tertiary sector of economy
c. Sale
b. Maturity
d. High yield stock

11. In finance, _____ is the process of estimating the potential market value of a financial asset or liability. They can be done on assets (for example, investments in marketable securities such as stocks, options, business enterprises, or intangible assets such as patents and trademarks) or on liabilities (e.g., Bonds issued by a company.) A _____ is required in many contexts including investment analysis, capital budgeting, merger and acquisition transactions, financial reporting, taxable events to determine the proper tax liability, and in litigation.

a. Disclosure
c. Daybook
b. Vyborg Appeal
d. Valuation

12. A _____ is an expenditure creating future benefits. A _____ is incurred when a business spends money either to buy fixed assets or to add to the value of an existing fixed asset with a useful life that extends beyond the taxable year. Capex are used by a company to acquire or upgrade physical assets such as equipment, property, or industrial buildings.

a. Capital expenditure
c. BMC Software, Inc.
b. Cost of capital
d. 3M Company

13. _____ is a term used in accounting, economics and finance to spread the cost of an asset over the span of several years.

Chapter 6. Accounting for and Presentation of Property, and Other Noncurrent Assets 67

In simple words we can say that _____ is the reduction in the value of an asset due to usage, passage of time, wear and tear, technological outdating or obsolescence, depletion, inadequacy, rot, rust, decay or other such factors.

In accounting, _____ is a term used to describe any method of attributing the historical or purchase cost of an asset across its useful life, roughly corresponding to normal wear and tear.

a. Current asset
b. Depreciation
c. Net profit
d. General ledger

14. An _____ is a tax levied on the financial income of people, corporations, or other legal entities. Various _____ systems exist, with varying degrees of tax incidence. Income taxation can be progressive, proportional, or regressive.

a. Individual Retirement Arrangement
b. Ordinary income
c. Implied level of government service
d. Income tax

15. _____ is a cornerstone of accrual accounting together with the revenue recognition principle. They both determine the accounting period, in which revenues and expenses are recognized. According to the principle, expenses are recognized when obligations are (1) incurred (usually when goods are transferred or services rendered, e.g. sold), and (2) offset against recognized revenues, which were generated from those expenses (related on the cause-and-effect basis), no matter when cash is paid out.

a. Payroll
b. Matching principle
c. Net sales
d. Current liabilities

16. In physics, and more specifically kinematics, _____ is the change in velocity over time. Because velocity is a vector, it can change in two ways: a change in magnitude and/or a change in direction. In one dimension, _____ is the rate at which something speeds up or slows down.

a. ABC Television Network
b. AMEX
c. AIG
d. Acceleration

17. _____, in accrual accounting, is any account where the asset or liability is not realized until a future date (accounting period), e.g. annuities, charges, taxes, income, etc. The _____ item may be carried, dependent on type of deferral, as either an asset or liability.

a. Cash basis accounting
b. Pro forma
c. Payroll
d. Deferred

18. In financial accounting, a _____ is defined as an obligation of an entity arising from past transactions or events, the settlement of which may result in the transfer or use of assets, provision of services or other yielding of economic benefits in the future.

a. Vested
b. Corporate governance
c. False Claims Act
d. Liability

19. _____ was a maxim coined by Josiah Warren, indicating a (prescriptive) version of the labor theory of value. Warren maintained that the just compensation for labor (or for its product) could only be an equivalent amount of labor (or a product embodying an equivalent amount.) Thus, profit, rent, and interest were considered unjust economic arrangements.

68 Chapter 6. Accounting for and Presentation of Property, and Other Noncurrent Assets

a. Cost the limit of price
c. 3M Company
b. Politicized issue
d. BMC Software, Inc.

20. _____ is a fee paid on borrowed assets. It is the price paid for the use of borrowed money, or, money earned by deposited funds. Assets that are sometimes lent with _____ include money, shares, consumer goods through hire purchase, major assets such as aircraft, and even entire factories in finance lease arrangements. The _____ is calculated upon the value of the assets in the same manner as upon money.
a. Insolvency
c. AIG
b. ABC Television Network
d. Interest

21. A _____ is any one of a variety of different systems, institutions, procedures, social relations and infrastructures whereby persons trade, and goods and services are exchanged, forming part of the economy. It is an arrangement that allows buyers and sellers to exchange things. _____s vary in size, range, geographic scale, location, types and variety of human communities, as well as the types of goods and services traded.
a. Market Failure
c. Recession
b. Market
d. Perfect competition

22. _____ is the price at which an asset would trade in a competitive Walrasian auction setting. _____ is often used interchangeably with open _____, fair value or fair _____, although these terms have distinct definitions in different standards, and may differ in some circumstances.

International Valuation Standards defines _____ as 'the estimated amount for which a property should exchange on the date of valuation between a willing buyer and a willing seller in an arme;s-length transaction after proper marketing wherein the parties had each acted knowledgeably, prudently, and without compulsion.'

_____ is a concept distinct from market price, which is e;the price at which one can transacte;, while _____ is e;the true underlying valuee; according to theoretical standards.

a. Debtor
c. Segregated portfolio company
b. Sinking fund
d. Market value

23. In business, _____, Overhead cost or _____ expense refers to an ongoing expense of operating a business. The term _____ is usually used to group expenses that are necessary to the continued functioning of the business, but do not directly generate profits.

_____ expenses are all costs on the income statement except for direct labor and direct materials.

a. AIG
c. Intangible assets
b. ABC Television Network
d. Overhead

24. _____ refers to services paid for in advance. Examples include tolls, pay as you go cell phones, and stored-value cards such as gift cards and preloaded credit cards. _____ accounts are assets, and they are increased by debiting the account(s.)
a. 3M Company
c. BNSF Railway
b. BMC Software, Inc.
d. Prepaid

Chapter 6. Accounting for and Presentation of Property, and Other Noncurrent Assets

25. In accounting, _____ has a very specific meaning. It is an outflow of cash or other valuable assets from a person or company to another person or company. This outflow of cash is generally one side of a trade for products or services that have equal or better current or future value to the buyer than to the seller.
   a. ABC Television Network
   b. Expense
   c. AMEX
   d. AIG

26. Book Value = Original Cost - _____

Book value at the end of year becomes book value at the beginning of next year. The asset is depreciated until the book value equals scrap value.

If the vehicle were to be sold and the sales price exceeded the depreciated value (net book value) then the excess would be considered a gain and subject to depreciation recapture.

   a. AMEX
   b. AIG
   c. Accumulated depreciation
   d. ABC Television Network

27. In accounting, _____ or carrying value is the value of an asset according to its balance sheet account balance. For assets, the value is based on the original cost of the asset less any depreciation, amortization or impairment costs made against the asset. Traditionally, a company's _____ is its total assets minus intangible assets and liabilities.
   a. Generally accepted accounting principles
   b. Matching principle
   c. Depreciation
   d. Book value

28. There are several methods for calculating depreciation, generally based on either the passage of time or the level of activity (or use) of the asset.

_____ is the simplest and most often used technique, in which the company estimates the salvage value of the asset at the end of the period during which it will be used to generate revenues (useful life), and will expense a portion of original cost in equal increments over that period.

   a. Pro forma
   b. Closing entries
   c. Current asset
   d. Straight-line depreciation

29. _____ refers to any one of several methods by which a company, for 'financial accounting' and/or tax purposes, depreciates a fixed asset in such a way that the amount of depreciation taken each year is higher during the earlier years of an assete;s life. For financial accounting purposes, _____ is generally used when an asset is expected to be much more productive during its early years, so that depreciation expense will more accurately represent how much of an assete;s usefulness is being used up each year. For tax purposes, _____ provides a way of deferring corporate income taxes by reducing taxable income in current years, in exchange for increased taxable income in future years.
   a. Accelerated depreciation
   b. Effective marginal tax rates
   c. Indirect tax
   d. User charge

30. Straight-line depreciation is the simplest and most often used technique, in which the company estimates the _____ of the asset at the end of the period during which it will be used to generate revenues (useful life), and will expense a portion of original cost in equal increments over that period. The _____ is an estimate of the value of the asset at the time it will be sold or disposed of; it may be zero. _____ is scrap value, by another name.

Chapter 6. Accounting for and Presentation of Property, and Other Noncurrent Assets

a. Closing entries
c. Salvage value

b. Generally accepted accounting principles
d. Net profit

31. A _____ proof is a mathematical proof that a particular theory is consistent. The early development of mathematical proof theory was driven by the desire to provide finitary _____ proofs for all of mathematics as part of Hilbert's program. Hilbert's program was strongly impacted by incompleteness theorems, which showed that sufficiently strong proof theories cannot prove their own _____.

a. Monte Carlo methods
c. Consistency

b. Daybook
d. Consumption

32. _____, making better, is a general term used particularly in connection with the increased value given to real property by causes for which a tenant or the public, but not the owner, is responsible; it is thus of the nature of unearned increment. When, for instance, some public improvement results in raising the value of a piece of private land, and the owner is thereby bettered through no merit of his own, he gains by the _____, and many economists and politicians have sought to arrange, by taxation or otherwise, that the increased value shall come into the pocket of the public rather than into the owner's. A _____ tax would be so assessed as to divert from the owner of the property the profit thus accruing unearned to him.

a. Malpractice
c. Fiduciary

b. Secondary authority
d. Betterment

33. The _____ is the current method of accelerated asset depreciation required by the United States income tax code. Under _____, all assets are divided into classes which dictate the number of years over which an asset's cost will be recovered.

Prior to the Accelerated Cost Recovery System (ACRS), most capital purchases were depreciated using a straight line technique, that allowed for the depreciation of the asset over its useful life.

a. 3M Company
c. Categorical grants

b. BMC Software, Inc.
d. Modified Accelerated Cost Recovery System

34. An _____ is a term used in behavioral economics to describe those types of behaviors that impose costs on a person in the long-run that are not taken into account when making decisions in the present. Classical Economics discourages government from creating legislation that targets internalities, because it is assumed that the consumer takes these personal costs into account when paying for the good that causes the _____. For example, cigarettes should be taxed because of the negative consumption externalities that they impose, such as second-hand smoke, not because the smoker harms him or herself by smoking.

a. Operating budget
c. Inventory turnover ratio

b. Authorised capital
d. Internality

35. The _____ is the main body of domestic statutory tax law of the United States organized topically, including laws covering the income tax , payroll taxes, gift taxes, estate taxes and statutory excise taxes. The _____ is published as Title 26 of the United States Code (USC), and is also known as the internal revenue title.

a. Internal Revenue Code
c. Income tax

b. Equity of condition
d. Ordinary income

36. _____ is the process of changing the way taxes are collected or managed by the government.

Chapter 6. Accounting for and Presentation of Property, and Other Noncurrent Assets 71

_____ers have different goals. Some seek to reduce the level of taxation of all people by the government.

a. Tax Reform
c. Tax exporting
b. Tax investigation
d. Franchise tax

37. The U.S. Congress passed the _____, (Pub.L. 99-514, 100 Stat. 2085, enacted October 22, 1986) to simplify the income tax code, broaden the tax base and eliminate many tax shelters and other preferences.

The tax reform was designed to be revenue neutral, but because individual taxes were decreased while corporate taxes were increased, Congressional Budget Office estimates (which ignore corporate taxes) suggested every tax payer saw a decrease in their tax bill. As of 2009, the _____ was the most recent major simplification of the tax code, drastically reducing the number of deductions and the number of tax brackets.

a. Tax Reform Act of 1986
c. 3M Company
b. BNSF Railway
d. BMC Software, Inc.

38. The _____ is the United States federal government agency that collects taxes and enforces the internal revenue laws. It is an agency within the U.S. Dept of the treasury responsible for interpretation and application of Federal tax law. The official U.S. Treasury regulations provide (in part):

The _____ is a bureau of the Department of the Treasury under the immediate direction of the Commissioner of Internal Revenue.

a. Internal Revenue Service
c. Use tax
b. Indirect tax
d. Income tax

39. An _____ is the buying of one company by another. An _____ may be friendly or hostile. In the former case, the companies cooperate in negotiations; in the latter case, the takeover target is unwilling to be bought or the target's board has no prior knowledge of the offer. _____ usually refers to a purchase of a smaller firm by a larger one. Sometimes, however, a smaller firm will acquire management control of a larger or longer established company and keep its name for the combined entity. This is known as a reverse takeover.
a. Acquisition
c. AMEX
b. AIG
d. ABC Television Network

40. An _____ is a lease whose term is short compared to the useful life of the asset or piece of equipment (an airliner, a ship etc.) being leased. An _____ is commonly used to acquire equipment on a relatively short-term basis.
a. Express warranty
c. Operating lease
b. Issued shares
d. Employee Retirement Income Security Act

41. _____ is the value on a given date of a future payment or series of future payments, discounted to reflect the time value of money and other factors such as investment risk. _____ calculations are widely used in business and economics to provide a means to compare cash flows at different times on a meaningful 'like to like' basis.

The most commonly applied model of the time value of money is compound interest.

a. Net present value
b. Present value
c. 3M Company
d. Future value

42. In economics, the _____, (or _____) measures the payments that flow between any individual country and all other countries. It is used to summarize all international economic transactions for that country during a specific time period, usually a year. The _____ is determined by the country's exports and imports of goods, services, and financial capital, as well as financial transfers.

a. Yield to maturity
b. Balance of payments
c. Moving average
d. Stock split

43. A _____ is the transfer of wealth from one party (such as a person or company) to another. A _____ is usually made in exchange for the provision of goods, services or both, or to fulfill a legal obligation.

The simplest and oldest form of _____ is barter, the exchange of one good or service for another.

a. BMC Software, Inc.
b. Payment
c. Payee
d. 3M Company

44. _____ is the term used to refer to the standard framework of guidelines for financial accounting used in any given jurisdiction. _____ includes the standards, conventions, and rules accountants follow in recording and summarizing transactions, and in the preparation of financial statements.

Financial accounting information must be assembled and reported objectively.

a. Generally accepted accounting principles
b. General ledger
c. Long-term liabilities
d. Current asset

45. _____ are defined as identifiable non-monetary assets that cannot be seen, touched or physically measured, which are created through time and/or effort and that are identifiable as a separate asset. There are two primary forms of intangibles - legal intangibles (such as trade secrets (e.g., customer lists), copyrights, patents, trademarks, and goodwill) and competitive intangibles (such as knowledge activities (know-how, knowledge), collaboration activities, leverage activities, and structural activities.) Legal intangibles are known under the generic term intellectual property and generate legal property rights defensible in a court of law.

a. ABC Television Network
b. Intangible assets
c. Overhead
d. AIG

Chapter 6. Accounting for and Presentation of Property, and Other Noncurrent Assets 73

46. _____ is the process of increasing, or accounting for, an amount over a period of time. Particular instances of the term include:

- _____, the allocation of a lump sum amount to different time periods, particularly for loans and other forms of finance, including related interest or other finance charges.
    - _____ schedule, a table detailing each periodic payment on a loan (typically a mortgage), as generated by an _____ calculator.
    - Negative _____, an _____ schedule where the loan amount actually increases through not paying the full interest
- Amortized analysis, analyzing the execution cost of algorithms over a sequence of operations.
- _____ of capital expenditures of certain assets under accounting rules, particularly intangible assets, in a manner analogous to depreciation.
- _____

a. EBIT
c. Amortization
b. Intangible
d. Annuity

47. The _____ is an independent agency of the United States government, established in 1914 by the _____ Act. Its principal mission is the promotion of 'consumer protection' and the elimination and prevention of what regulators perceive to be harmfully 'anti-competitive' business practices, such as coercive monopoly.

The _____ Act was one of President Wilson's major acts against trusts.

a. 3M Company
c. BNSF Railway
b. BMC Software, Inc.
d. Federal Trade Commission

48. A _____ estate is an ownership interest in land in which a lessee or a tenant holds real property by some form of title from a lessor or landlord.

_____ is a form of property tenure where one party buys the right to occupy land or a building for a given length of time. As lease is a legal estate, _____ estate can be bought and sold on the open market.

a. Leasehold
c. Liquidation value
b. 3M Company
d. Real Estate Investment Trust

49. A _____ is a set of exclusive rights granted by a state to an inventor or his assignee for a limited period of time in exchange for a disclosure of an invention.

The procedure for granting _____s, the requirements placed on the _____ee and the extent of the exclusive rights vary widely between countries according to national laws and international agreements. Typically, however, a _____ application must include one or more claims defining the invention which must be new, inventive, and useful or industrially applicable.

a. Trust indenture
c. Negligence
b. FLSA
d. Patent

Chapter 6. Accounting for and Presentation of Property, and Other Noncurrent Assets

50. A _____ or trade mark, identified by the symbols â„¢ (not yet registered) and Â® (registered), is a distinctive sign or indicator used by an individual, business organization or other legal entity to identify that the products and/or services to consumers with which the _____ appears originate from a unique source, and to distinguish its products or services from those of other entities. A _____ is a type of intellectual property, and typically a name, word, phrase, logo, symbol, design, image, or a combination of these elements. There is also a range of non-conventional _____s comprising marks which do not fall into these standard categories.
- a. Kanban
- b. FIFO
- c. Risk management
- d. Trademark

51. _____ is a term in both law and accounting that is based on the economics term of 'market value.' It is also a common basis for assessing damages to be awarded for the loss of or damage to the property, generally in a claim under tort or a contract of insurance.

A _____ is often an estimate of what a willing buyer would pay to a willing seller, both in a free market, for an asset or any piece of property. If such a transaction actually occurs, then the actual transaction price is usually the _____.

- a. Cash and cash equivalents
- b. Shares authorized
- c. Disposal tax effect
- d. Fair market value

52. _____ measures the nominal future sum of money that a given sum of money is 'worth' at a specified time in the future assuming a certain interest rate rate of return; it is the present value multiplied by the accumulation function.

The value does not include corrections for inflation or other factors that affect the true value of money in the future. This is used in time value of money calculations.

- a. Present value
- b. 3M Company
- c. Future value
- d. Net present value

53. _____ are sometimes the same as net worth, or shareholders' equity - assets minus liabilities. The term _____ is commonly used with charities or not for profit entities. Although these entities don't make money, it is important to maintain reasonable reserves to help future growth.
- a. Sortino ratio
- b. Net interest spread
- c. Debtor days
- d. Net assets

54. A _____ is used in research to outline possible courses of action or to present a preferred approach to an idea or thought. For example, the philosopher Isaiah Berlin used the 'hedgehogs' versus 'foxes' approach; a 'hedgehog' might approach the world in terms of a single organizing principle; a 'fox' might pursue multiple conflicting goals simultaneously. Alternatively, an empiricist might approach a subject by direct examination, whereas an intuitionist might simply intuit what's next.
- a. 3M Company
- b. BNSF Railway
- c. BMC Software, Inc.
- d. Conceptual Framework

55. The _____ founded on April 1, 2001 is the successor of the International Accounting Standards Committee (IASC) founded in June 1973 in London. It is responsible for developing the International Financial Reporting Standards (new name for the International Accounting Standards issued after 2001), and promoting the use and application of these standards.

Chapter 6. Accounting for and Presentation of Property, and Other Noncurrent Assets

The _____ is an independent, privately-funded accounting standard-setter based in London, UK.

a. Institute of Management Accountants
b. Information Systems Audit and Control Association
c. Emerging technologies
d. International Accounting Standards Board

56. An _____ is the price a borrower pays for the use of money they do not own, for instance a small company might borrow from a bank to kick start their business, and the return a lender receives for deferring the use of funds, by lending it to the borrower. _____s are normally expressed as a percentage rate over the period of one year.

_____s targets are also a vital tool of monetary policy and are used to control variables like investment, inflation, and unemployment.

a. Interest rate
b. AMEX
c. ABC Television Network
d. AIG

57. Simply put, _____ is the value of money figuring in a given amount of interest for a given amount of time. For example 100 dollars of todays money held for a year at 5 percent interest is worth 105 dollars, therefore 100 dollars paid now or 105 dollars paid exactly one year from now is the same amount of payment of money with that given intersest at that given amount of time. This notion dates at least to Martín de Azpilcueta of the School of Salamanca.

a. Collusion
b. Competition law
c. Merck ' Co., Inc.
d. Time value of money

58. Discounting is a financial mechanism in which a debtor obtains the right to delay payments to a creditor, for a defined period of time, in exchange for a charge or fee. Essentially, the party that owes money in the present purchases the right to delay the payment until some future date. The _____, or charge, is simply the difference between the original amount owed in the present and the amount that has to be paid in the future to settle the debt.

a. Discount
b. Discount factor
c. Risk aversion
d. Discounting

59. The _____ is an interest rate a central bank charges depository institutions that borrow reserves from it.

The term _____ has two meanings:

- the same as interest rate; the term 'discount' does not refer to the meaning of the word, but to the purpose of using the quantity, such as computations of present value, e.g. net present value or discounted cash flow

- the annual effective _____, which is the annual interest divided by the capital including that interest; this rate is lower than the interest rate; it corresponds to using the value after a year as the nominal value, and seeing the initial value as the nominal value minus a discount; it is used for Treasury Bills and similar financial instruments

The annual effective _____ is the annual interest divided by the capital including that interest, which is the interest rate divided by 100% plus the interest rate. It is the annual discount factor to be applied to the future cash flow, to find the discount, subtracted from a future value to find the value one year earlier.

Chapter 6. Accounting for and Presentation of Property, and Other Noncurrent Assets

For example, suppose there is a government bond that sells for $95 and pays $100 in a year's time.

a. Discount rate
b. Process time
c. Convertible bond
d. Municipal bond

60. _____ is one of a series of accounting transactions dealing with the billing of customers who owe money to a person, company or organization for goods and services that have been provided to the customer. In most business entities this is typically done by generating an invoice and mailing or electronically delivering it to the customer, who in turn must pay it within an established timeframe called credit or payment terms.

An example of a common payment term is Net 30, meaning payment is due in the amount of the invoice 30 days from the date of invoice.

a. Accrual
b. Accrued revenue
c. Adjusting entries
d. Accounts receivable

Chapter 7. Accounting for and Presentation of Liabilities

1. _____, is a liability with an uncertain timing or amount, but where the uncertainty is not significant enough to qualify it as a provision. An example is an unpaid obligation to pay for goods or services received FROM a counterpart, while cash for them is to be paid out in a latter accounting period when its amount is deducted from _____s.
   a. Accrual basis accounting
   b. Accounts receivable
   c. Assets
   d. Accrued expense

2. In financial accounting, a _____ or statement of financial position is a summary of a person's or organization's balances. Assets, liabilities and ownership equity are listed as of a specific date, such as the end of its financial year. A _____ is often described as a snapshot of a company's financial condition.
   a. Statement of retained earnings
   b. Financial statements
   c. Balance sheet
   d. 3M Company

3. In accounting, _____ are considered liabilities of the business that are to be settled in cash within the fiscal year or the operating cycle, whichever period is longer.

For example accounts payable for goods, services or supplies that were purchased for use in the operation of the business and payable within a normal period of time would be _____.

Bonds, mortgages and loans that are payable over a term exceeding one year would be fixed liabilities.

   a. Payroll
   b. Treasury stock
   c. Closing entries
   d. Current liabilities

4. In financial accounting, a _____ is defined as an obligation of an entity arising from past transactions or events, the settlement of which may result in the transfer or use of assets, provision of services or other yielding of economic benefits in the future.
   a. Corporate governance
   b. Liability
   c. Vested
   d. False Claims Act

5. An _____, operating expenditure, operational expense, operational expenditure or OPEX is an on-going cost for running a product, business, or system. Its counterpart, a capital expenditure (CAPEX), is the cost of developing or providing non-consumable parts for the product or system. For example, the purchase of a photocopier is the CAPEX, and the annual paper and toner cost is the OPEX.
   a. Operating expense
   b. AMEX
   c. AIG
   d. ABC Television Network

6. In accounting, _____ has a very specific meaning. It is an outflow of cash or other valuable assets from a person or company to another person or company. This outflow of cash is generally one side of a trade for products or services that have equal or better current or future value to the buyer than to the seller.
   a. ABC Television Network
   b. Expense
   c. AMEX
   d. AIG

7. _____ is a fee paid on borrowed assets. It is the price paid for the use of borrowed money, or, money earned by deposited funds. Assets that are sometimes lent with _____ include money, shares, consumer goods through hire purchase, major assets such as aircraft, and even entire factories in finance lease arrangements. The _____ is calculated upon the value of the assets in the same manner as upon money.

Chapter 7. Accounting for and Presentation of Liabilities

a. AIG
c. ABC Television Network
b. Insolvency
d. Interest

8. _____ relates to the cost of borrowing money. It is the price that a lender charges a borrower for the use of the lender's money. _____ is different from OPEX and CAPEX, for it relates to the capital structure of a company.
   a. Interest
   c. Interest expense
   b. ABC Television Network
   d. AIG

9. _____ is a life of security. It may also refer to the final payment date of a loan or other financial instrument, at which point all remaining interest and principal is due to be paid.

1, 3, 6 months _____ band can be calculated by using 30-day per month periods. For _____ bands over a year it is acceptable to use 365 day per year. For example with a Treasury Bond, its _____ is the date on which the principal is paid.

a. The Goodyear Tire ' Rubber Company
c. Factor
b. Statements of Financial Accounting Standards No. 133, Accounting for Derivative Instruments and Hedging Activities
d. Maturity

10. A _____, also referred to as a note payable in accounting, is a contract where one party (the maker or issuer) makes an unconditional promise in writing to pay a sum of money to the other (the payee), either at a fixed or determinable future time or on demand of the payee, under specific terms. They differ from IOUs in that they contain a specific promise to pay, rather than simply acknowledging that a debt exists.

The terms of a note typically include the principal amount, the interest rate if any, and the maturity date.

a. 3M Company
c. BMC Software, Inc.
b. BNSF Railway
d. Promissory note

11. _____ is a term applied in many countries to a reference interest rate used by banks. The term originally indicated the rate of interest at which banks lent to favored customers, i.e., those with high credibility, though this is no longer always the case. Some variable interest rates may be expressed as a percentage above or below _____.
   a. Transactional account
   c. Reserve requirement
   b. Variable rate mortgage
   d. Prime rate

12. In economics, the concept of the _____ refers to the decision-making time frame of a firm in which at least one factor of production is fixed. Costs which are fixed in the _____ have no impact on a firms decisions. For example a firm can raise output by increasing the amount of labour through overtime.
   a. BMC Software, Inc.
   c. Long-run
   b. 3M Company
   d. Short-run

13. _____ is a financial metric which represents operating liquidity available to a business. Along with fixed assets such as plant and equipment, _____ is considered a part of operating capital. It is calculated as current assets minus current liabilities.

Chapter 7. Accounting for and Presentation of Liabilities

a. Working capital
c. BMC Software, Inc.
b. Working capital management
d. 3M Company

14. In economics, _____ or _____ goods or real _____ refers to factors of production used to create goods or services that are not themselves significantly consumed (though they may depreciate) in the production process. _____ goods may be acquired with money or financial _____. In finance and accounting, _____ generally refers to financial wealth, especially that used to start or maintain a business.
a. Capital
c. Screening
b. Vyborg Appeal
d. Disclosure

15. _____ is that which is owed; usually referencing assets owed, but the term can also cover moral obligations and other interactions not requiring money. In the case of assets, _____ is a means of using future purchasing power in the present before a summation has been earned. Some companies and corporations use _____ as a part of their overall corporate finance strategy.
a. Loan
c. Debenture
b. Debt
d. Lender

16. A _____ is any credit facility extended to a business by a bank or financial institution. A _____ may take several forms such as cash credit, overdraft, demand loan, export packing credit, term loan, discounting or purchase of commercial bills etc. It is like an account that can readily be tapped into if the need arises or not touched at all and saved for emergencies.
a. BMC Software, Inc.
c. Line of credit
b. Simple interest
d. 3M Company

17. A _____ is a type of debt Like all debt instruments, a _____ entails the redistribution of financial assets over time, between the lender and the borrower.
a. Loan
c. Lender
b. Loan to value
d. Debenture

18. In finance, _____ is the interest that has accumulated since the principal investment, or since the previous interest payment if there has been one already. For a financial instrument such as a bond, interest is calculated and paid in set intervals.

The primary formula for calculating the interest accrued in a given period is:

$$I_A = T \times P \times R$$

where I_A is the _____, T is the fraction of the year, P is the principal, and R is the annualized interest rate.

a. ABC Television Network
c. Interest
b. AIG
d. Accrued interest

19. The terms _____, nominal _____, and effective _____ describe the interest rate for a whole year (annualized), rather than just a monthly fee/rate, as applied on a loan, mortgage, credit card, etc. It is a finance charge expressed as an annual rate. Those terms have formal, legal definitions in some countries or legal jurisdictions, but in general:

- The nominal _____ is the simple-interest rate (for a year.)
- The effective _____ is the fee+compound interest rate (calculated across a year.)

The nominal _____ is calculated as: the rate, for a payment period, multiplied by the number of payment periods in a year. However, the exact legal definition of 'effective _____', or EAR in short, can vary greatly in each jurisdiction, depending on the type of fees included, such as participation fees, loan origination fees, monthly service charges, or late fees. The effective _____ has been called the 'mathematically-true' interest rate for each year.

a. ABC Television Network
b. AIG
c. Annual percentage rate
d. AMEX

20. Discounting is a financial mechanism in which a debtor obtains the right to delay payments to a creditor, for a defined period of time, in exchange for a charge or fee. Essentially, the party that owes money in the present purchases the right to delay the payment until some future date. The _____, or charge, is simply the difference between the original amount owed in the present and the amount that has to be paid in the future to settle the debt.

a. Discounting
b. Discount factor
c. Risk aversion
d. Discount

21. An _____ is the price a borrower pays for the use of money they do not own, for instance a small company might borrow from a bank to kick start their business, and the return a lender receives for deferring the use of funds, by lending it to the borrower. _____s are normally expressed as a percentage rate over the period of one year.

_____s targets are also a vital tool of monetary policy and are used to control variables like investment, inflation, and unemployment.

a. AIG
b. ABC Television Network
c. AMEX
d. Interest rate

22. _____ is the value on a given date of a future payment or series of future payments, discounted to reflect the time value of money and other factors such as investment risk. _____ calculations are widely used in business and economics to provide a means to compare cash flows at different times on a meaningful 'like to like' basis.

The most commonly applied model of the time value of money is compound interest.

a. Future value
b. Net present value
c. 3M Company
d. Present value

23. _____ is interest calculated only on the principal amount, or on that portion of the principal amount which remains unpaid.

Chapter 7. Accounting for and Presentation of Liabilities   81

The amount of _____ is calculated according to the following formula:

$$I_{simp} = (r \cdot B_0) \cdot m$$

where r is the period interest rate , B_0 the initial balance and m the number of time periods elapsed.

a. Simple interest
b. Line of credit
c. BMC Software, Inc.
d. 3M Company

24. An _____ is a loan that is repaid over time with a set number of scheduled payments. The term of loan may be as little as a few months and as long as 30 years. A mortgage, for example, may be considered a type of _____.

a. ABC Television Network
b. AIG
c. AMEX
d. Installment loan

25. In the mathematical subfield of numerical analysis, _____ is a method of constructing new data points within the range of a discrete set of known data points.

In engineering and science one often has a number of data points, as obtained by sampling or experimentation, and tries to construct a function which closely fits those data points. This is called curve fitting or regression analysis.

a. AMEX
b. ABC Television Network
c. Interpolation
d. AIG

26. An _____ is a loan in which for a set term the borrower pays only the interest on the principal balance, with the principal balance unchanged. At the end of the interest-only term the borrower may enter an interest-only mortgage, pay the principal, or (with some lenders) convert the loan to a principal and interest payment (or amortized) loan at his/her option.

In the United States, a five- or ten-year interest-only period is typical.

a. AIG
b. ABC Television Network
c. Interest-only loan
d. AMEX

Chapter 7. Accounting for and Presentation of Liabilities

27. _____ is the process of increasing, or accounting for, an amount over a period of time. Particular instances of the term include:

- _____, the allocation of a lump sum amount to different time periods, particularly for loans and other forms of finance, including related interest or other finance charges.
  - _____ schedule, a table detailing each periodic payment on a loan (typically a mortgage), as generated by an _____ calculator.
  - Negative _____, an _____ schedule where the loan amount actually increases through not paying the full interest
- Amortized analysis, analyzing the execution cost of algorithms over a sequence of operations.
- _____ of capital expenditures of certain assets under accounting rules, particularly intangible assets, in a manner analogous to depreciation.
- _____

a. EBIT
c. Annuity
b. Intangible
d. Amortization

28. In economic models, the _____ time frame assumes no fixed factors of production. Firms can enter or leave the marketplace, and the cost (and availability) of land, labor, raw materials, and capital goods can be assumed to vary. In contrast, in the short-run time frame, certain factors are assumed to be fixed, because there is not sufficient time for them to change.
a. 3M Company
c. Short-run
b. BMC Software, Inc.
d. Long-run

29. In business and accounting, _____ are everything of value that is owned by a person or company. It is a claim on the property your income of a borrower. The balance sheet of a firm records the monetary value of the _____ owned by the firm.
a. Earnings before interest, taxes, depreciation and amortization
b. Accounts receivable
c. Accrual basis accounting
d. Assets

30. _____ are defined as identifiable non-monetary assets that cannot be seen, touched or physically measured, which are created through time and/or effort and that are identifiable as a separate asset. There are two primary forms of intangibles - legal intangibles (such as trade secrets (e.g., customer lists), copyrights, patents, trademarks, and goodwill) and competitive intangibles (such as knowledge activities (know-how, knowledge), collaboration activities, leverage activities, and structural activities.) Legal intangibles are known under the generic term intellectual property and generate legal property rights defensible in a court of law.
a. AIG
c. Overhead
b. ABC Television Network
d. Intangible assets

31. _____ is a file or account that contains money that a person or company owes to suppliers, but has not paid yet (a form of debt.) When you receive an invoice you add it to the file, and then you remove it when you pay. Thus, the A/P is a form of credit that suppliers offer to their purchasers by allowing them to pay for a product or service after it has already been received.

Chapter 7. Accounting for and Presentation of Liabilities

a. Earnings before interest, taxes, depreciation and amortization
b. Accounts receivable
c. Accrual
d. Accounts payable

32. _____ are reductions to a basic price of goods or services. They can occur anywhere in the distribution channel, modifying either the manufacturer's list price (determined by the manufacturer and often printed on the package), the retail price (set by the retailer and often attached to the product with a sticker), or the list price (which is quoted to a potential buyer, usually in written form.) The market price (also called effective price) is the amount actually paid.
   a. Discounts and allowances
   b. Resale price maintenance
   c. Target costing
   d. Pricing

33. _____, in accrual accounting, is any account where the asset or liability is not realized until a future date (accounting period), e.g. annuities, charges, taxes, income, etc. The _____ item may be carried, dependent on type of deferral, as either an asset or liability.
   a. Cash basis accounting
   b. Deferred
   c. Pro forma
   d. Payroll

34. _____ refers to income that is not a wage.

It includes interest, dividends or realized capital gains from investments, rent from land or property ownership, and any other income that does not derive from work.

_____ has often been treated differently for tax purposes than earned income, in order to redistribute income or to recognize its qualitative difference from income derived from work.

   a. ABC Television Network
   b. AMEX
   c. AIG
   d. Unearned income

35. In economics, the _____, (or _____) measures the payments that flow between any individual country and all other countries. It is used to summarize all international economic transactions for that country during a specific time period, usually a year. The _____ is determined by the country's exports and imports of goods, services, and financial capital, as well as financial transfers.
   a. Moving average
   b. Balance of payments
   c. Yield to maturity
   d. Stock split

36. _____ refers to a business or organization attempting to acquire goods or services to accomplish the goals of the enterprise. Though there are several organizations that attempt to set standards in the _____ process, processes can vary greatly between organizations. Typically the word e;_____e; is not used interchangeably with the word e;procuremente;, since procurement typically includes Expediting, Supplier Quality, and Traffic and Logistics (T'L) in addition to _____.
   a. Consignor
   b. Free port
   c. Supply chain
   d. Purchasing

37. _____, in accrual accounting, (e.g. advance payment received from a client) is, according to revenue recognition, revenue not earned until the delivery of goods or services, which until then, is still owed to the payer, hence remaining a liability.

_____, sometimes referred to as deferred revenue or unearned revenue, shares characteristics with accrued expense with the difference that a liability to be covered latter is cash received FROM a counterpart, while goods or services are to be delivered in a latter period, when such income item is earned, the related revenue item is recognized, and the same amount is deducted from deferred revenues.

a. Treasury stock
b. Deferred income
c. Gross sales
d. Matching principle

38. _____ is the term used to refer to the standard framework of guidelines for financial accounting used in any given jurisdiction. _____ includes the standards, conventions, and rules accountants follow in recording and summarizing transactions, and in the preparation of financial statements.

Financial accounting information must be assembled and reported objectively.

a. Current asset
b. General ledger
c. Long-term liabilities
d. Generally accepted accounting principles

39. A _____ is a form of periodic payment from an employer to an employee, which may be specified in an employment contract. It is contrasted with piece wages, where each job, hour or other unit is paid separately, rather than on a periodic basis.

From the point of a view of running a business, _____ can also be viewed as the cost of acquiring human resources for running operations, and is then termed personnel expense or _____ expense.

a. BMC Software, Inc.
b. Separation of duties
c. 3M Company
d. Salary

40. An _____ is a tax levied on the financial income of people, corporations, or other legal entities. Various _____ systems exist, with varying degrees of tax incidence. Income taxation can be progressive, proportional, or regressive.

a. Income tax
b. Implied level of government service
c. Individual Retirement Arrangement
d. Ordinary income

41. _____ is the remaining amount after deductions from the gross salary, where net means ultimate.

Example deductions: income taxes, trade union dues, authorized deduction for a retirement fund.

_____ is the amount left over after deductions from the gross salary.

a. Residual value
b. 3M Company
c. Net pay
d. Round-tripping

42. In a company, _____ is the sum of all financial records of salaries, wages, bonuses and deductions.

Chapter 7. Accounting for and Presentation of Liabilities

A paycheck, is traditionally a paper document issued by an employer to pay an employee for services rendered. While most commonly used in the United States, recently the physical paycheck has been increasingly replaced by electronic direct deposit to bank accounts.

a. Tax expense
c. 3M Company
b. Total Expense Ratio
d. Payroll

43. _____ generally refers to two kinds of taxes: Taxes which employers are required to withhold from employees' pay Pay-As-You-Earn or Pay-As-You-Go tax; and taxes which are paid from the employer's own funds and which are directly related to employing a worker, which may be either fixed charges or proportionally linked to an employee's pay.

In Australia, the _____ is a specific tax which is paid to states and territories by employers, not by employees. The tax is not deducted from the worker's pay.

a. Payroll tax
c. Passive foreign investment company
b. Federal Unemployment Tax Act
d. Nonbusiness Energy Property Tax Credit

44. _____ principle is a cornerstone of accrual accounting together with matching principle. They both determine the accounting period, in which revenues and expenses are recognized. According to the principle, revenues are recognized when they are (1) realized or realizable, and are (2) earned (usually when goods are transferred or services rendered), no matter when cash is received.

a. Revenue recognition
c. BMC Software, Inc.
b. Net realizable value
d. 3M Company

45. A _____ is a compensation, usually financial, received by a worker in exchange for their labor.

Compensation in terms of _____s is given to worker and compensation in terms of salary is given to employees. Compensation is a monetary benefits given to employees in returns of the services provided by them.

a. BMC Software, Inc.
c. Wage
b. 3M Company
d. Retirement plan

46. _____ is an amount withheld by the party making a payment to another (payee) and paid to the taxation authorities. The amount the payer deducts may vary, depending on the nature of the product or service being paid for. The payee is assessed on the gross amount, and the tax to be withheld (the _____) is computed in that assessment.

a. Tax wedge
c. Withholding tax
b. Tax advantage
d. Salaries tax

47. _____ are liabilities which have occurred, but have not been paid or logged under accounts payable during an accounting period; in other words, obligations for goods and services provided to a company for which invoices have not yet been received. Examples would include accrued wages payable, accrued sales tax payable, and accrued rent payable.

Chapter 7. Accounting for and Presentation of Liabilities

There are two general types of _____ :

- Routine and recurring
- Infrequent or non-routine

Most companies pay their employees on a predetermined schedule. Let's say that the 'Imaginary company Ltd.' pays its employees each Friday for the hours worked that week.

a. Accrued liabilities   b. AIG
c. ABC Television Network   d. AMEX

48. _____ is any physical or virtual entity that is owned by an individual or jointly by a group of individuals. An owner of _____ has the right to consume, sell, rent, mortgage, transfer and exchange his or her _____. Important widely-recognized types of _____ include real _____, personal _____ (other physical possessions), and intellectual _____ (rights over artistic creations, inventions, etc.), although the latter is not always as widely recognized or enforced.

a. Disclosure requirement   b. Property
c. Fiduciary   d. Primary authority

49. _____ is a cornerstone of accrual accounting together with the revenue recognition principle. They both determine the accounting period, in which revenues and expenses are recognized. According to the principle, expenses are recognized when obligations are (1) incurred (usually when goods are transferred or services rendered, e.g. sold), and (2) offset against recognized revenues, which were generated from those expenses (related on the cause-and-effect basis), no matter when cash is paid out.

a. Net sales   b. Current liabilities
c. Payroll   d. Matching principle

50. An _____ is quite usually a standard guarantee from the seller of a product that specifies the extent to which the quality or performance of the product is assured and states the conditions under which the product can be returned, replaced, or repaired. It is often given in the form of a specific, written 'Warranty' document. However, a warranty may also arise by operation of law based upon the seller's description of the goods, and perhaps their source and quality, and any material deviation from that specification would violate the guarantee.

a. Escheat   b. Operating Lease
c. Exclusive right   d. Express warranty

51. _____ are formal records of a business' financial activities.

In British English, including United Kingdom company law, _____ are often referred to as accounts, although the term _____ is also used, particularly by accountants.

_____ provide an overview of a business' financial condition in both short and long term.

a. Financial statements   b. Notes to the financial statements
c. 3M Company   d. Statement of retained earnings

Chapter 7. Accounting for and Presentation of Liabilities

52. _____ are additional notes and information added to the end of the financial statements to supplement the reader with more information. Notes to Financial Statements help explain the computation of specific items in the financial statements as well as provide a more comprehensive assessment of a company's financial condition. Notes to Financial Statements can include information on debt, going concern, accounts, contingent liabilities, or contextual information explaining the financial numbers (e.g. to indicate a lawsuit.)
   a. 3M Company
   b. Statement of retained earnings
   c. Financial statements
   d. Notes to the financial statements

53. In finance, _____ refers to the way a corporation finances its assets through some combination of equity, debt, or hybrid securities. A firm's _____ is then the composition or 'structure' of its liabilities. For example, a firm that sells $20 billion in equity and $80 billion in debt is said to be 20% equity-financed and 80% debt-financed.
   a. Gross income
   b. Restricted stock
   c. Flow-through entity
   d. Capital structure

54. _____ measures the rate of return on the ownership interest (shareholders' equity) of the common stock owners. It measures a firm's efficiency at generating profits from every dollar of shareholders' equity (also known as net assets or assets minus liabilities.) It shows how well a company uses investment dollars to generate earnings growth.
   a. Sortino ratio
   b. Return on capital employed
   c. Like for like
   d. Return on equity

55. In economics, business, retail, and accounting, a _____ is the value of money that has been used up to produce something, and hence is not available for use anymore. In economics, a _____ is an alternative that is given up as a result of a decision. In business, the _____ may be one of acquisition, in which case the amount of money expended to acquire it is counted as _____.
   a. Cost allocation
   b. Prime cost
   c. Cost of quality
   d. Cost

56. In accounting, _____ or carrying value is the value of an asset according to its balance sheet account balance. For assets, the value is based on the original cost of the asset less any depreciation, amortization or impairment costs made against the asset. Traditionally, a company's _____ is its total assets minus intangible assets and liabilities.
   a. Book value
   b. Generally accepted accounting principles
   c. Depreciation
   d. Matching principle

57. An _____ is the buying of one company by another. An _____ may be friendly or hostile. In the former case, the companies cooperate in negotiations; in the latter case, the takeover target is unwilling to be bought or the target's board has no prior knowledge of the offer. _____ usually refers to a purchase of a smaller firm by a larger one. Sometimes, however, a smaller firm will acquire management control of a larger or longer established company and keep its name for the combined entity. This is known as a reverse takeover.
   a. ABC Television Network
   b. AIG
   c. Acquisition
   d. AMEX

58. In finance, a _____ is a debt security, in which the authorized issuer owes the holders a debt and, depending on the terms of the _____, is obliged to pay interest (the coupon) and/or to repay the principal at a later date, termed maturity. It is a formal contract to repay borrowed money with interest at fixed intervals.

Thus a _____ is like a loan: the issuer is the borrower, the _____ holder is the lender, and the coupon is the interest.

a. Bond
b. Zero-coupon bond
c. Coupon rate
d. Revenue bonds

59. The _____ is a financial market where participants buy and sell debt securities, usually in the form of bonds. As of 2006, the size of the international _____ is an estimated $44.9 trillion, of which the size of the outstanding U.S. _____ debt was $25.2 trillion.

Nearly all of the $923 billion average daily trading volume in the U.S. _____ takes place between broker-dealers and large institutions in a decentralized, over-the-counter market.

a. Bond market
b. Convertible bond
c. Demand curve
d. Variance

60. A _____ is any one of a variety of different systems, institutions, procedures, social relations and infrastructures whereby persons trade, and goods and services are exchanged, forming part of the economy. It is an arrangement that allows buyers and sellers to exchange things. _____s vary in size, range, geographic scale, location, types and variety of human communities, as well as the types of goods and services traded.

a. Market
b. Perfect competition
c. Recession
d. Market Failure

61. _____ in economics and business is the result of an exchange and from that trade we assign a numerical monetary value to a good, service or asset. If Alice trades Bob 4 apples for an orange, the _____ of an orange is 4 apples. Inversely, the _____ of an apple is 1/4 oranges.

a. Price
b. Discounts and allowances
c. Price discrimination
d. Transactional Net Margin Method

62. In marketing a _____ is a ticket or document that can be exchanged for a financial discount or rebate when purchasing a product. Customarily, _____s are issued by manufacturers of consumer packaged goods or by retailers, to be used in retail stores as a part of sales promotions. They are often widely distributed through mail, magazines, newspapers, the Internet, and mobile devices such as cell phones.

a. BMC Software, Inc.
b. 3M Company
c. Merchandising
d. Coupon

63. The _____ of a bond is the amount of interest paid per year expressed as a percentage of the face value of the bond. It is the interest rate that a bond issuer will pay to a bondholder.

For example if you hold $10,000 nominal of a bond described as a 4.5% loan stock, you will receive $450 in interest each year (probably in two installments of $225 each.)

a. Convertible bond
b. Callable bond
c. Revenue bonds
d. Coupon rate

Chapter 7. Accounting for and Presentation of Liabilities 89

64. _____ is the balance of the amounts of cash being received and paid by a business during a defined period of time, sometimes tied to a specific project. Measurement of _____ can be used

- to evaluate the state or performance of a business or project.
- to determine problems with liquidity. Being profitable does not necessarily mean being liquid. A company can fail because of a shortage of cash, even while profitable.
- to project rate of returns. The time of _____s into and out of projects are used as inputs to financial models such as internal rate of return, and net present value.
- to examine income or growth of a business when it is believed that accrual accounting concepts do not represent economic realities. Alternately, _____ can be used to 'validate' the net income generated by accrual accounting.

_____ as a generic term may be used differently depending on context, and certain _____ definitions may be adapted by analysts and users for their own uses. Common terms include operating _____ and free _____.

a. Flow-through entity
b. Commercial paper
c. Controlling interest
d. Cash flow

65. _____ is one of the four Ps of the marketing mix. The other three aspects are product, promotion, and place. It is also a key variable in microeconomic price allocation theory.
a. Pricing
b. Price
c. Target costing
d. Cost-plus pricing

66. In finance, _____ also known as return on investment, rate of profit or sometimes just return, is the ratio of money gained or lost on an investment relative to the amount of money invested. The amount of money gained or lost may be referred to as interest, profit/loss, gain/loss, or net income/loss. The money invested may be referred to as the asset, capital, principal, or the cost basis of the investment.
a. Rate of return
b. Debt to capital ratio
c. Theoretical ex-rights price
d. Capital employed

67. The term _____ is used in finance theory to refer to any terminating stream of fixed payments over a specified period of time. This usage is most commonly seen in academic discussions of finance, usually in connection with the valuation of the stream of payments, taking into account time value of money concepts such as interest rate and future value.

Examples of these are regular deposits to a savings account, monthly home mortgage payments and monthly insurance payments.

a. Appropriation
b. Improvement
c. Annuity
d. Intangible

68. A _____ is a type of bond that allows the issuer of the bond to retain the privilege of redeeming the bond at some point before the bond reaches the date of maturity. In other words, on the call dates, the issuer has the right, but not the obligation, to buy back the bonds from the bond holders at the call price. Technically speaking, the bonds are not really bought and held by the issuer but cancelled immediately.

a. Catastrophe bonds
c. Coupon rate
b. Zero-coupon
d. Callable bond

69. _____ is a legal document issued to lenders and describes key terms such as the interest rate, maturity date, convertibility, pledge, promises, representations, covenants, and other terms of the bond offering. When the Offering Memorandum is prepared in advance of marketing a Bond, the indenture will typically be summarised in the 'Description of Notes' section.
  a. Leasing
  b. Consumer protection laws
  c. Malpractice
  d. Bond indenture

70. _____ is a legal term that refers to a holder of property on behalf of a beneficiary. A trust can be set up either to benefit particular persons, or for any charitable purposes (but not generally for non-charitable purposes): typical examples are a will trust for the testator's children and family, a pension trust (to confer benefits on employees and their families), and a charitable trust. In all cases, the _____ may be a person or company, whether or not they are a prospective beneficiary.
  a. Trustee
  b. Cash cow
  c. Performance measurement
  d. Management by exception

71. An _____ is a legal contract between two parties, particularly for indentured labour or a term of apprenticeship but also for certain land transactions. The term comes from the medieval English '_____ of retainer' -- a legal contract written in duplicate on the same sheet, with the copies separated by cutting along a jagged line so that the teeth of the two parts could later be refitted to confirm authenticity. Each party to the deed would then retain a part.
  a. Operating Lease
  b. Employee Retirement Income Security Act
  c. Impracticability
  d. Indenture

72. A _____ is like a lottery bond issued by the United Kingdom government's National Savings and Investments scheme. The government promises to buy back the bond, on request, for its original price.

_____s were introduced by the government in 1956, with the aim of encouraging saving and controlling inflation, with the first bonds going on sale on 1 November of that year.

  a. Zero-coupon bond
  b. Premium Bond
  c. Revenue bonds
  d. Callable bond

73. _____ is a form of corporation equity ownership represented in the securities. It is a stock whose dividends are based on market fluctuations. It is dangerous in comparison to preferred shares and some other investment options, in that in the event of bankruptcy, _____ investors receive their funds after preferred stock holders, bondholders, creditors, etc. On the other hand, common shares on average perform better than preferred shares or bonds over time.
  a. Growth investing
  b. Stock split
  c. 3M Company
  d. Common stock

74. In finance, a _____ is a type of bond that can be converted into shares of stock in the issuing company, usually at some pre-announced ratio. It is a hybrid security with debt- and equity-like features. Although it typically has a low coupon rate, the holder is compensated with the ability to convert the bond to common stock, usually at a substantial discount to the stock's market value.

Chapter 7. Accounting for and Presentation of Liabilities

a. Zero-coupon bond
c. Zero-coupon
b. Coupon rate
d. Convertible bond

75. A _____ is defined as a certificate of agreement of loans which is given under the company's stamp and carries an undertaking that the _____ holder will get a fixed return (fixed on the basis of interest rates) and the principal amount whenever the _____ matures.

In finance, a _____ is a long-term debt instrument used by governments and large companies to obtain funds. It is defined as 'any form of borrowing that commits a firm to pay interest and repay capital.

a. Loan to value
c. Loan
b. Credit rating
d. Debenture

76. _____ is an accounting concept, meaning a future tax liability or asset, resulting from temporary differences between book (accounting) value of assets and liabilities and their tax value, or timing differences between the recognition of gains and losses in financial statements and their recognition in a tax computation.

Temporary differences are differences between the carrying amount of an asset or liability recognised in the balance sheet and the amount attributed to that asset or liability for tax purposes (the tax base.)

a. Federal tax revenue by state
c. Deficit
b. Tax refund
d. Deferred tax

77. _____ is a term used in accounting, economics and finance to spread the cost of an asset over the span of several years.

In simple words we can say that _____ is the reduction in the value of an asset due to usage, passage of time, wear and tear, technological outdating or obsolescence, depletion, inadequacy, rot, rust, decay or other such factors.

In accounting, _____ is a term used to describe any method of attributing the historical or purchase cost of an asset across its useful life, roughly corresponding to normal wear and tear.

a. Net profit
c. Depreciation
b. General ledger
d. Current asset

78. The _____ is the current method of accelerated asset depreciation required by the United States income tax code. Under _____, all assets are divided into classes which dictate the number of years over which an asset's cost will be recovered.

Prior to the Accelerated Cost Recovery System (ACRS), most capital purchases were depreciated using a straight line technique, that allowed for the depreciation of the asset over its useful life.

Chapter 7. Accounting for and Presentation of Liabilities

a. Categorical grants
c. BMC Software, Inc.
b. Modified accelerated cost recovery system
d. 3M Company

79. A _____ is the transfer of an interest in property (or the equivalent in law - a charge) to a lender as a security for a debt - usually a loan of money. While a _____ in itself is not a debt, it is the lender's security for a debt. It is a transfer of an interest in land (or the equivalent) from the owner to the _____ lender, on the condition that this interest will be returned to the owner when the terms of the _____ have been satisfied or performed.
a. Mortgage
c. 3M Company
b. BMC Software, Inc.
d. BNSF Railway

80. _____ is typically a 'higher ranking' stock than voting shares, and its terms are negotiated between the corporation and the investor.

_____ usually carries no voting rights, but may carry superior priority over common stock in the payment of dividends and upon liquidation. _____ may carry a dividend that is paid out prior to any dividends being paid to common stock holders.

a. Cash flow
c. Restricted stock
b. Gross income
d. Preferred stock

81. _____ are financial bonds that mature in installments over a period of time. In effect, a $100,000, 5-year serial bond would mature in a $20,000 annuity over a 5-year interval. Bond issues consisting of a series of blocks of securities maturing in sequence, the coupon rate can be different.
a. Serial bonds
c. Just-in-time
b. Household and Dependent Care Credit
d. Low Income Housing Tax Credit

82. In physics, and more specifically kinematics, _____ is the change in velocity over time. Because velocity is a vector, it can change in two ways: a change in magnitude and/or a change in direction. In one dimension, _____ is the rate at which something speeds up or slows down.
a. AIG
c. ABC Television Network
b. AMEX
d. Acceleration

83. A _____ or a tax-deductible expense affects a taxpayer's income tax. A _____ represents an expense incurred by a taxpayer. They are variable amounts that you can subtract, or deduct, from your gross income.It is subtracted from gross income when the taxpayer computes his or her income taxes.
a. Tax avoidance
c. Tax protester constitutional arguments
b. Tax incidence
d. Tax deduction

84. There are several methods for calculating depreciation, generally based on either the passage of time or the level of activity (or use) of the asset.

_____ is the simplest and most often used technique, in which the company estimates the salvage value of the asset at the end of the period during which it will be used to generate revenues (useful life), and will expense a portion of original cost in equal increments over that period.

Chapter 7. Accounting for and Presentation of Liabilities

a. Pro forma
c. Straight-line depreciation
b. Closing entries
d. Current asset

85. A _____ is used in research to outline possible courses of action or to present a preferred approach to an idea or thought. For example, the philosopher Isaiah Berlin used the 'hedgehogs' versus 'foxes' approach; a 'hedgehog' might approach the world in terms of a single organizing principle; a 'fox' might pursue multiple conflicting goals simultaneously. Alternatively, an empiricist might approach a subject by direct examination, whereas an intuitionist might simply intuit what's next.
   a. 3M Company
   c. BNSF Railway
   b. Conceptual Framework
   d. BMC Software, Inc.

86. A _____ is a pool of assets forming an independent legal entity that are bought with the contributions to a pension plan for the exclusive purpose of financing pension plan benefits.

_____s are important shareholders of listed and private companies. They are especially important to the stock market where large institutional investors like the Ontario Teachers' Pension Plan dominate.

   a. Public offering
   c. Return on assets
   b. Limited liability company
   d. Pension fund

87. _____ are financial statements that factor the holding company's subsidiaries into its aggregated accounting figure. It is a representation of how the holding company is doing as a group. The consolidated accounts should provide a true and fair view of the financial and operating conditions of the group.
   a. Committee on Accounting Procedure
   c. Redemption value
   b. Consolidated financial statements
   d. Replacement cost

88. _____ that may or may not be incurred by an entity depending on the outcome of a future event such as a court case. These liabilities are recorded in a company's accounts and shown in the balance sheet when both probable and reasonably estimable. A footnote to the balance sheet describes the nature and extent of the _____.
   a. Tangible
   c. Headnote
   b. Contingent liabilities
   d. Nonacquiescence

89. _____ in business is an accounting concept that refers to ownership of a company (subsidiary) that is less than 50% of outstanding shares. _____ belongs to other investors and is reported on the consolidated balance sheet of the owning company to reflect the claim on assets belonging to other, non-controlling shareholders. Also, _____ is reported on the consolidated income statement as a share of profit belonging to minority shareholders.
   a. Subledger
   c. Bankruptcy prediction
   b. Credit memo
   d. Minority interest

90. _____ means the giving out of information, either voluntarily or to be in compliance with legal regulations or workplace rules.

- In Computer security, full _____ means disclosing full information about vulnerabilities.
- In computing, _____ widget
- Journalism, full _____ refers to disclosing the interests of the writer which may bear on the subject being written about, for example, if the writer has worked with an interview subject in the past.

- In law:
    - The law of England and Wales, _____ refers to a process that may form part of legal proceedings, whereby parties inform to other parties the existence of any relevant documents that are, or have been, in their control. This compares with the process known as discovery in the course of legal proceedings in the United States.
    - In U.S. civil procedure (litigation rules for civil cases), _____ is a stage prior to trial. In civil cases, each party must disclose to the opposing party the following: names of witnesses which it may use to support its side, copies of documents (or mere description of these documents) in its control which it may use to support its side, computation of damages claimed, and certain insurance information. _____ is related to, but technically prior to, the discovery stage.
    - In Company law (known as 'corporate law' in the United States), _____ refers to giving out information about public or limited companies or their officers, which might be kept secret if the company was a private company or a partnership.

- In real property transactions, _____ refers to providing to a buyer information known to the seller or broker/agent concerning the condition or other aspects of real property that would affect the property's value or desirability. These rules regarding what information must be disclosed, and whether the information must be disclosed even if a buyer does not ask, vary from one jurisdiction to the next.

a. Trailing
c. Controlled Foreign Corporations
b. Tax harmonisation
d. Disclosure

Chapter 8. Accounting for and Presentation of Owners' Equity　　　　95

1. _____ are sometimes the same as net worth, or shareholders' equity - assets minus liabilities. The term _____ is commonly used with charities or not for profit entities. Although these entities don't make money, it is important to maintain reasonable reserves to help future growth.

   a. Net interest spread　　　　　　　　　b. Debtor days
   c. Net assets　　　　　　　　　　　　　d. Sortino ratio

2. In business and accounting, _____ are everything of value that is owned by a person or company. It is a claim on the property your income of a borrower. The balance sheet of a firm records the monetary value of the _____ owned by the firm.

   a. Assets　　　　　　　　　　　　　　b. Earnings before interest, taxes, depreciation and amortization
   c. Accounts receivable　　　　　　　　d. Accrual basis accounting

3. In financial accounting, a _____ or statement of financial position is a summary of a person's or organization's balances. Assets, liabilities and ownership equity are listed as of a specific date, such as the end of its financial year. A _____ is often described as a snapshot of a company's financial condition.

   a. Financial statements　　　　　　　　b. Balance sheet
   c. 3M Company　　　　　　　　　　　d. Statement of retained earnings

4. In economics, _____ or _____ goods or real _____ refers to factors of production used to create goods or services that are not themselves significantly consumed (though they may depreciate) in the production process. _____ goods may be acquired with money or financial _____. In finance and accounting, _____ generally refers to financial wealth, especially that used to start or maintain a business.

   a. Screening　　　　　　　　　　　　b. Vyborg Appeal
   c. Capital　　　　　　　　　　　　　d. Disclosure

5. _____ is a specific term used in companies' financial reporting from the company-whole point of view. Because that use excludes the effects of changing ownership interest, an economic measure of _____ is necessary for financial analysis from the shareholders' point of view

   _____ is defined by the Financial Accounting Standards Board, or FASB, as 'the change in equity [net assets] of a business enterprise during a period from transactions and other events and circumstances from nonowner sources. It includes all changes in equity during a period except those resulting from investments by owners and distributions to owners.'

   _____ is the sum of net income and other items that must bypass the income statement because they have not been realized, including items like an unrealized holding gain or loss from available for sale securities and foreign currency translation gains or losses.

   a. 3M Company　　　　　　　　　　　b. BNSF Railway
   c. Comprehensive income　　　　　　　d. BMC Software, Inc.

6. A _____ is a type of business entity in which partners (owners) share with each other the profits or losses of the business undertaking in which all have invested. _____s are often favored over corporations for taxation purposes, as the _____ structure does not generally incur a tax on profits before it is distributed to the partners (i.e. there is no dividend tax levied.) However, depending on the _____ structure and the jurisdiction in which it operates, owners of a _____ may be exposed to greater personal liability than they would as shareholders of a corporation.

a. Resource Conservation and Recovery Act
b. National Information Infrastructure Protection Act
c. Corporate governance
d. Partnership

7. A sole _____, or simply _____ is a type of business entity which legally has no separate existence from its owner. Hence, the limitations of liability enjoyed by a corporation and limited liability partnerships do not apply to sole proprietors. All debts of the business are debts of the owner.
   a. Free cash flow
   b. Safety stock
   c. Pre-determined overhead rate
   d. Proprietorship

8. _____ is a legally declared inability or impairment of ability of an individual or organization to pay its creditors. Creditors may file a _____ petition against a debtor ('involuntary _____') in an effort to recoup a portion of what they are owed or initiate a restructuring. In the majority of cases, however, _____ is initiated by the debtor (a 'voluntary _____' that is filed by the bankrupt individual or organization.)
   a. Bankruptcy protection
   b. 3M Company
   c. BMC Software, Inc.
   d. Bankruptcy

9. A _____ is a body of elected or appointed members who jointly oversee the activities of a company or organization. The body sometimes has a different name, such as board of trustees, board of governors, board of managers, or executive board. It is often simply referred to as 'the board.'

A board's activities are determined by the powers, duties, and responsibilities delegated to it or conferred on it by an authority outside itself.

   a. Chief Financial Officers Act of 1990
   b. Board of directors
   c. Hospital Survey and Construction Act
   d. Consumer protection laws

10. _____ is a form of corporation equity ownership represented in the securities. It is a stock whose dividends are based on market fluctuations. It is dangerous in comparison to preferred shares and some other investment options, in that in the event of bankruptcy, _____ investors receive their funds after preferred stock holders, bondholders, creditors, etc. On the other hand, common shares on average perform better than preferred shares or bonds over time.
   a. 3M Company
   b. Growth investing
   c. Stock split
   d. Common stock

11. In law, _____ refers to the process by which a company (or part of a company) is brought to an end, and the assets and property of the company redistributed. _____ can also be referred to as winding-up or dissolution, although dissolution technically refers to the last stage of _____. The process of _____ also arises when customs, an authority or agency in a country responsible for collecting and safeguarding customs duties, determines the final computation or ascertainment of the duties or drawback accruing on an entry.
   a. 3M Company
   b. Bankruptcy protection
   c. BMC Software, Inc.
   d. Liquidation

12. A _____ is any one of a variety of different systems, institutions, procedures, social relations and infrastructures whereby persons trade, and goods and services are exchanged, forming part of the economy. It is an arrangement that allows buyers and sellers to exchange things. _____s vary in size, range, geographic scale, location, types and variety of human communities, as well as the types of goods and services traded.

Chapter 8. Accounting for and Presentation of Owners' Equity

a. Market Failure
b. Market
c. Recession
d. Perfect competition

13. _____ is the price at which an asset would trade in a competitive Walrasian auction setting. _____ is often used interchangeably with open _____, fair value or fair _____, although these terms have distinct definitions in different standards, and may differ in some circumstances.

International Valuation Standards defines _____ as 'the estimated amount for which a property should exchange on the date of valuation between a willing buyer and a willing seller in an arme;s-length transaction after proper marketing wherein the parties had each acted knowledgeably, prudently, and without compulsion.'

_____ is a concept distinct from market price, which is e;the price at which one can transacte;, while _____ is e;the true underlying valuee; according to theoretical standards.

a. Sinking fund
b. Market value
c. Debtor
d. Segregated portfolio company

14. A mutual shareholder or _____ is an individual or company (including a corporation) that legally owns one or more shares of stock in a joint stock company. A company's shareholders collectively own that company. Thus, the typical goal of such companies is to enhance shareholder value.

a. Growth investing
b. Stock split
c. Stockholder
d. 3M Company

15. _____ is the planning process used to determine whether a firm's long term investments such as new machinery, replacement machinery, new plants, new products, and research development projects are worth pursuing. It is budget for major capital, or investment, expenditures.

Many formal methods are used in _____, including the techniques such as

- Net present value
- Profitability index
- Internal rate of return
- Modified Internal Rate of Return
- Equivalent annuity

These methods use the incremental cash flows from each potential investment, or project. Techniques based on accounting earnings and accounting rules are sometimes used - though economists consider this to be improper - such as the accounting rate of return, and 'return on investment.' Simplified and hybrid methods are used as well, such as payback period and discounted payback period.

a. Preferred stock
b. Cash flow
c. Gross profit
d. Capital budgeting

Chapter 8. Accounting for and Presentation of Owners' Equity

16. In financial accounting, a _____ is defined as an obligation of an entity arising from past transactions or events, the settlement of which may result in the transfer or use of assets, provision of services or other yielding of economic benefits in the future.
    a. Vested
    b. Corporate governance
    c. False Claims Act
    d. Liability

17. _____ is the state or fact of exclusive rights and control over property, which may be an object, land/real estate or intellectual property. An _____ right is also referred to as title.

    _____ is the key building block in the development of the capitalist socio-economic system.

    a. Encumbrance
    b. ABC Television Network
    c. Administrative proceeding
    d. Ownership

18. _____, in finance and accounting, means stated value or face value. From this comes the expressions at par (at the _____), over par (over _____) and under par (under _____).

    _____ is a nominal value of a security which is determined by an issuer company at a minimum price. _____ of an equity (a stock) is a somewhat archaic concept. The _____ of a stock was the share price upon initial offering; the issuing company promised not to issue further shares below _____, so investors could be confident that no one else was receiving a more favorable issue price. This was far more important in unregulated equity markets than in the regulated markets that exist today.

    a. Net worth
    b. Creditor
    c. Par value
    d. Restructuring

19. _____ is a multiple-winner voting system intended to promote proportional representation while also being simple to understand.

    _____ is used frequently in corporate governance, where it is mandated by many U.S. states, and it was used to elect the Illinois House of Representatives from 1870 until its repeal in 1980. It was used in England in the late 19th century to elect school boards.

    a. BNSF Railway
    b. 3M Company
    c. Cumulative voting
    d. BMC Software, Inc.

20. _____ is the maximum number of shares that a company can issue. This number is specified in the company's articles of association but can be changed by shareholder approval. A company usually authorizes a higher number of shares than required to be able to issue stock in the future.
    a. Restructuring
    b. Fair market value
    c. Shares authorized
    d. Disposal tax effect

21. _____ is a term of law and finance for the quantity of shares of a corporation, which have been sold or awarded and are subsequently held by the shareholders.

Chapter 8. Accounting for and Presentation of Owners' Equity

The number of _____ usually a subset of the total authorized shares, which the board of directors and/or shareholders have agreed to distribute under certain circumstances.

- Shares authorized = Shares issued + Shares unissued
- Shares issued = Shares outstanding + Treasury stock

a. Exclusive right
b. Operating Lease
c. Investment Advisers Act of 1940
d. Issued shares

22. _____ are common shares that have been authorized, issued, and purchased by investors. They have voting rights and represent ownership in the corporation by the person or institution that holds the shares. They should be distinguished from treasury shares, which are common stock repurchased by the corporation.
a. Participating preferred stock
b. Preferred stock
c. Shares outstanding
d. Controlling interest

23. A _____ is a right to acquire certain property in preference to any other person. It usually refers to property newly coming into existence. A right to acquire existing property in preference to any other person is usually referred to as a right of first refusal.

In practice, the most common form of _____ is the right of existing shareholders to acquire newly issued shares issued by a company in a rights issue, a usually but not always public offering.

a. Disclosure requirement
b. Fiduciary
c. Pre-emption right
d. Corporate governance

24. A _____ or reacquired stock is stock which is bought back by the issuing company, reducing the amount of outstanding stock on the open market ('open market' including insiders' holdings).

Stock repurchases are often used as a tax-efficient method to put cash into shareholders' hands, rather than pay dividends. Sometimes, companies do this when they feel that their stock is undervalued on the open market.

a. Net profit
b. Treasury stock
c. Cost of goods sold
d. Matching principle

25. _____ are payments made by a corporation to its shareholder members. It is the portion of corporate profits paid out to stockholders. When a corporation earns a profit or surplus, that money can be put to two uses: it can either be re-invested in the business (called retained earnings), or it can be paid to the shareholders as a dividend.
a. Dividend payout ratio
b. Dividend yield
c. Dividend stripping
d. Dividends

26. _____ is typically a 'higher ranking' stock than voting shares, and its terms are negotiated between the corporation and the investor.

_____ usually carries no voting rights, but may carry superior priority over common stock in the payment of dividends and upon liquidation. _____ may carry a dividend that is paid out prior to any dividends being paid to common stock holders.

a. Restricted stock
b. Cash flow
c. Preferred stock
d. Gross income

27. _____ is the price at which the issuing company may choose to repurchase a security before its maturity date.

A bond is purchased at a discount if its _____ exceeds its purchase price. It is purchased at a premium if its purchase price exceeds its _____.

a. Consolidated financial statements
b. Redemption value
c. Trade name
d. Lump sum

28. _____ is the likely price of an asset when it is allowed insufficient time to sell on the open market, thereby reducing its exposure to potential buyers. _____ is typically lower than fair market value. Unlike cash or securities, certain illiquid assets, like real estate, often require a period of several months in order to obtain their fair market value in a sale, and will generally sell for a significantly lower price if a sale is forced to occur in a shorter time period.

a. 3M Company
b. Real Estate Investment Trust
c. REIT
d. Liquidation value

29. An _____ is a practitioner of accountancy, which is the measurement, disclosure or provision of assurance about financial information that helps managers, investors, tax authorities and other decision makers make resource allocation decisions.

The word '_____' is derived from the French 'Compter' which took its origin from the Latin 'Computare'. The word was formerly written in English as 'Accomptant', but in process of time the word, which was always pronounced by dropping the 'p', became gradually changed both in pronunciation and in orthography to its present form.

a. ABC Television Network
b. AIG
c. AMEX
d. Accountant

30. The _____ is the national, professional association of CPAs in the United States, with more than 330,000 members, including CPAs in business and industry, public practice, government, and education; student affiliates; and international associates. It sets ethical standards for the profession and U.S. auditing standards for audits of private companies; federal, state and local governments; and non-profit organizations.

Approximately 40% of its members are engaged in the practice of public accounting, in areas such as auditing, accounting, taxation, general business consulting, business valuation, personal financial planning and business technology.

Chapter 8. Accounting for and Presentation of Owners' Equity 101

a. ABC Television Network
c. Other postemployment benefits
b. AIG
d. American Institute of Certified Public Accountants

31. In finance, a _____ is a debt security, in which the authorized issuer owes the holders a debt and, depending on the terms of the _____, is obliged to pay interest (the coupon) and/or to repay the principal at a later date, termed maturity. It is a formal contract to repay borrowed money with interest at fixed intervals.

Thus a _____ is like a loan: the issuer is the borrower, the _____ holder is the lender, and the coupon is the interest.

a. Zero-coupon bond
c. Revenue bonds
b. Bond
d. Coupon rate

32. A _____ is a type of bond that allows the issuer of the bond to retain the privilege of redeeming the bond at some point before the bond reaches the date of maturity. In other words, on the call dates, the issuer has the right, but not the obligation, to buy back the bonds from the bond holders at the call price. Technically speaking, the bonds are not really bought and held by the issuer but cancelled immediately.

a. Coupon rate
c. Catastrophe bonds
b. Zero-coupon
d. Callable bond

33. _____ is the statutory title of qualified accountants in the United States who have passed the Uniform _____ Examination and have met additional state education and experience requirements for certification as a _____. Individuals who have passed the Exam but have not either accomplished the required on-the-job experience or have previously met it but in the meantime have lapsed their continuing professional education are, in many states, permitted the designation '_____ Inactive' or an equivalent phrase. In most U.S. states, only _____s who are licensed are able to provide to the public attestation (including auditing) opinions on financial statements.

a. Chartered Certified Accountant
c. Certified General Accountant
b. Chartered Accountant
d. Certified Public Accountant

34. In finance, a _____ is a type of bond that can be converted into shares of stock in the issuing company, usually at some pre-announced ratio. It is a hybrid security with debt- and equity-like features. Although it typically has a low coupon rate, the holder is compensated with the ability to convert the bond to common stock, usually at a substantial discount to the stock's market value.

a. Zero-coupon
c. Zero-coupon bond
b. Coupon rate
d. Convertible bond

35. A _____ is a party (e.g. person, organization, company, or government) that has a claim to the services of a second party. It is a person or institution to whom money is owed. The first party, in general, has provided some property or service to the second party under the assumption (usually enforced by contract) that the second party will return an equivalent property or service.

a. Treasury company
c. Creditor
b. Payback period
d. Par value

36. In accounting, _____ or carrying value is the value of an asset according to its balance sheet account balance. For assets, the value is based on the original cost of the asset less any depreciation, amortization or impairment costs made against the asset. Traditionally, a company's _____ is its total assets minus intangible assets and liabilities.

a. Book value
c. Depreciation
b. Matching principle
d. Generally accepted accounting principles

37. _____ is an accounting term which frequently appears as a balance sheet item as a component of shareholders' equity. _____ is used to account for any funds the issuing firm has received over and above the par value of the common stock. It may also be used to account for any gains the firm may derive from selling treasury stock, although this is less commonly seen.

a. Replacement cost
c. Liquidating dividend
b. Realization
d. Capital surplus

38. _____ means the giving out of information, either voluntarily or to be in compliance with legal regulations or workplace rules.

- In Computer security, full _____ means disclosing full information about vulnerabilities.
- In computing, _____ widget
- Journalism, full _____ refers to disclosing the interests of the writer which may bear on the subject being written about, for example, if the writer has worked with an interview subject in the past.

- In law:
    - The law of England and Wales, _____ refers to a process that may form part of legal proceedings, whereby parties inform to other parties the existence of any relevant documents that are, or have been, in their control. This compares with the process known as discovery in the course of legal proceedings in the United States.
    - In U.S. civil procedure (litigation rules for civil cases), _____ is a stage prior to trial. In civil cases, each party must disclose to the opposing party the following: names of witnesses which it may use to support its side, copies of documents (or mere description of these documents) in its control which it may use to support its side, computation of damages claimed, and certain insurance information. _____ is related to, but technically prior to, the discovery stage.
    - In Company law (known as 'corporate law' in the United States), _____ refers to giving out information about public or limited companies or their officers, which might be kept secret if the company was a private company or a partnership.

- In real property transactions, _____ refers to providing to a buyer information known to the seller or broker/agent concerning the condition or other aspects of real property that would affect the property's value or desirability. These rules regarding what information must be disclosed, and whether the information must be disclosed even if a buyer does not ask, vary from one jurisdiction to the next.

a. Tax harmonisation
c. Trailing
b. Controlled Foreign Corporations
d. Disclosure

39. _____ is the term used to refer to the standard framework of guidelines for financial accounting used in any given jurisdiction. _____ includes the standards, conventions, and rules accountants follow in recording and summarizing transactions, and in the preparation of financial statements.

Financial accounting information must be assembled and reported objectively.

Chapter 8. Accounting for and Presentation of Owners' Equity

a. General ledger
c. Current asset
b. Generally accepted accounting principles
d. Long-term liabilities

40. A budget _____ occurs when an entity spends more money than it takes in. The opposite of a budget _____ is a budget surplus. Debt is essentially an accumulated flow of _____s.

a. Progressive tax
c. Land value taxation
b. Windfall profits tax
d. Deficit

41. _____ are formal records of a business' financial activities.

In British English, including United Kingdom company law, _____ are often referred to as accounts, although the term _____ is also used, particularly by accountants.

_____ provide an overview of a business' financial condition in both short and long term.

a. 3M Company
c. Financial statements
b. Statement of retained earnings
d. Notes to the financial statements

42. _____ is a company's financial statement that indicates how the revenue is transformed into the net income The purpose of the _____ is to show managers and investors whether the company made or lost money during the period being reported.

The important thing to remember about an _____ is that it represents a period of time.

a. AIG
c. ABC Television Network
b. AMEX
d. Income statement

43.

The key date to remember for dividend paying stocks is the _____. The Record Date, or Date of Record determines the _____, when you must own the stock.

In order to receive the upcoming dividend payment pay-out you must already own or you must purchase the stock prior to the _____.

a. AMEX
c. AIG
b. ABC Television Network
d. Ex-dividend date

44. A _____ is the transfer of wealth from one party (such as a person or company) to another. A _____ is usually made in exchange for the provision of goods, services or both, or to fulfill a legal obligation.

The simplest and oldest form of _____ is barter, the exchange of one good or service for another.

Chapter 8. Accounting for and Presentation of Owners' Equity

a. 3M Company
c. Payee
b. BMC Software, Inc.
d. Payment

45. On a stock exchange, a _____ or reverse split is the opposite of a stock split, i.e. a stock merge - a reduction in the number of shares and an accompanying increase in the share price. The ratio is also reversed: 1-for-2, 1-for-3 and so on.

There is a stigma attached to doing this so it is not initiated without very good reason.

a. Public good
c. Cost of capital
b. Discount rate
d. Reverse stock split

46. A _____ or stock divide increases or decreases the number of shares in a public company. The price is adjusted such that the before and after market capitalization of the company remains the same and dilution does not occur. Options and warrants are included.

a. 3M Company
c. Stockholder
b. Growth investing
d. Stock split

47. _____ is a subsection in equity where 'other comprehensive income' is accumulated (summed or 'aggregated'.)

The balance of _____ is presented in the Equity section of the Balance Sheet as is the Retained Earnings balance, which aggregates past and current Earnings, and past and current Dividends.

Other comprehensive income is the difference between net income and comprehensive income and represents the certain gains and losses of the enterprise.

a. Inventory turnover ratio
c. Operating budget
b. Authorised capital
d. Accumulated other comprehensive income

48. The _____ is a private, not-for-profit organization whose primary purpose is to develop generally accepted accounting principles (GAAP) within the United States in the public's interest. The Securities and Exchange Commission (SEC) designated the _____ as the organization responsible for setting accounting standards for public companies in the U.S. It was created in 1973, replacing the Accounting Principles Board and the Committee on Accounting Procedure of the American Institute of Certified Public Accountants. The _____'s mission is 'to establish and improve standards of financial accounting and reporting for the guidance and education of the public, including issuers, auditors, and users of financial information.'

The _____ is not a governmental body.

a. Public company
c. Governmental Accounting Standards Board
b. Fannie Mae
d. Financial Accounting Standards Board

Chapter 8. Accounting for and Presentation of Owners' Equity

49. In monetary economics _____ can refer either to a particular _____, for example British Pounds or United States Dollars, or, to the coins and banknotes of a particular _____, which actually form only a small part of the monetary base of a nation's money supply. The other part of a nation's money supply consists of money deposited in banks (sometimes called deposit money), ownership of which can be transferred by means of checks (cheques in the United Kingdom and Australia) or other forms of money transfer such as credit and debit cards. Deposit money and _____ are 'money' in the sense that both are acceptable as a means of exchange, but money need not necessarily be '_____'.
   a. 3M Company
   b. Currency
   c. BNSF Railway
   d. BMC Software, Inc.

50. The Exxon Mobil Corporation is an American oil and gas corporation. It is a direct descendant of John D. Rockefeller's Standard Oil company, formed on November 30, 1999, by the merger of Exxon and Mobil.

_____ is the world's largest publicly traded company when measured by either revenue or market capitalization.

   a. Arthur Betz Laffer
   b. Alan Greenspan
   c. Abby Joseph Cohen
   d. ExxonMobil

51. _____ is a fee paid on borrowed assets. It is the price paid for the use of borrowed money , or, money earned by deposited funds .Assets that are sometimes lent with _____ include money, shares, consumer goods through hire purchase, major assets such as aircraft, and even entire factories in finance lease arrangements. The _____ is calculated upon the value of the assets in the same manner as upon money.
   a. ABC Television Network
   b. Insolvency
   c. Interest
   d. AIG

52. The _____ is one of the basic financial statements as per Generally Accepted Accounting Principles, and it explains the changes in a company's retained earnings over the reporting period. It breaks down changes affecting the account, such as profits or losses from operations, dividends paid, and any other items charged or credited to retained earnings. A retained earnings statement is required by Generally Accepted Accounting Principles whenever comparative balance sheets and income statements are presented.
   a. Financial statements
   b. Statement of retained earnings
   c. 3M Company
   d. Notes to the financial statements

53. An _____ is a company whose main business is holding securities of other companies purely for investment purposes. The _____ invests money on behalf of its shareholders who in turn share in the profits and losses.

In United States securities law, there are at least three types of investment companies :

- Open-End Management Investment Companies (mutual funds)
- Closed-End Management Investment Companies (closed-end funds)
- UITs (unit investment trusts)

A fourth and lesser-known type of _____ under the _____ Act of 1940 is a Face-Amount Certificate Company.

a. AMEX
b. ABC Television Network
c. AIG
d. Investment company

54. A _____ is a professionally managed type of collective investment scheme that pools money from many investors and invests it in stocks, bonds, short-term money market instruments, and/or other securities. The _____ will have a fund manager that trades the pooled money on a regular basis. As of early 2008, the worldwide value of all _____s totals more than $26 trillion.

a. Laffer curve
b. Moving average
c. Mutual fund
d. Competition law

55. NYSE Amex Equities, formerly known as the _____ is an _____ situated in New York. AMEX was a mutual organization, owned by its members. Until 1953 it was known as the New York Curb Exchange.

a. AIG
b. AMEX
c. ABC Television Network
d. American Stock Exchange

56. The _____ is an investment strategy popularized by Michael Oe;Higgins in 1991 which proposes that an investor annually select for investment the ten Dow Jones Industrial Average stocks whose dividend is the highest fraction of their price.

Proponents of the _____ strategy argue that blue chip companies do not alter their dividend to reflect trading conditions and, therefore, the dividend is a measure of the average worth of the company; the stock price, in contrast, fluctuates through the business cycle. This should mean that companies with a high yield, with high dividend relative to price, are near the bottom of their business cycle and are likely to see their stock price increase faster than low yield companies.

a. Value based pricing
b. BMC Software, Inc.
c. 3M Company
d. Dogs of the Dow

57. _____ is an American publishing and financial information firm.

The company was founded in 1882 by three reporters: Charles Dow, Edward Jones, and Charles Bergstresser. Like The New York Times and the Washington Post, the company was in recent years publicly traded but privately controlled.

a. Dow Jones ' Company
b. Professional association
c. Multinational corporation
d. MicroStrategy

58. The _____ (acronym of National Association of Securities Dealers Automated Quotations) is an American stock exchange. It is the largest electronic screen-based equity securities trading market in the United States. With approximately 3,800 companies, it has more trading volume per hour than any other stock exchange in the world.

a. Variance
b. Sale of goods
c. Sustainability measurement
d. NASDAQ

59. _____ is an equity (stock) exchange located at 11 Wall Street in lower Manhattan, New York, USA.) It is the largest stock exchange in the world by dollar value of its listed companies' securities. As of October 2008, the combined capitalization of all domestic _____ listed companies was US$10.1 trillion.

Chapter 8. Accounting for and Presentation of Owners' Equity

a. BMC Software, Inc.
c. BNSF Railway
b. 3M Company
d. New York Stock Exchange

60. A _____, (formerly a securities exchange) is a corporation or mutual organization which provides 'trading' facilities for stock brokers and traders, to trade stocks and other securities. _____s also provide facilities for the issue and redemption of securities as well as other financial instruments and capital events including the payment of income and dividends. The securities traded on a _____ include: shares issued by companies, unit trusts, derivatives, pooled investment products and bonds.

a. BMC Software, Inc.
c. 3M Company
b. BNSF Railway
d. Stock Exchange

Chapter 9. The Income Statement and the Statement of Cash Flows

1. Net income is informally called the _____ because it is typically found on the last line of a company's income statement. A related term is top line, meaning revenue, which forms the first line of the account statement.

An equation for net income in merchandising:

Net income or net loss = Revenue - Cost of goods sold - Sales discounts - Sales returns and allowances - Expenses - Minority interest - Preferred stock dividends

   a. Current asset
   c. Payroll
   b. Pro forma
   d. Bottom line

2. In accounting, _____ or sales profit is the difference between revenue and the cost of making a product or providing a service, before deducting overhead, payroll, taxation, and interest payments. Note that this is different from operating profit (earnings before interest and taxes.)

Net sales are calculated:

   Net sales = Sales - Sales returns and allowances.

   a. Participating preferred stock
   c. Capital structure
   b. Commercial paper
   d. Gross profit

3. _____ is a company's financial statement that indicates how the revenue is transformed into the net income The purpose of the _____ is to show managers and investors whether the company made or lost money during the period being reported.

The important thing to remember about an _____ is that it represents a period of time.

   a. ABC Television Network
   c. AMEX
   b. AIG
   d. Income statement

4. _____ is equal to the income that a firm has after subtracting costs and expenses from the total revenue. _____ can be distributed among holders of common stock as a dividend or held by the firm as retained earnings.

The items deducted will typically include tax expense, financing expense (interest expense), and minority interest. Likewise, preferred stock dividends will be subtracted too, though they are not an expense.

   a. Matching principle
   c. Generally accepted accounting principles
   b. Net income
   d. Long-term liabilities

5. _____ is the difference between operating revenues and operating expenses, but it is also sometimes used as a synonym for EBIT and operating profit. This is true if the firm has no non-_____.

A professional investor contemplating a change to the capital structure of a firm first evaluates a firm's fundamental earnings potential (reflected by Earnings Before Interest, Taxes, Depreciation and Amortization EBITDA and EBIT), and then determines the optimal use of debt vs. equity.

Chapter 9. The Income Statement and the Statement of Cash Flows

a. ABC Television Network
b. Operating income
c. AMEX
d. AIG

6. In financial accounting, a _____ or statement of financial position is a summary of a person's or organization's balances. Assets, liabilities and ownership equity are listed as of a specific date, such as the end of its financial year. A _____ is often described as a snapshot of a company's financial condition.

a. Financial statements
b. Balance sheet
c. Statement of retained earnings
d. 3M Company

7. _____ is the balance of the amounts of cash being received and paid by a business during a defined period of time, sometimes tied to a specific project. Measurement of _____ can be used

- to evaluate the state or performance of a business or project.
- to determine problems with liquidity. Being profitable does not necessarily mean being liquid. A company can fail because of a shortage of cash, even while profitable.
- to project rate of returns. The time of _____s into and out of projects are used as inputs to financial models such as internal rate of return, and net present value.
- to examine income or growth of a business when it is believed that accrual accounting concepts do not represent economic realities. Alternately, _____ can be used to 'validate' the net income generated by accrual accounting.

_____ as a generic term may be used differently depending on context, and certain _____ definitions may be adapted by analysts and users for their own uses. Common terms include operating _____ and free _____.

a. Commercial paper
b. Cash flow
c. Flow-through entity
d. Controlling interest

8. _____, Gross profit margin or Gross Profit Rate can be defined as the amount of contribution to the business enterprise, after paying for direct-fixed and direct-variable unit costs, required to cover overheads (fixed commitments) and provide a buffer for unknown items. It expresses the relationship between gross profit and sales revenue.

It can be expressed in absolute terms:

Gross Profit = Revenue − Cost of Goods Sold

or as the ratio of gross profit to sales revenue, usually in the form of a percentage:

_____ Percentage = (Revenue-Cost of Goods Sold)/Revenue

Cost of goods sold includes variable costs and fixed costs directly linked to the product, such as material and labor.

a. BMC Software, Inc.
b. BNSF Railway
c. 3M Company
d. Gross margin

9. _____ is a cornerstone of accrual accounting together with the revenue recognition principle. They both determine the accounting period, in which revenues and expenses are recognized. According to the principle, expenses are recognized when obligations are (1) incurred (usually when goods are transferred or services rendered, e.g. sold), and (2) offset against recognized revenues, which were generated from those expenses (related on the cause-and-effect basis), no matter when cash is paid out.

    a. Payroll
    b. Net sales
    c. Current liabilities
    d. Matching principle

10. A _____ is used in research to outline possible courses of action or to present a preferred approach to an idea or thought. For example, the philosopher Isaiah Berlin used the 'hedgehogs' versus 'foxes' approach; a 'hedgehog' might approach the world in terms of a single organizing principle; a 'fox' might pursue multiple conflicting goals simultaneously. Alternatively, an empiricist might approach a subject by direct examination, whereas an intuitionist might simply intuit what's next.

    a. BNSF Railway
    b. BMC Software, Inc.
    c. Conceptual Framework
    d. 3M Company

11. _____ is generally understood in financial circles as the point at which revenue is recognized, typically through a transaction which involves the exchange of an asset, product, or service for cash or its equivalents.

This approach gives the accounting division a strictly objective basis for changing the books. For example, a homeowner may believe that his house has grown in value during a strong market, or fallen in value during a weak market, but until the house is actually sold for a specific price to a specific buyer, the change in value can only be estimated and is considered unrealized.

    a. Merck ' Co., Inc.
    b. Total-factor productivity
    c. Valuation
    d. Realization

12. _____ principle is a cornerstone of accrual accounting together with matching principle. They both determine the accounting period, in which revenues and expenses are recognized. According to the principle, revenues are recognized when they are (1) realized or realizable, and are (2) earned (usually when goods are transferred or services rendered), no matter when cash is received.

    a. Net realizable value
    b. 3M Company
    c. Revenue recognition
    d. BMC Software, Inc.

13. In bookkeeping, accounting, and finance, _____ are operating revenues earned by a company when it sells its products. Revenue (_____) are reported directly on the income statement as Sales or _____.

In financial ratios that use income statement sales values, 'sales' refers to _____, not gross sales.

    a. Historical cost
    b. Matching principle
    c. Deferred
    d. Net sales

14. A _____ is the pinnacle activity involved in selling products or services in return for money or other compensation. It is an act of completion of a commercial activity.

A _____ is completed by the seller, the owner of the goods.

Chapter 9. The Income Statement and the Statement of Cash Flows

a. Tertiary sector of economy
c. Maturity

b. High yield stock
d. Sale

15. In economics, the _____, (or _____) measures the payments that flow between any individual country and all other countries. It is used to summarize all international economic transactions for that country during a specific time period, usually a year. The _____ is determined by the country's exports and imports of goods, services, and financial capital, as well as financial transfers.

a. Stock split
c. Yield to maturity

b. Balance of payments
d. Moving average

16. _____ refers to services paid for in advance. Examples include tolls, pay as you go cell phones, and stored-value cards such as gift cards and preloaded credit cards. _____ accounts are assets, and they are increased by debiting the account(s.)

a. 3M Company
c. BNSF Railway

b. BMC Software, Inc.
d. Prepaid

17. _____ is a form of corporation equity ownership represented in the securities. It is a stock whose dividends are based on market fluctuations. It is dangerous in comparison to preferred shares and some other investment options, in that in the event of bankruptcy, _____ investors receive their funds after preferred stock holders, bondholders, creditors, etc. On the other hand, common shares on average perform better than preferred shares or bonds over time.

a. 3M Company
c. Growth investing

b. Stock split
d. Common stock

18. A _____ is an annual report required by the U.S. Securities and Exchange Commission (SEC), that gives a comprehensive summary of a public company's performance. Although similarly named, the annual report on _____ is distinct from the often glossy 'annual report to shareholders', which a company must send to its shareholders when it holds an annual meeting to elect directors (though some companies combine the annual report and the 10-K into one document.) The 10-K includes information such as company history, organizational structure, executive compensation, equity, subsidiaries, and audited financial statements, among other information.

a. 3M Company
c. Form 10-K

b. Form 10-Q
d. Form 8-K

19. An _____, operating expenditure, operational expense, operational expenditure or OPEX is an on-going cost for running a product, business, or system. Its counterpart, a capital expenditure (CAPEX), is the cost of developing or providing non-consumable parts for the product or system. For example, the purchase of a photocopier is the CAPEX, and the annual paper and toner cost is the OPEX.

a. AIG
c. ABC Television Network

b. AMEX
d. Operating expense

20. _____ is typically a 'higher ranking' stock than voting shares, and its terms are negotiated between the corporation and the investor.

_____ usually carries no voting rights, but may carry superior priority over common stock in the payment of dividends and upon liquidation. _____ may carry a dividend that is paid out prior to any dividends being paid to common stock holders.

a. Gross income
b. Cash flow
c. Restricted stock
d. Preferred stock

21. In finance, a _____ is a debt security, in which the authorized issuer owes the holders a debt and, depending on the terms of the _____, is obliged to pay interest (the coupon) and/or to repay the principal at a later date, termed maturity. It is a formal contract to repay borrowed money with interest at fixed intervals.

Thus a _____ is like a loan: the issuer is the borrower, the _____ holder is the lender, and the coupon is the interest.

a. Coupon rate
b. Bond
c. Revenue bonds
d. Zero-coupon bond

22. In finance, a _____ is a type of bond that can be converted into shares of stock in the issuing company, usually at some pre-announced ratio. It is a hybrid security with debt- and equity-like features. Although it typically has a low coupon rate, the holder is compensated with the ability to convert the bond to common stock, usually at a substantial discount to the stock's market value.

a. Convertible bond
b. Zero-coupon
c. Coupon rate
d. Zero-coupon bond

23. In accounting, _____ has a very specific meaning. It is an outflow of cash or other valuable assets from a person or company to another person or company. This outflow of cash is generally one side of a trade for products or services that have equal or better current or future value to the buyer than to the seller.

a. AIG
b. Expense
c. AMEX
d. ABC Television Network

24. In economics, business, retail, and accounting, a _____ is the value of money that has been used up to produce something, and hence is not available for use anymore. In economics, a _____ is an alternative that is given up as a result of a decision. In business, the _____ may be one of acquisition, in which case the amount of money expended to acquire it is counted as _____.

a. Prime cost
b. Cost of quality
c. Cost allocation
d. Cost

25. In financial accounting, _____ or cost of sales includes the direct costs attributable to the production of the goods sold by a company. This amount includes the materials cost used in creating the goods along with the direct labor costs used to produce the good. It excludes indirect expenses such as distribution costs and sales force costs.

a. FIFO and LIFO accounting
b. 3M Company
c. Cost of goods sold
d. Reorder point

26. In financial accounting the term inventory _____ is the loss of products between point of manufacture or purchase from supplier and point of sale. The term relates to the difference in the amount of margin or profit a retailer can obtain. If the amount of _____ is large, then profits go down which results in increased costs to the consumer to meet the needs of the retailer.

a. Maturity
b. Screening
c. Shrinkage
d. Homogeneous

Chapter 9. The Income Statement and the Statement of Cash Flows

27. _____ refers to a business or organization attempting to acquire goods or services to accomplish the goals of the enterprise. Though there are several organizations that attempt to set standards in the _____ process, processes can vary greatly between organizations. Typically the word e;_____e; is not used interchangeably with the word e;procuremente;, since procurement typically includes Expediting, Supplier Quality, and Traffic and Logistics (T'L) in addition to _____.
   a. Supply chain
   b. Free port
   c. Consignor
   d. Purchasing

28. _____ is the calculated approximation of a result which is usable even if input data may be incomplete or uncertain.

In statistics, see _____ theory, estimator.

In mathematics, approximation or _____ typically means finding upper or lower bounds of a quantity that cannot readily be computed precisely and is also an educated guess .

   a. ABC Television Network
   b. Estimation
   c. AIG
   d. AMEX

29. _____ in economics and business is the result of an exchange and from that trade we assign a numerical monetary value to a good, service or asset. If Alice trades Bob 4 apples for an orange, the _____ of an orange is 4 apples. Inversely, the _____ of an apple is 1/4 oranges.
   a. Price
   b. Price discrimination
   c. Discounts and allowances
   d. Transactional Net Margin Method

30. _____ are formal records of a business' financial activities.

In British English, including United Kingdom company law, _____ are often referred to as accounts, although the term _____ is also used, particularly by accountants.

_____ provide an overview of a business' financial condition in both short and long term.

   a. Financial statements
   b. 3M Company
   c. Statement of retained earnings
   d. Notes to the financial statements

31. _____ are additional notes and information added to the end of the financial statements to supplement the reader with more information. Notes to Financial Statements help explain the computation of specific items in the financial statements as well as provide a more comprehensive assessment of a company's financial condition. Notes to Financial Statements can include information on debt, going concern, accounts, contingent liabilities, or contextual information explaining the financial numbers (e.g. to indicate a lawsuit.)
   a. Financial statements
   b. 3M Company
   c. Notes to the financial statements
   d. Statement of retained earnings

32. In business and accounting, _____ are everything of value that is owned by a person or company. It is a claim on the property your income of a borrower. The balance sheet of a firm records the monetary value of the _____ owned by the firm.

Chapter 9. The Income Statement and the Statement of Cash Flows

a. Accounts receivable
b. Accrual basis accounting
c. Earnings before interest, taxes, depreciation and amortization
d. Assets

33. _____ is a fee paid on borrowed assets. It is the price paid for the use of borrowed money, or, money earned by deposited funds. Assets that are sometimes lent with _____ include money, shares, consumer goods through hire purchase, major assets such as aircraft, and even entire factories in finance lease arrangements. The _____ is calculated upon the value of the assets in the same manner as upon money.
   a. ABC Television Network
   b. Insolvency
   c. AIG
   d. Interest

34. _____ relates to the cost of borrowing money. It is the price that a lender charges a borrower for the use of the lender's money. _____ is different from OPEX and CAPEX, for it relates to the capital structure of a company.
   a. ABC Television Network
   b. AIG
   c. Interest
   d. Interest expense

35. _____ is the corporate management term for the act of partially dismantling or otherwise reorganizing a company for the purpose of making it more profitable. Also known as corporate _____, debt _____ and financial _____.

_____ is often done as part of a bankruptcy or of a strategic takeover by another firm, such as a leveraged buyout by a private equity firm.

   a. Payback period
   b. Net worth
   c. Restructuring
   d. Fair market value

36. In finance, _____ is the interest that has accumulated since the principal investment, or since the previous interest payment if there has been one already. For a financial instrument such as a bond, interest is calculated and paid in set intervals.

The primary formula for calculating the interest accrued in a given period is:

$$I_A = T \times P \times R$$

where I_A is the _____, T is the fraction of the year, P is the principal, and R is the annualized interest rate.

   a. Interest
   b. Accrued interest
   c. AIG
   d. ABC Television Network

37. _____ is a company's earnings per share (EPS) calculated using fully diluted shares outstanding. _____ indicates a 'worst case' scenario, one in which everyone who could have received stock without purchasing it directly for the full market value did so.

Chapter 9. The Income Statement and the Statement of Cash Flows 115

To find _____, basic EPS is calculated for each of the categories on the income statement first. Then each of the dilutive securities are ranked based on their effects, from most dilutive to least dilutive and antidilutive. Then the basic EPS number is diluted one by one by applying each one, skipping any instruments that have an antidilutive effect.

a. Diluted earnings per share
b. Cash conversion cycle
c. Financial ratio
d. Return on assets Du Pont

38. _____ is a specific term used in companies' financial reporting from the company-whole point of view. Because that use excludes the effects of changing ownership interest, an economic measure of _____ is necessary for financial analysis from the shareholders' point of view

_____ is defined by the Financial Accounting Standards Board, or FASB, as 'the change in equity [net assets] of a business enterprise during a period from transactions and other events and circumstances from nonowner sources. It includes all changes in equity during a period except those resulting from investments by owners and distributions to owners.'

_____ is the sum of net income and other items that must bypass the income statement because they have not been realized, including items like an unrealized holding gain or loss from available for sale securities and foreign currency translation gains or losses.

a. BMC Software, Inc.
b. Comprehensive income
c. BNSF Railway
d. 3M Company

39. _____ are the earnings returned on the initial investment amount.

In the US, the Financial Accounting Standards Board (FASB) requires companies' income statements to report _____ for each of the major categories of the income statement: continuing operations, discontinued operations, extraordinary items, and net income.

The _____ formula does not include preferred dividends for categories outside of continued operations and net income.

a. Average accounting return
b. Earnings yield
c. Invested capital
d. Earnings per share

40. In computer security, _____ means to disclose all the details of a security problem which are known. It is a philosophy of security management completely opposed to the idea of security through obscurity. The concept of _____ is controversial, but not new; it has been an issue for locksmiths since the 19th century.

a. 3M Company
b. Full disclosure
c. BNSF Railway
d. BMC Software, Inc.

Chapter 9. The Income Statement and the Statement of Cash Flows

41. An _____ is a tax levied on the financial income of people, corporations, or other legal entities. Various _____ systems exist, with varying degrees of tax incidence. Income taxation can be progressive, proportional, or regressive.

    a. Individual Retirement Arrangement
    b. Income tax
    c. Implied level of government service
    d. Ordinary income

42. _____ is a rent received on a regular basis, with little effort required to maintain it.

Some examples of _____ are:

- Repeated regular income, earned by a sales person, generated from the payment of a product or service that must be renewed on a regular basis, in order to continue receiving its benefits - also called residual income.
- Rental from property;
- Royalties from publishing a book or from licensing a patent or other form of intellectual property;
- Earnings from internet advertisement on your websites;
- Earnings from a business that does not require direct involvement from the owner or merchant;
- Dividend and interest income from owning securities, such as stocks and bonds, are usually referred to as portfolio income, which can be considered a form of _____;
- Pensions.

_____ is usually taxable. The American Internal Revenue Service defines _____ as 'any activity... in which the taxpayer does not materially participate.' Other financial and government institutions also recognize it as an income obtained as a result of capital growth or in relation to negative gearing.

   a. BNSF Railway
   b. 3M Company
   c. BMC Software, Inc.
   d. Passive income

Chapter 9. The Income Statement and the Statement of Cash Flows 117

43. _____ means the giving out of information, either voluntarily or to be in compliance with legal regulations or workplace rules.

- In Computer security, full _____ means disclosing full information about vulnerabilities.
- In computing, _____ widget
- Journalism, full _____ refers to disclosing the interests of the writer which may bear on the subject being written about, for example, if the writer has worked with an interview subject in the past.

- In law:
    - The law of England and Wales, _____ refers to a process that may form part of legal proceedings, whereby parties inform to other parties the existence of any relevant documents that are, or have been, in their control. This compares with the process known as discovery in the course of legal proceedings in the United States.
    - In U.S. civil procedure (litigation rules for civil cases), _____ is a stage prior to trial. In civil cases, each party must disclose to the opposing party the following: names of witnesses which it may use to support its side, copies of documents (or mere description of these documents) in its control which it may use to support its side, computation of damages claimed, and certain insurance information. _____ is related to, but technically prior to, the discovery stage.
    - In Company law (known as 'corporate law' in the United States), _____ refers to giving out information about public or limited companies or their officers, which might be kept secret if the company was a private company or a partnership.

- In real property transactions, _____ refers to providing to a buyer information known to the seller or broker/agent concerning the condition or other aspects of real property that would affect the property's value or desirability. These rules regarding what information must be disclosed, and whether the information must be disclosed even if a buyer does not ask, vary from one jurisdiction to the next.

a. Controlled Foreign Corporations
c. Tax harmonisation
b. Trailing
d. Disclosure

44. _____ are common shares that have been authorized, issued, and purchased by investors. They have voting rights and represent ownership in the corporation by the person or institution that holds the shares. They should be distinguished from treasury shares, which are common stock repurchased by the corporation.
    a. Shares outstanding
    c. Preferred stock
    b. Controlling interest
    d. Participating preferred stock

45. At its simplest, a company's _____ as it sometimes called, is computed in by multiplying the income before tax number, as reported to shareholders, by the appropriate tax rate. In reality, the computation is typically considerably more complex due to things such as expenses considered not deductible by taxing authorities ('add backs'), the range of tax rates applicable to various levels of income, different tax rates in different jurisdictions, multiple layers of tax on income, and other issues.

Historically, in many places, a revenue-expense method was used, in which the income statement was seen as primary, and the balance sheet as secondary.

a. Total Expense Ratio
b. 3M Company
c. Payroll
d. Tax expense

46. _____ are payments made by a corporation to its shareholder members. It is the portion of corporate profits paid out to stockholders. When a corporation earns a profit or surplus, that money can be put to two uses: it can either be re-invested in the business (called retained earnings), or it can be paid to the shareholders as a dividend.
   a. Dividend yield
   b. Dividend stripping
   c. Dividend payout ratio
   d. Dividends

47. _____ is a term used with respect to a retailed product, indicating that the product is in the end of its product lifetime and a vendor will no longer be marketing, selling, or promoting a particular product and may also be limiting or ending support for the product. In the specific case of product sales, the term end-of-sale (EOS) has also been used. The term lifetime, after the last production date, depends on the product and is related to a customer's expected product lifetime.
   a. AIG
   b. ABC Television Network
   c. AMEX
   d. End-of-life

48. The _____ is a private, not-for-profit organization whose primary purpose is to develop generally accepted accounting principles (GAAP) within the United States in the public's interest. The Securities and Exchange Commission (SEC) designated the _____ as the organization responsible for setting accounting standards for public companies in the U.S. It was created in 1973, replacing the Accounting Principles Board and the Committee on Accounting Procedure of the American Institute of Certified Public Accountants. The _____'s mission is 'to establish and improve standards of financial accounting and reporting for the guidance and education of the public, including issuers, auditors, and users of financial information.'

The _____ is not a governmental body.

   a. Governmental Accounting Standards Board
   b. Public company
   c. Fannie Mae
   d. Financial Accounting Standards Board

49. _____ in business is an accounting concept that refers to ownership of a company (subsidiary) that is less than 50% of outstanding shares. _____ belongs to other investors and is reported on the consolidated balance sheet of the owning company to reflect the claim on assets belonging to other, non-controlling shareholders. Also, _____ is reported on the consolidated income statement as a share of profit belonging to minority shareholders.
   a. Subledger
   b. Bankruptcy prediction
   c. Credit memo
   d. Minority interest

Chapter 9. The Income Statement and the Statement of Cash Flows 119

50. _____ is the process of increasing, or accounting for, an amount over a period of time. Particular instances of the term include:

- _____, the allocation of a lump sum amount to different time periods, particularly for loans and other forms of finance, including related interest or other finance charges.
    - _____ schedule, a table detailing each periodic payment on a loan (typically a mortgage), as generated by an _____ calculator.
    - Negative _____, an _____ schedule where the loan amount actually increases through not paying the full interest
- Amortized analysis, analyzing the execution cost of algorithms over a sequence of operations.
- _____ of capital expenditures of certain assets under accounting rules, particularly intangible assets, in a manner analogous to depreciation.
- _____

a. Annuity
c. Intangible
b. EBIT
d. Amortization

51. In economics, _____ or _____ goods or real _____ refers to factors of production used to create goods or services that are not themselves significantly consumed (though they may depreciate) in the production process. _____ goods may be acquired with money or financial _____. In finance and accounting, _____ generally refers to financial wealth, especially that used to start or maintain a business.

a. Screening
c. Vyborg Appeal
b. Disclosure
d. Capital

52. _____ is a term used in accounting, economics and finance to spread the cost of an asset over the span of several years.

In simple words we can say that _____ is the reduction in the value of an asset due to usage, passage of time, wear and tear, technological outdating or obsolescence, depletion, inadequacy, rot, rust, decay or other such factors.

In accounting, _____ is a term used to describe any method of attributing the historical or purchase cost of an asset across its useful life, roughly corresponding to normal wear and tear.

a. Depreciation
c. General ledger
b. Current asset
d. Net profit

53. An _____ is a practitioner of accountancy, which is the measurement, disclosure or provision of assurance about financial information that helps managers, investors, tax authorities and other decision makers make resource allocation decisions.

The word '_____' is derived from the French 'Compter' which took its origin from the Latin 'Computare'. The word was formerly written in English as 'Accomptant', but in process of time the word, which was always pronounced by dropping the 'p', became gradually changed both in pronunciation and in orthography to its present form.

Chapter 9. The Income Statement and the Statement of Cash Flows

a. ABC Television Network
c. AMEX

b. AIG
d. Accountant

54. The _____ is the national, professional association of CPAs in the United States, with more than 330,000 members, including CPAs in business and industry, public practice, government, and education; student affiliates; and international associates. It sets ethical standards for the profession and U.S. auditing standards for audits of private companies; federal, state and local governments; and non-profit organizations.

Approximately 40% of its members are engaged in the practice of public accounting, in areas such as auditing, accounting, taxation, general business consulting, business valuation, personal financial planning and business technology.

a. Other postemployment benefits
c. American Institute of Certified Public Accountants

b. AIG
d. ABC Television Network

55. _____ is the statutory title of qualified accountants in the United States who have passed the Uniform _____ Examination and have met additional state education and experience requirements for certification as a _____. Individuals who have passed the Exam but have not either accomplished the required on-the-job experience or have previously met it but in the meantime have lapsed their continuing professional education are, in many states, permitted the designation '_____ Inactive' or an equivalent phrase. In most U.S. states, only _____s who are licensed are able to provide to the public attestation (including auditing) opinions on financial statements.

a. Certified Public Accountant
c. Certified General Accountant

b. Chartered Accountant
d. Chartered Certified Accountant

56. In financial accounting, a _____ or Statement of cash flows is a financial statement that shows a company's flow of cash. The money coming into the business is called cash inflow, and money going out from the business is called cash outflow. The statement shows how changes in balance sheet and income accounts affect cash and cash equivalents, and breaks the analysis down to operating, investing, and financing activities.

a. BNSF Railway
c. BMC Software, Inc.

b. 3M Company
d. Cash flow statement

57. _____ is a business, economics or investment term that refers to an asset's ability to be easily converted through an act of buying or selling without causing a significant movement in the price and with minimum loss of value. Money, or cash on hand, is the most liquid asset. An act of exchange of a less liquid asset with a more liquid asset is called liquidation.

a. Financial instruments
c. Transfer agent

b. Spot rate
d. Market liquidity

Chapter 10. Corporate Governance, Explanatory Notes, and Other Disclosures

1. The general definition of an _____ is an evaluation of a person, organization, system, process, project or product. _____s are performed to ascertain the validity and reliability of information; also to provide an assessment of a system's internal control. The goal of an _____ is to express an opinion on the person/organization/system (etc) in question, under evaluation based on work done on a test basis.
    a. Institute of Chartered Accountants of India
    b. Audit regime
    c. Assurance service
    d. Audit

2. _____ is the set of processes, customs, policies, laws, and institutions affecting the way a corporation is directed, administered or controlled. _____ also includes the relationships among the many stakeholders involved and the goals for which the corporation is governed. The principal stakeholders are the shareholders/members, management, and the board of directors.
    a. Patent
    b. FLSA
    c. Trust indenture
    d. Corporate governance

3. In computer security, _____ means to disclose all the details of a security problem which are known. It is a philosophy of security management completely opposed to the idea of security through obscurity. The concept of _____ is controversial, but not new; it has been an issue for locksmiths since the 19th century.
    a. BNSF Railway
    b. BMC Software, Inc.
    c. 3M Company
    d. Full disclosure

4. The term _____ usually refers to a company that is permitted to offer its registered securities (stock, bonds, etc.) for sale to the general public, typically through a stock exchange, or occasionally a company whose stock is traded over the counter (OTC) via market makers who use non-exchange quotation services.

    The term '_____' may also refer to a company owned by the government.

    a. MicroStrategy
    b. Public Company
    c. Professional association
    d. Governmental Accounting Standards Board

5. The _____ (sometimes called 'Peekaboo') is a private-sector, non-profit corporation created by the Sarbanes-Oxley Act, a 2002 United States federal law, to oversee the auditors of public companies. Its stated purpose is to 'protect the interests of investors and further the public interest in the preparation of informative, fair, and independent audit reports'. Although a private entity, the _____ has many government-like regulatory functions, making it in some ways similar to the private Self Regulatory Organizations (SROs) that regulate stock markets and other aspects of the financial markets in the United States.
    a. Financial Crimes Enforcement Network
    b. 3M Company
    c. Pension Benefit Guaranty Corporation
    d. Public Company Accounting Oversight Board

6. A _____ is a fungible, negotiable instrument representing financial value. they are broadly categorized into debt securities (such as banknotes, bonds and debentures), and equity securities; e.g., common stocks. The company or other entity issuing the _____ is called the issuer.
    a. Security
    b. Tracking stock
    c. BMC Software, Inc.
    d. 3M Company

122 Chapter 10. Corporate Governance, Explanatory Notes, and Other Disclosures

7. The U.S. _____ is an independent agency of the United States government which holds primary responsibility for enforcing the federal securities laws and regulating the securities industry, the nation's stock and options exchanges, and other electronic securities markets. The SEC was created by section 4 of the Securities Exchange Act of 1934 (now codified as 15 U.S.C. ÂÂ§ 78d and commonly referred to as the 1934 Act.)

   a. BNSF Railway
   b. 3M Company
   c. BMC Software, Inc.
   d. Securities and Exchange Commission

8. _____ means the giving out of information, either voluntarily or to be in compliance with legal regulations or workplace rules.

- In Computer security, full _____ means disclosing full information about vulnerabilities.
- In computing, _____ widget
- Journalism, full _____ refers to disclosing the interests of the writer which may bear on the subject being written about, for example, if the writer has worked with an interview subject in the past.

- In law:
    - The law of England and Wales, _____ refers to a process that may form part of legal proceedings, whereby parties inform to other parties the existence of any relevant documents that are, or have been, in their control. This compares with the process known as discovery in the course of legal proceedings in the United States.
    - In U.S. civil procedure (litigation rules for civil cases), _____ is a stage prior to trial. In civil cases, each party must disclose to the opposing party the following: names of witnesses which it may use to support its side, copies of documents (or mere description of these documents) in its control which it may use to support its side, computation of damages claimed, and certain insurance information. _____ is related to, but technically prior to, the discovery stage.
    - In Company law (known as 'corporate law' in the United States), _____ refers to giving out information about public or limited companies or their officers, which might be kept secret if the company was a private company or a partnership.

- In real property transactions, _____ refers to providing to a buyer information known to the seller or broker/agent concerning the condition or other aspects of real property that would affect the property's value or desirability. These rules regarding what information must be disclosed, and whether the information must be disclosed even if a buyer does not ask, vary from one jurisdiction to the next.

   a. Trailing
   b. Controlled Foreign Corporations
   c. Disclosure
   d. Tax harmonisation

9. _____ are formal records of a business' financial activities.

In British English, including United Kingdom company law, _____ are often referred to as accounts, although the term _____ is also used, particularly by accountants.

_____ provide an overview of a business' financial condition in both short and long term.

Chapter 10. Corporate Governance, Explanatory Notes, and Other Disclosures

a. Statement of retained earnings
c. Notes to the financial statements
b. 3M Company
d. Financial statements

10. _____ are additional notes and information added to the end of the financial statements to supplement the reader with more information. Notes to Financial Statements help explain the computation of specific items in the financial statements as well as provide a more comprehensive assessment of a company's financial condition. Notes to Financial Statements can include information on debt, going concern, accounts, contingent liabilities, or contextual information explaining the financial numbers (e.g. to indicate a lawsuit.)

a. Statement of retained earnings
c. Notes to the financial statements
b. 3M Company
d. Financial statements

11. _____ is a legally declared inability or impairment of ability of an individual or organization to pay its creditors. Creditors may file a _____ petition against a debtor ('involuntary _____') in an effort to recoup a portion of what they are owed or initiate a restructuring. In the majority of cases, however, _____ is initiated by the debtor (a 'voluntary _____' that is filed by the bankrupt individual or organization.)

a. BMC Software, Inc.
c. Bankruptcy
b. Bankruptcy protection
d. 3M Company

12. _____ asserts that there is a technique, method, process, activity, incentive or reward that is more effective at delivering a particular outcome than any other technique, method, process, etc. The idea is that with proper processes, checks, and testing, a desired outcome can be delivered with fewer problems and unforeseen complications. _____s can also be defined as the most efficient (least amount of effort) and effective (best results) way of accomplishing a task, based on repeatable procedures that have proven themselves over time for large numbers of people.

a. Best practice
c. Management by objectives
b. Cash cow
d. Performance measurement

13. The _____ is a private, not-for-profit organization whose primary purpose is to develop generally accepted accounting principles (GAAP) within the United States in the public's interest. The Securities and Exchange Commission (SEC) designated the _____ as the organization responsible for setting accounting standards for public companies in the U.S. It was created in 1973, replacing the Accounting Principles Board and the Committee on Accounting Procedure of the American Institute of Certified Public Accountants. The _____'s mission is 'to establish and improve standards of financial accounting and reporting for the guidance and education of the public, including issuers, auditors, and users of financial information.'

The _____ is not a governmental body.

a. Governmental Accounting Standards Board
c. Public company
b. Fannie Mae
d. Financial Accounting Standards Board

14. A _____ is an annual report required by the U.S. Securities and Exchange Commission (SEC), that gives a comprehensive summary of a public company's performance. Although similarly named, the annual report on _____ is distinct from the often glossy 'annual report to shareholders', which a company must send to its shareholders when it holds an annual meeting to elect directors (though some companies combine the annual report and the 10-K into one document.) The 10-K includes information such as company history, organizational structure, executive compensation, equity, subsidiaries, and audited financial statements, among other information.

a. Form 10-Q
b. Form 10-K
c. 3M Company
d. Form 8-K

15. The _____ of 2002 (Pub.L. 107-204, 116 Stat. 745, enacted July 30, 2002), also known as the Public Company Accounting Reform and Investor Protection Act of 2002, is a United States federal law enacted on July 30, 2002 in response to a number of major corporate and accounting scandals including those affecting Enron, Tyco International, Adelphia, Peregrine Systems and WorldCom. The legislation establishes new or enhanced standards for all U.S. public company boards, management, and public accounting firms. It does not apply to privately held companies.

a. Fair Labor Standards Act
b. FCPA
c. Lease
d. Sarbanes-Oxley Act

16. _____ of something is, in finance, the adding together of interest or different investments over a period of time such as atoms (1 - the act or process of accruing; 2 - the amount that accrues.) It holds specific meanings in accounting and payroll.

_____, in accounting, describes the accounting method known as _____ basis, whereby revenues and expenses are recognized when they are accrued, i.e. accumulated (earned or incurred), regardless when the actual cash is received or paid out.

a. Accrual
b. Assets
c. Earnings before interest, taxes, depreciation and amortization
d. Accounts receivable

17. In the technical language of the World Trade Organization (WTO) system, a _____ is used to restrain international trade in order to protect a certain home industry from foreign competition. A member may take a e; _____ e; action (i.e., restrict importation of a product temporarily) to protect a specific domestic industry from an increase in imports of any product which is causing, or which is threatening to cause, serious injury to the domestic industry that produces like or directly-competitive products.

_____ measures were always available under the General Agreement on Tariffs and Trade (GATT) (Article XIX.)

a. BMC Software, Inc.
b. 3M Company
c. Safeguard
d. BNSF Railway

18. _____ LLP, based in Chicago, was once one of the 'Big Five' accounting firms among PricewaterhouseCoopers, Deloitte Touche Tohmatsu, Ernst ' Young and KPMG, providing auditing, tax, and consulting services to large corporations. In 2002, the firm voluntarily surrendered its licenses to practice as Certified Public Accountants in the United States after being found guilty of criminal charges relating to the firm's handling of the auditing of Enron, the energy corporation, resulting in the loss of 85,000 jobs. Although the verdict was subsequently overturned by the Supreme Court of the United States, it has not returned as a viable business.

a. ABC Television Network
b. AIG
c. AMEX
d. Arthur Andersen

Chapter 10. Corporate Governance, Explanatory Notes, and Other Disclosures 125

19. _____, the Electronic Data-Gathering, Analysis, and Retrieval system, performs automated collection, validation, indexing, acceptance, and forwarding of submissions by companies and others who are required by law to file forms with the U.S. Securities and Exchange Commission (the 'SEC'.) The database is freely available to the public via Web or FTP, typically posting in excess of 3,000 filings per day.

Not all SEC filings by public companies are available on _____.

a. AMEX
b. AIG
c. ABC Television Network
d. EDGAR

20. A mutual shareholder or _____ is an individual or company (including a corporation) that legally owns one or more shares of stock in a joint stock company. A company's shareholders collectively own that company. Thus, the typical goal of such companies is to enhance shareholder value.

a. Stockholder
b. 3M Company
c. Growth investing
d. Stock split

21. _____ is a term used in accounting, economics and finance to spread the cost of an asset over the span of several years.

In simple words we can say that _____ is the reduction in the value of an asset due to usage, passage of time, wear and tear, technological outdating or obsolescence, depletion, inadequacy, rot, rust, decay or other such factors.

In accounting, _____ is a term used to describe any method of attributing the historical or purchase cost of an asset across its useful life, roughly corresponding to normal wear and tear.

a. General ledger
b. Net profit
c. Current asset
d. Depreciation

22. In physics, and more specifically kinematics, _____ is the change in velocity over time. Because velocity is a vector, it can change in two ways: a change in magnitude and/or a change in direction. In one dimension, _____ is the rate at which something speeds up or slows down.

a. AIG
b. ABC Television Network
c. AMEX
d. Acceleration

23. In economics, business, retail, and accounting, a _____ is the value of money that has been used up to produce something, and hence is not available for use anymore. In economics, a _____ is an alternative that is given up as a result of a decision. In business, the _____ may be one of acquisition, in which case the amount of money expended to acquire it is counted as _____.

a. Cost of quality
b. Cost allocation
c. Cost
d. Prime cost

24. _____ are financial statements that factor the holding company's subsidiaries into its aggregated accounting figure. It is a representation of how the holding company is doing as a group. The consolidated accounts should provide a true and fair view of the financial and operating conditions of the group.

Chapter 10. Corporate Governance, Explanatory Notes, and Other Disclosures

a. Replacement cost
b. Redemption value
c. Committee on Accounting Procedure
d. Consolidated financial statements

25. In accounting, _____ are considered liabilities of the business that are to be settled in cash within the fiscal year or the operating cycle, whichever period is longer.

For example accounts payable for goods, services or supplies that were purchased for use in the operation of the business and payable within a normal period of time would be _____.

Bonds, mortgages and loans that are payable over a term exceeding one year would be fixed liabilities.

a. Payroll
b. Closing entries
c. Treasury stock
d. Current liabilities

26. _____, in accrual accounting, is any account where the asset or liability is not realized until a future date (accounting period), e.g. annuities, charges, taxes, income, etc. The _____ item may be carried, dependent on type of deferral, as either an asset or liability.
a. Deferred
b. Cash basis accounting
c. Pro forma
d. Payroll

27. _____ is an accounting concept, meaning a future tax liability or asset, resulting from temporary differences between book (accounting) value of assets and liabilities and their tax value, or timing differences between the recognition of gains and losses in financial statements and their recognition in a tax computation.

Temporary differences are differences between the carrying amount of an asset or liability recognised in the balance sheet and the amount attributed to that asset or liability for tax purposes (the tax base.)

a. Federal tax revenue by state
b. Deferred tax
c. Tax refund
d. Deficit

28. Employment is a contract between two parties, one being the employer and the other being the _____. An _____ may be defined as: 'A person in the service of another under any contract of hire, express or implied, oral or written, where the employer has the power or right to control and direct the _____ in the material details of how the work is to be performed.' Black's Law Dictionary page 471 (5th ed. 1979.)
a. ABC Television Network
b. AMEX
c. AIG
d. Employee

29. _____ and benefits in kind are various non-wage compensations provided to employees in addition to their normal wages or salaries. Where an employee exchanges (cash) wages for some other form of benefit, this is generally referred to as a 'salary sacrifice' arrangement. In most countries, most kinds of _____ are taxable to at least some degree.
a. ABC Television Network
b. AMEX
c. Employee benefits
d. AIG

Chapter 10. Corporate Governance, Explanatory Notes, and Other Disclosures

30. An _____ is a tax levied on the financial income of people, corporations, or other legal entities. Various _____ systems exist, with varying degrees of tax incidence. Income taxation can be progressive, proportional, or regressive.
    a. Implied level of government service
    b. Income tax
    c. Individual Retirement Arrangement
    d. Ordinary income

31. An _____ allows a company to provide a monetary value for items that make up their inventory. Inventories are usually the largest current asset of a business, and proper measurement of them is necessary to assure accurate financial statements. If inventory is not properly measured, expenses and revenues cannot be properly matched and a company could make poor business decisions.
    a. AIG
    b. AMEX
    c. ABC Television Network
    d. Inventory valuation

32. An _____, operating expenditure, operational expense, operational expenditure or OPEX is an on-going cost for running a product, business, or system. Its counterpart, a capital expenditure (CAPEX), is the cost of developing or providing non-consumable parts for the product or system. For example, the purchase of a photocopier is the CAPEX, and the annual paper and toner cost is the OPEX.
    a. ABC Television Network
    b. AIG
    c. AMEX
    d. Operating expense

33. _____ is one of a series of accounting transactions dealing with the billing of customers who owe money to a person, company or organization for goods and services that have been provided to the customer. In most business entities this is typically done by generating an invoice and mailing or electronically delivering it to the customer, who in turn must pay it within an established timeframe called credit or payment terms.

An example of a common payment term is Net 30, meaning payment is due in the amount of the invoice 30 days from the date of invoice.

    a. Accrual
    b. Accrued revenue
    c. Adjusting entries
    d. Accounts receivable

34. In business and accounting, _____ are everything of value that is owned by a person or company. It is a claim on the property your income of a borrower. The balance sheet of a firm records the monetary value of the _____ owned by the firm.
    a. Accrual basis accounting
    b. Accounts receivable
    c. Earnings before interest, taxes, depreciation and amortization
    d. Assets

35. _____, in accrual accounting, (e.g. advance payment received from a client) is, according to revenue recognition, revenue not earned until the delivery of goods or services, which until then, is still owed to the payer, hence remaining a liability.

_____, sometimes referred to as deferred revenue or unearned revenue, shares characteristics with accrued expense with the difference that a liability to be covered latter is cash received FROM a counterpart, while goods or services are to be delivered in a latter period, when such income item is earned, the related revenue item is recognized, and the same amount is deducted from deferred revenues.

| a. Deferred income | b. Gross sales |
| c. Treasury stock | d. Matching principle |

36. In accounting, _____ has a very specific meaning. It is an outflow of cash or other valuable assets from a person or company to another person or company. This outflow of cash is generally one side of a trade for products or services that have equal or better current or future value to the buyer than to the seller.

| a. AMEX | b. Expense |
| c. ABC Television Network | d. AIG |

37. In financial accounting, a _____ is defined as an obligation of an entity arising from past transactions or events, the settlement of which may result in the transfer or use of assets, provision of services or other yielding of economic benefits in the future.

| a. Vested | b. Corporate governance |
| c. False Claims Act | d. Liability |

38. In finance, _____ is the process of estimating the potential market value of a financial asset or liability. They can be done on assets (for example, investments in marketable securities such as stocks, options, business enterprises, or intangible assets such as patents and trademarks) or on liabilities (e.g., Bonds issued by a company.) A _____ is required in many contexts including investment analysis, capital budgeting, merger and acquisition transactions, financial reporting, taxable events to determine the proper tax liability, and in litigation.

| a. Valuation | b. Daybook |
| c. Vyborg Appeal | d. Disclosure |

39. _____ is a form of corporation equity ownership represented in the securities. It is a stock whose dividends are based on market fluctuations. It is dangerous in comparison to preferred shares and some other investment options, in that in the event of bankruptcy, _____ investors receive their funds after preferred stock holders, bondholders, creditors, etc. On the other hand, common shares on average perform better than preferred shares or bonds over time.

| a. Stock split | b. Common stock |
| c. 3M Company | d. Growth investing |

40. _____ is a company's earnings per share (EPS) calculated using fully diluted shares outstanding. _____ indicates a 'worst case' scenario, one in which everyone who could have received stock without purchasing it directly for the full market value did so.

To find _____, basic EPS is calculated for each of the categories on the income statement first. Then each of the dilutive securities are ranked based on their effects, from most dilutive to least dilutive and antidilutive. Then the basic EPS number is diluted one by one by applying each one, skipping any instruments that have an antidilutive effect.

| a. Cash conversion cycle | b. Return on assets Du Pont |
| c. Diluted earnings per share | d. Financial ratio |

41. _____ is a specific term used in companies' financial reporting from the company-whole point of view. Because that use excludes the effects of changing ownership interest, an economic measure of _____ is necessary for financial analysis from the shareholders' point of view

Chapter 10. Corporate Governance, Explanatory Notes, and Other Disclosures 129

_____ is defined by the Financial Accounting Standards Board, or FASB, as 'the change in equity [net assets] of a business enterprise during a period from transactions and other events and circumstances from nonowner sources. It includes all changes in equity during a period except those resulting from investments by owners and distributions to owners.'

_____ is the sum of net income and other items that must bypass the income statement because they have not been realized, including items like an unrealized holding gain or loss from available for sale securities and foreign currency translation gains or losses.

- a. BNSF Railway
- c. 3M Company
- b. Comprehensive income
- d. BMC Software, Inc.

42. _____ are the earnings returned on the initial investment amount.

In the US, the Financial Accounting Standards Board (FASB) requires companies' income statements to report _____ for each of the major categories of the income statement: continuing operations, discontinued operations, extraordinary items, and net income.

The _____ formula does not include preferred dividends for categories outside of continued operations and net income.

- a. Earnings per share
- c. Invested capital
- b. Average accounting return
- d. Earnings yield

43. _____, also called fair price (in a commonplace conflation of the two distinct concepts), is a concept used in finance and economics, defined as a rational and unbiased estimate of the potential market price of a good, service, or asset, taking into account such objective factors as:

- acquisition/production/distribution costs, replacement costs, or costs of close substitutes
- actual utility at a given level of development of social productive capability
- supply vs. demand

and subjective factors such as

- risk characteristics
- cost of capital
- individually perceived utility

Chapter 10. Corporate Governance, Explanatory Notes, and Other Disclosures

In accounting, _____ is used as an estimate of the market value of an asset (or liability) for which a market price cannot be determined (usually because there is no established market for the asset.) Under GAAP (FAS 157), _____ is the amount at which the asset could be bought or sold in a current transaction between willing parties, or transferred to an equivalent party, other than in a liquidation sale. This is used for assets whose carrying value is based on mark-to-market valuations; for assets carried at historical cost, the _____ of the asset is not used. One example of where _____ is an issue is a College kitchen with a cost of $2 million which was built 5 years ago.

a. BMC Software, Inc.
b. Fair value
c. 3M Company
d. BNSF Railway

44. _____ are defined as identifiable non-monetary assets that cannot be seen, touched or physically measured, which are created through time and/or effort and that are identifiable as a separate asset. There are two primary forms of intangibles - legal intangibles (such as trade secrets (e.g., customer lists), copyrights, patents, trademarks, and goodwill) and competitive intangibles (such as knowledge activities (know-how, knowledge), collaboration activities, leverage activities, and structural activities.) Legal intangibles are known under the generic term intellectual property and generate legal property rights defensible in a court of law.

a. Overhead
b. ABC Television Network
c. AIG
d. Intangible assets

45. _____ refers to services paid for in advance. Examples include tolls, pay as you go cell phones, and stored-value cards such as gift cards and preloaded credit cards. _____ accounts are assets, and they are increased by debiting the account(s.)

a. 3M Company
b. BNSF Railway
c. BMC Software, Inc.
d. Prepaid

46. _____ is the process of increasing, or accounting for, an amount over a period of time. Particular instances of the term include:

- _____, the allocation of a lump sum amount to different time periods, particularly for loans and other forms of finance, including related interest or other finance charges.
  - _____ schedule, a table detailing each periodic payment on a loan (typically a mortgage), as generated by an _____ calculator.
  - Negative _____, an _____ schedule where the loan amount actually increases through not paying the full interest
- Amortized analysis, analyzing the execution cost of algorithms over a sequence of operations.
- _____ of capital expenditures of certain assets under accounting rules, particularly intangible assets, in a manner analogous to depreciation.
- _____

a. EBIT
b. Intangible
c. Annuity
d. Amortization

Chapter 10. Corporate Governance, Explanatory Notes, and Other Disclosures

47. In finance, an _____ is a contract between a buyer and a seller that gives the buyer the right--but not the obligation--to buy or to sell a particular asset (the underlying asset) at a later time at an agreed price. In return for granting the _____, the seller collects a payment (the premium) from the buyer. A call _____ gives the buyer the right to buy the underlying asset; a put _____ gives the buyer of the _____ the right to sell the underlying asset.

   a. AIG   b. AMEX
   c. ABC Television Network   d. Option

48. In economic models, the _____ time frame assumes no fixed factors of production. Firms can enter or leave the marketplace, and the cost (and availability) of land, labor, raw materials, and capital goods can be assumed to vary. In contrast, in the short-run time frame, certain factors are assumed to be fixed, because there is not sufficient time for them to change.

   a. BMC Software, Inc.   b. 3M Company
   c. Short-run   d. Long-run

49. The _____ (acronym of National Association of Securities Dealers Automated Quotations) is an American stock exchange. It is the largest electronic screen-based equity securities trading market in the United States. With approximately 3,800 companies, it has more trading volume per hour than any other stock exchange in the world.

   a. Sustainability measurement   b. NASDAQ
   c. Sale of goods   d. Variance

50. _____ is that which is owed; usually referencing assets owed, but the term can also cover moral obligations and other interactions not requiring money. In the case of assets, _____ is a means of using future purchasing power in the present before a summation has been earned. Some companies and corporations use _____ as a part of their overall corporate finance strategy.

   a. Loan   b. Debenture
   c. Lender   d. Debt

51. _____ is one of the four Ps of the marketing mix. The other three aspects are product, promotion, and place. It is also a key variable in microeconomic price allocation theory.

   a. Price   b. Cost-plus pricing
   c. Target costing   d. Pricing

52. An _____ is a practitioner of accountancy, which is the measurement, disclosure or provision of assurance about financial information that helps managers, investors, tax authorities and other decision makers make resource allocation decisions.

The word '_____' is derived from the French 'Compter' which took its origin from the Latin 'Computare'. The word was formerly written in English as 'Accomptant', but in process of time the word, which was always pronounced by dropping the 'p', became gradually changed both in pronunciation and in orthography to its present form.

   a. Accountant   b. ABC Television Network
   c. AMEX   d. AIG

53. The _____ is the national, professional association of CPAs in the United States, with more than 330,000 members, including CPAs in business and industry, public practice, government, and education; student affiliates; and international associates. It sets ethical standards for the profession and U.S. auditing standards for audits of private companies; federal, state and local governments; and non-profit organizations.

Approximately 40% of its members are engaged in the practice of public accounting, in areas such as auditing, accounting, taxation, general business consulting, business valuation, personal financial planning and business technology.

  a. Other postemployment benefits
  b. AIG
  c. ABC Television Network
  d. American Institute of Certified Public Accountants

54. An _____ is a meeting that official bodies, and associations involving the public, are often required by law to hold.

An _____ is generally held every year to inform their members of previous and future activities.

  a. AMEX
  b. ABC Television Network
  c. AIG
  d. Annual general meeting

55. An _____ is a comprehensive report on a company's activities throughout the preceding year. _____s are intended to give shareholders and other interested persons information about the company's activities and financial performance. Most jurisdictions require companies to prepare and disclose _____s, and many require the _____ to be filed at the company's registry.
  a. AMEX
  b. AIG
  c. Annual report
  d. ABC Television Network

56. _____ is the statutory title of qualified accountants in the United States who have passed the Uniform _____ Examination and have met additional state education and experience requirements for certification as a _____. Individuals who have passed the Exam but have not either accomplished the required on-the-job experience or have previously met it but in the meantime have lapsed their continuing professional education are, in many states, permitted the designation '_____ Inactive' or an equivalent phrase. In most U.S. states, only _____s who are licensed are able to provide to the public attestation (including auditing) opinions on financial statements.
  a. Certified Public Accountant
  b. Certified General Accountant
  c. Chartered Accountant
  d. Chartered Certified Accountant

57. Congress enacted the _____, in the aftermath of the stock market crash of 1929 and during the ensuing Great Depression.
  a. Securities Act of 1933
  b. Monte Carlo methods
  c. Bookkeeping
  d. Sustainability measurement

58. The _____ of 1934 is a law governing the secondary trading of securities (stocks, bonds, and debentures) in the United States of America. The Act, 48 Stat. 881 (enacted June 6, 1934), codified at 15 U.S.C.
  a. BMC Software, Inc.
  b. BNSF Railway
  c. 3M Company
  d. Securities Exchange Act

Chapter 10. Corporate Governance, Explanatory Notes, and Other Disclosures

59. The _____ is a law governing the secondary trading of securities (stocks, bonds, and debentures) in the United States of America. The Act, 48 Stat. 881 (enacted June 6, 1934), codified at 15 U.S.C.
   a. 3M Company
   b. BNSF Railway
   c. BMC Software, Inc.
   d. Securities Exchange Act of 1934

60. In accounting, _____ or carrying value is the value of an asset according to its balance sheet account balance. For assets, the value is based on the original cost of the asset less any depreciation, amortization or impairment costs made against the asset. Traditionally, a company's _____ is its total assets minus intangible assets and liabilities.
   a. Matching principle
   b. Depreciation
   c. Generally accepted accounting principles
   d. Book value

61. _____ is a term in both law and accounting that is based on the economics term of 'market value.' It is also a common basis for assessing damages to be awarded for the loss of or damage to the property, generally in a claim under tort or a contract of insurance.

A _____ is often an estimate of what a willing buyer would pay to a willing seller, both in a free market, for an asset or any piece of property. If such a transaction actually occurs, then the actual transaction price is usually the _____.

   a. Fair market value
   b. Shares authorized
   c. Cash and cash equivalents
   d. Disposal tax effect

62. _____ is a cornerstone of accrual accounting together with the revenue recognition principle. They both determine the accounting period, in which revenues and expenses are recognized. According to the principle, expenses are recognized when obligations are (1) incurred (usually when goods are transferred or services rendered, e.g. sold), and (2) offset against recognized revenues, which were generated from those expenses (related on the cause-and-effect basis), no matter when cash is paid out.
   a. Current liabilities
   b. Payroll
   c. Net sales
   d. Matching principle

63. In business or economics a _____ is a combination of two companies into one larger company. Such actions are commonly voluntary and involve stock swap or cash payment to the target. Stock swap is often used as it allows the shareholders of the two companies to share the risk involved in the deal. A _____ can resemble a takeover but result in a new company name (often combining the names of the original companies) and in new branding; in some cases, terming the combination a '_____' rather than an acquisition is done purely for political or marketing reasons.
   a. BNSF Railway
   b. Merger
   c. 3M Company
   d. BMC Software, Inc.

64. The phrase _____ refers to the aspect of corporate strategy, corporate finance and management dealing with the buying, selling and combining of different companies that can aid, finance, or help a growing company in a given industry grow rapidly without having to create another business entity.
   a. 3M Company
   b. BMC Software, Inc.
   c. BNSF Railway
   d. Mergers and acquisitions

65. An _____ is the buying of one company by another. An _____ may be friendly or hostile. In the former case, the companies cooperate in negotiations; in the latter case, the takeover target is unwilling to be bought or the target's board has no prior knowledge of the offer. _____ usually refers to a purchase of a smaller firm by a larger one. Sometimes, however, a smaller firm will acquire management control of a larger or longer established company and keep its name for the combined entity. This is known as a reverse takeover.
   a. AMEX
   b. AIG
   c. ABC Television Network
   d. Acquisition

66. In economics, _____ or _____ goods or real _____ refers to factors of production used to create goods or services that are not themselves significantly consumed (though they may depreciate) in the production process. _____ goods may be acquired with money or financial _____. In finance and accounting, _____ generally refers to financial wealth, especially that used to start or maintain a business.
   a. Vyborg Appeal
   b. Disclosure
   c. Screening
   d. Capital

67. _____ is a type of lease - the other being an operating lease. A _____ effectively allows a firm to finance the purchase of an asset, even if, strictly speaking, the firm never acquires the asset. Typically, a _____ will give the lessee control over an asset for a large proportion of the asset's useful life, providing them the benefits and risks of ownership.
   a. Profitability index
   b. 3M Company
   c. Debt ratio
   d. Finance lease

68. _____ is a fee paid on borrowed assets. It is the price paid for the use of borrowed money, or, money earned by deposited funds. Assets that are sometimes lent with _____ include money, shares, consumer goods through hire purchase, major assets such as aircraft, and even entire factories in finance lease arrangements. The _____ is calculated upon the value of the assets in the same manner as upon money.
   a. Insolvency
   b. ABC Television Network
   c. Interest
   d. AIG

69. A _____ is a contract conferring a right on one person to possess property belonging to another person (called a landlord or lessor) to the exclusion of the owner landlord. It is a rental agreement between landlord and tenant. The relationship between the tenant and the landlord is called a tenancy, and the right to possession by the tenant is sometimes called a leasehold interest.
   a. Lease
   b. Model Code of Professional Responsibility
   c. Robinson-Patman Act
   d. Federal Sentencing Guidelines

70. A _____ is any one of a variety of different systems, institutions, procedures, social relations and infrastructures whereby persons trade, and goods and services are exchanged, forming part of the economy. It is an arrangement that allows buyers and sellers to exchange things. _____s vary in size, range, geographic scale, location, types and variety of human communities, as well as the types of goods and services traded.
   a. Recession
   b. Market Failure
   c. Market
   d. Perfect competition

71. _____ is the price at which an asset would trade in a competitive Walrasian auction setting. _____ is often used interchangeably with open _____, fair value or fair _____, although these terms have distinct definitions in different standards, and may differ in some circumstances.

International Valuation Standards defines _____ as 'the estimated amount for which a property should exchange on the date of valuation between a willing buyer and a willing seller in an arme;s-length transaction after proper marketing wherein the parties had each acted knowledgeably, prudently, and without compulsion.'

_____ is a concept distinct from market price, which is e;the price at which one can transacte;, while _____ is e;the true underlying valuee; according to theoretical standards.

   a. Sinking fund
   c. Debtor
   b. Segregated portfolio company
   d. Market value

72.   In financial accounting, a _____ or statement of financial position is a summary of a person's or organization's balances. Assets, liabilities and ownership equity are listed as of a specific date, such as the end of its financial year. A _____ is often described as a snapshot of a company's financial condition.
   a. Financial statements
   c. 3M Company
   b. Balance sheet
   d. Statement of retained earnings

73.   _____ is the term used to refer to the standard framework of guidelines for financial accounting used in any given jurisdiction. _____ includes the standards, conventions, and rules accountants follow in recording and summarizing transactions, and in the preparation of financial statements.

Financial accounting information must be assembled and reported objectively.

   a. General ledger
   c. Generally accepted accounting principles
   b. Long-term liabilities
   d. Current asset

74.   In accounting, _____ is the original monetary value of an economic item. In some circumstances, assets and liabilities may be shown at their _____, as if there had been no change in value since the date of acquisition. The balance sheet value of the item may therefore differ from the 'true' value.
   a. Matching principle
   c. Bottom line
   b. Cost of goods sold
   d. Historical cost

75.   In economics, _____ is a rise in the general level of prices of goods and services in an economy over a period of time. When the general price level rises, each unit of currency buys fewer goods and services; consequently, _____ is also a decline in the real value of money--a loss of purchasing power in the medium of exchange which is also the monetary unit of account in the economy. A chief measure of general price-level _____ is the general _____ rate, which is the percentage change in a general price index (normally the Consumer Price Index) over time.
   a. Opportunity cost
   c. ABC Television Network
   b. AIG
   d. Inflation

76.   A _____ is the pinnacle activity involved in selling products or services in return for money or other compensation. It is an act of completion of a commercial activity.

A _____ is completed by the seller, the owner of the goods.

a. High yield stock
b. Maturity
c. Tertiary sector of economy
d. Sale

77. In the United States, the _____ is the senior technical committee designated by the American Institute of Certified Public Accountants (AICPA) to issue auditing, attestation, and quality control statements, standards and guidance to certified public accountants (CPAs) for non-public company audits. Created in October 1978, it is composed of 19 members representing various industries and sectors, including public accountants and private, educational, and governmental entities. It issues pronouncements in the form of statements, interpretations, and guidelines, which all CPAs must adhere to when performing audits and attestations.

a. Assurance service
b. Information audit
c. Auditing Standards Board
d. Engagement Letter

78. In finance, _____ also known as return on investment, rate of profit or sometimes just return, is the ratio of money gained or lost on an investment relative to the amount of money invested. The amount of money gained or lost may be referred to as interest, profit/loss, gain/loss, or net income/loss. The money invested may be referred to as the asset, capital, principal, or the cost basis of the investment.

a. Capital employed
b. Debt to capital ratio
c. Theoretical ex-rights price
d. Rate of return

Chapter 11. Financial Statement Analysis

1. In finance, _____ also known as return on investment, rate of profit or sometimes just return, is the ratio of money gained or lost on an investment relative to the amount of money invested. The amount of money gained or lost may be referred to as interest, profit/loss, gain/loss, or net income/loss. The money invested may be referred to as the asset, capital, principal, or the cost basis of the investment.
   - a. Capital employed
   - b. Debt to capital ratio
   - c. Theoretical ex-rights price
   - d. Rate of return

2. _____ of a business involves analyzing its financial statements and health, its management and competitive advantages, and its competitors and markets. The term is used to distinguish such analysis from other types of investment analysis, such as quantitative analysis and technical analysis.

   _____ is performed on historical and present data, but with the goal of making financial forecasts.

   - a. BMC Software, Inc.
   - b. 3M Company
   - c. BNSF Railway
   - d. Fundamental analysis

3. _____ is a business, economics or investment term that refers to an asset's ability to be easily converted through an act of buying or selling without causing a significant movement in the price and with minimum loss of value. Money, or cash on hand, is the most liquid asset. An act of exchange of a less liquid asset with a more liquid asset is called liquidation.
   - a. Spot rate
   - b. Transfer agent
   - c. Financial instruments
   - d. Market liquidity

4. The term '_____' refers to the concept of collecting information and attempting to spot a pattern in the information. In some fields of study, the term '_____' has more formally-defined meanings.

   In project management _____ is a mathematical technique that uses historical results to predict future outcome.

   - a. Multicollinearity
   - b. Regression analysis
   - c. 3M Company
   - d. Trend analysis

5. _____ is a financial metric which represents operating liquidity available to a business. Along with fixed assets such as plant and equipment, _____ is considered a part of operating capital. It is calculated as current assets minus current liabilities.
   - a. Working capital
   - b. BMC Software, Inc.
   - c. Working capital management
   - d. 3M Company

6. In accounting, _____ or carrying value is the value of an asset according to its balance sheet account balance. For assets, the value is based on the original cost of the asset less any depreciation, amortization or impairment costs made against the asset. Traditionally, a company's _____ is its total assets minus intangible assets and liabilities.
   - a. Depreciation
   - b. Matching principle
   - c. Generally accepted accounting principles
   - d. Book value

7. In economics, _____ or _____ goods or real _____ refers to factors of production used to create goods or services that are not themselves significantly consumed (though they may depreciate) in the production process. _____ goods may be acquired with money or financial _____. In finance and accounting, _____ generally refers to financial wealth, especially that used to start or maintain a business.

a. Disclosure
b. Vyborg Appeal
c. Screening
d. Capital

8. _____ is a form of corporation equity ownership represented in the securities. It is a stock whose dividends are based on market fluctuations. It is dangerous in comparison to preferred shares and some other investment options, in that in the event of bankruptcy, _____ investors receive their funds after preferred stock holders, bondholders, creditors, etc. On the other hand, common shares on average perform better than preferred shares or bonds over time.
   a. Growth investing
   b. Stock split
   c. 3M Company
   d. Common stock

9. In finance, a _____ is a debt security, in which the authorized issuer owes the holders a debt and, depending on the terms of the _____, is obliged to pay interest (the coupon) and/or to repay the principal at a later date, termed maturity. It is a formal contract to repay borrowed money with interest at fixed intervals.

Thus a _____ is like a loan: the issuer is the borrower, the _____ holder is the lender, and the coupon is the interest.

   a. Revenue bonds
   b. Coupon rate
   c. Zero-coupon bond
   d. Bond

10. In investment, the _____ assesses the credit worthiness of a corporation's debt issues. It is analogous to credit ratings for individuals and countries. The credit rating is a financial indicator to potential investors of debt securities such as bonds.
    a. Treasury company
    b. Holding gains
    c. Market value
    d. Bond credit rating

11. A _____ assesses the credit worthiness of an individual, corporation, or even a country. It is an evaluation made by credit bureaus of a borrower's overall credit history. They are calculated from financial history and current assets and liabilities.
    a. Credit rating
    b. Debt
    c. Loan
    d. Debenture

12. In economics, business, retail, and accounting, a _____ is the value of money that has been used up to produce something, and hence is not available for use anymore. In economics, a _____ is an alternative that is given up as a result of a decision. In business, the _____ may be one of acquisition, in which case the amount of money expended to acquire it is counted as _____.
    a. Prime cost
    b. Cost of quality
    c. Cost allocation
    d. Cost

13. In business, _____, Overhead cost or _____ expense refers to an ongoing expense of operating a business. The term _____ is usually used to group expenses that are necessary to the continued functioning of the business, but do not directly generate profits.

_____ expenses are all costs on the income statement except for direct labor and direct materials.

Chapter 11. Financial Statement Analysis

a. Intangible assets
c. ABC Television Network
b. AIG
d. Overhead

14. In business and accounting, _____ are everything of value that is owned by a person or company. It is a claim on the property your income of a borrower. The balance sheet of a firm records the monetary value of the _____ owned by the firm.

a. Earnings before interest, taxes, depreciation and amortization
b. Accounts receivable
c. Accrual basis accounting
d. Assets

15. _____ is a financial ratio that measures the efficiency of a company's use of its assets in generating sales revenue or sales income to the company.

$$Asset\ Turnover = \frac{Sales}{Average Total Assets}$$

- 'Sales' is the value of 'Net Sales' or 'Sales' from the company's income statement
- 'Average Total Assets' is the value of 'Total assets' from the company's balance sheet in the beginning and the end of the fiscal period divided by 2.

a. Information ratio
c. Average propensity to consume
b. Enterprise Value/Sales
d. Asset turnover

16. In financial accounting, _____ or cost of sales includes the direct costs attributable to the production of the goods sold by a company. This amount includes the materials cost used in creating the goods along with the direct labor costs used to produce the good. It excludes indirect expenses such as distribution costs and sales force costs.

a. Reorder point
c. 3M Company
b. Cost of goods sold
d. FIFO and LIFO accounting

17. _____ is a term used in accounting, economics and finance to spread the cost of an asset over the span of several years.

In simple words we can say that _____ is the reduction in the value of an asset due to usage, passage of time, wear and tear, technological outdating or obsolescence, depletion, inadequacy, rot, rust, decay or other such factors.

In accounting, _____ is a term used to describe any method of attributing the historical or purchase cost of an asset across its useful life, roughly corresponding to normal wear and tear.

a. Net profit
c. Current asset
b. General ledger
d. Depreciation

Chapter 11. Financial Statement Analysis

18. _____ methods are means of managing inventory and financial matters involving the money a company ties up within inventory of produced goods, raw materials, parts, components, or feed stocks. FIFO stands for first-in, first-out, meaning that the oldest inventory items are recorded as sold first. LIFO stands for last-in, first-out, meaning that the most recently purchased items are recorded as sold first.

    a. 3M Company
    b. Finished good
    c. Reorder point
    d. FIFO and LIFO accounting

19. In physics, and more specifically kinematics, _____ is the change in velocity over time. Because velocity is a vector, it can change in two ways: a change in magnitude and/or a change in direction. In one dimension, _____ is the rate at which something speeds up or slows down.

    a. AIG
    b. AMEX
    c. ABC Television Network
    d. Acceleration

20. Just in Time could refer to the following:

- _____, an inventory strategy that reduces in-process inventory
- _____ compilation, a technique for improving the performance of bytecode-compiled programming systems

    a. Comparable
    b. Fiscal
    c. Help desk and incident reporting auditing
    d. Just-in-time

21. _____ is one of a series of accounting transactions dealing with the billing of customers who owe money to a person, company or organization for goods and services that have been provided to the customer. In most business entities this is typically done by generating an invoice and mailing or electronically delivering it to the customer, who in turn must pay it within an established timeframe called credit or payment terms.

An example of a common payment term is Net 30, meaning payment is due in the amount of the invoice 30 days from the date of invoice.

    a. Accrued revenue
    b. Accrual
    c. Adjusting entries
    d. Accounts receivable

22. A _____ is the pinnacle activity involved in selling products or services in return for money or other compensation. It is an act of completion of a commercial activity.

A _____ is completed by the seller, the owner of the goods.

    a. High yield stock
    b. Tertiary sector of economy
    c. Sale
    d. Maturity

23. _____ is a fee paid on borrowed assets. It is the price paid for the use of borrowed money , or, money earned by deposited funds .Assets that are sometimes lent with _____ include money, shares, consumer goods through hire purchase, major assets such as aircraft, and even entire factories in finance lease arrangements. The _____ is calculated upon the value of the assets in the same manner as upon money.

Chapter 11. Financial Statement Analysis

a. Insolvency
c. AIG
b. ABC Television Network
d. Interest

24. _____ relates to the cost of borrowing money. It is the price that a lender charges a borrower for the use of the lender's money. _____ is different from OPEX and CAPEX, for it relates to the capital structure of a company.
   a. Interest
   c. Interest expense
   b. AIG
   d. ABC Television Network

25. _____ is the difference between operating revenues and operating expenses, but it is also sometimes used as a synonym for EBIT and operating profit. This is true if the firm has no non-_____.

A professional investor contemplating a change to the capital structure of a firm first evaluates a firm's fundamental earnings potential (reflected by Earnings Before Interest, Taxes, Depreciation and Amortization EBITDA and EBIT), and then determines the optimal use of debt vs. equity.

   a. AMEX
   c. ABC Television Network
   b. Operating income
   d. AIG

26. _____ measures the rate of return on the ownership interest (shareholders' equity) of the common stock owners. It measures a firm's efficiency at generating profits from every dollar of shareholders' equity (also known as net assets or assets minus liabilities.) It shows how well a company uses investment dollars to generate earnings growth.
   a. Return on capital employed
   c. Sortino ratio
   b. Like for like
   d. Return on equity

27. In accounting, _____ has a very specific meaning. It is an outflow of cash or other valuable assets from a person or company to another person or company. This outflow of cash is generally one side of a trade for products or services that have equal or better current or future value to the buyer than to the seller.
   a. AMEX
   c. ABC Television Network
   b. AIG
   d. Expense

28. _____ is a company's earnings per share (EPS) calculated using fully diluted shares outstanding. _____ indicates a 'worst case' scenario, one in which everyone who could have received stock without purchasing it directly for the full market value did so.

To find _____, basic EPS is calculated for each of the categories on the income statement first. Then each of the dilutive securities are ranked based on their effects, from most dilutive to least dilutive and antidilutive. Then the basic EPS number is diluted one by one by applying each one, skipping any instruments that have an antidilutive effect.

   a. Return on assets Du Pont
   c. Cash conversion cycle
   b. Financial ratio
   d. Diluted earnings per share

29. _____ is a specific term used in companies' financial reporting from the company-whole point of view. Because that use excludes the effects of changing ownership interest, an economic measure of _____ is necessary for financial analysis from the shareholders' point of view

_____ is defined by the Financial Accounting Standards Board, or FASB, as 'the change in equity [net assets] of a business enterprise during a period from transactions and other events and circumstances from nonowner sources. It includes all changes in equity during a period except those resulting from investments by owners and distributions to owners.'

_____ is the sum of net income and other items that must bypass the income statement because they have not been realized, including items like an unrealized holding gain or loss from available for sale securities and foreign currency translation gains or losses.

   a. BNSF Railway
   c. BMC Software, Inc.
   b. 3M Company
   d. Comprehensive income

30. In economics, _____ is the difference between a company's total revenue and its opportunity costs. It is the increase in wealth that an investor has from making an investment, taking into consideration all costs associated with that investment including the opportunity cost of capital.

Profit is the factor income of the entrepreneur.

   a. AMEX
   c. ABC Television Network
   b. Economic profit
   d. AIG

31. _____ are the earnings returned on the initial investment amount.

In the US, the Financial Accounting Standards Board (FASB) requires companies' income statements to report _____ for each of the major categories of the income statement: continuing operations, discontinued operations, extraordinary items, and net income.

The _____ formula does not include preferred dividends for categories outside of continued operations and net income.

   a. Earnings per share
   c. Average accounting return
   b. Invested capital
   d. Earnings yield

32. _____ in economics and business is the result of an exchange and from that trade we assign a numerical monetary value to a good, service or asset. If Alice trades Bob 4 apples for an orange, the _____ of an orange is 4 apples. Inversely, the _____ of an apple is 1/4 oranges.
   a. Transactional Net Margin Method
   c. Discounts and allowances
   b. Price discrimination
   d. Price

33. The _____ of a stock is a measure of the price paid for a share relative to the annual net income or profit earned by the firm per share. It is a financial ratio used for valuation: a higher _____ means that investors are paying more for each unit of net income, so the stock is more expensive compared to one with lower _____. The _____ has units of years, which can be interpreted as 'number of years of earnings to pay back purchase price', ignoring the time value of money.

Chapter 11. Financial Statement Analysis

a. P/E ratio
c. Rate of return
b. Sharpe ratio
d. Capital employed

34. _____ is the difference between a lower selling price and a higher purchase price, resulting in a financial loss for the seller. Pursuant to IRS TAX TIP 2009-35 'If your _____es exceed your capital gains, the excess can be deducted on your tax return, up to an annual limit of $3,000 ($1,500 if you are married filing separately.)'.
   a. Transactional Net Margin Method
   c. Price discrimination
   b. Penetration pricing
   d. Capital loss

35. A _____ has several related meanings:

   - a daily record of events or business; a private _____ is usually referred to as a diary.
   - a newspaper or other periodical, in the literal sense of one published each day;
   - many publications issued at stated intervals, such as magazines, or scholarly academic _____s, or the record of the transactions of a society, are often called _____s. Although _____ is sometimes used, erroneously, as a synonym for 'magazine,' in academic use, a _____ refers to a serious, scholarly publication, most often peer-reviewed. A non-scholarly magazine written for an educated audience about an industry or an area of professional activity is usually called a professional magazine.

The word 'journalist' for one whose business is writing for the public press has been in use since the end of the 17th century.

Open access _____s are scholarly _____s that are available to the reader without financial or other barrier other than access to the internet itself. Some are subsidized, and some require payment on behalf of the author. Subsidized _____s are financed by an academic institution or a government information center.

   a. 3M Company
   c. BNSF Railway
   b. BMC Software, Inc.
   d. Journal

36. A _____ is the dividend paid to common stock owners from the profits of the company. Like other dividends, the payout is in the form of cash or other like stock. The law may regulate the size of the _____ particularly when the payout is a cash distribution tantamount to a liquidation.
   a. Common stock dividend
   c. Due diligence
   b. Disclosure requirement
   d. Foreign Corrupt Practices Act

37. _____ are payments made by a corporation to its shareholder members. It is the portion of corporate profits paid out to stockholders. When a corporation earns a profit or surplus, that money can be put to two uses: it can either be re-invested in the business (called retained earnings), or it can be paid to the shareholders as a dividend.
   a. Dividend stripping
   c. Dividends
   b. Dividend yield
   d. Dividend payout ratio

38. _____ is the fraction of net income a firm pays to its stockholders in dividends:

The part of the earnings not paid to investors is left for investment to provide for future earnings growth. Investors seeking high current income and limited capital growth prefer companies with high _____. However investors seeking capital growth may prefer lower payout ratio because capital gains are taxed at a lower rate.

a. Dividends
b. Dividend payout ratio
c. Dividend yield
d. Dividend stripping

39. The _____ on a company stock is the company's annual dividend payments divided by its market cap, or the dividend per share divided by the price per share. It is often expressed as a percentage.

Dividend payments on preferred shares are stipulated by the prospectus.

a. Dividends
b. Dividend stripping
c. Dividend payout ratio
d. Dividend yield

40. In finance, the term _____ describes the amount in cash that returns to the owners of a security. Normally it does not include the price variations, at the difference of the total return. _____ applies to various stated rates of return on stocks (common and preferred, and convertible), fixed income instruments (bonds, notes, bills, strips, zero coupon), and some other investment type insurance products (e.g. annuities.)

a. Pension System
b. Residence trusts
c. Disclosure
d. Yield

41. In economic models, the _____ time frame assumes no fixed factors of production. Firms can enter or leave the marketplace, and the cost (and availability) of land, labor, raw materials, and capital goods can be assumed to vary. In contrast, in the short-run time frame, certain factors are assumed to be fixed, because there is not sufficient time for them to change.

a. 3M Company
b. Short-run
c. BMC Software, Inc.
d. Long-run

42. In economics, the concept of the _____ refers to the decision-making time frame of a firm in which at least one factor of production is fixed. Costs which are fixed in the _____ have no impact on a firms decisions. For example a firm can raise output by increasing the amount of labour through overtime.

a. 3M Company
b. Long-run
c. BMC Software, Inc.
d. Short-run

43. _____ is that which is owed; usually referencing assets owed, but the term can also cover moral obligations and other interactions not requiring money. In the case of assets, _____ is a means of using future purchasing power in the present before a summation has been earned. Some companies and corporations use _____ as a part of their overall corporate finance strategy.

a. Loan
b. Debt
c. Debenture
d. Lender

44. In financial accounting, a _____ or statement of financial position is a summary of a person's or organization's balances. Assets, liabilities and ownership equity are listed as of a specific date, such as the end of its financial year. A _____ is often described as a snapshot of a company's financial condition.

a. Statement of retained earnings
c. 3M Company

b. Financial statements
d. Balance sheet

45. _____ is a company's financial statement that indicates how the revenue is transformed into the net income The purpose of the _____ is to show managers and investors whether the company made or lost money during the period being reported.

The important thing to remember about an _____ is that it represents a period of time.

a. AMEX
c. Income statement

b. AIG
d. ABC Television Network

46. _____ is typically a 'higher ranking' stock than voting shares, and its terms are negotiated between the corporation and the investor.

_____ usually carries no voting rights, but may carry superior priority over common stock in the payment of dividends and upon liquidation. _____ may carry a dividend that is paid out prior to any dividends being paid to common stock holders.

a. Restricted stock
c. Cash flow

b. Gross income
d. Preferred stock

47. _____ are formal records of a business' financial activities.

In British English, including United Kingdom company law, _____ are often referred to as accounts, although the term _____ is also used, particularly by accountants.

_____ provide an overview of a business' financial condition in both short and long term.

a. 3M Company
c. Notes to the financial statements

b. Statement of retained earnings
d. Financial statements

48. In finance, _____ refers to the way a corporation finances its assets through some combination of equity, debt, or hybrid securities. A firm's _____ is then the composition or 'structure' of its liabilities. For example, a firm that sells $20 billion in equity and $80 billion in debt is said to be 20% equity-financed and 80% debt-financed.

a. Flow-through entity
c. Gross income

b. Restricted stock
d. Capital structure

49. _____ is a financial ratio that indicates the percentage of a company's assets are provided via debt. It is the ratio of total debt (the sum of current liabilities and long-term liabilities) and total assets (the sum of current assets, fixed assets, and other assets such as 'goodwill'.)

$$\text{Debt ratio} = \frac{\text{Total Debt}}{\text{Total Assets}}$$

or alternatively:

$$\text{Debt ratio} = \frac{\text{Total Liability}}{\text{Total Assets}}$$

For example, a company with $2 million in total assets and $500,000 in total liabilities would have a _____ of 25%

Like all financial ratios, a company's _____ should be compared with their industry average or other competing firms.

a. 3M Company
b. Debt ratio
c. Finance lease
d. Profitability index

50. _____ or interest coverage ratio is a measure of a company's ability to honor its debt payments. It may be calculated as either EBIT or EBITDA divided by the total interest payable.

a. Return of capital
b. Yield Gap
c. Capital recovery factor
d. Times interest earned

51. A _____ occurs when a financial sponsor acquires a controlling interest in a company's equity and where a significant percentage of the purchase price is financed through leverage (borrowing.) The assets of the acquired company are used as collateral for the borrowed capital, sometimes with assets of the acquiring company. The bonds or other paper issued for a _____ is commonly considered not to be investment grade because of the significant risks involved.

a. BMC Software, Inc.
b. BNSF Railway
c. 3M Company
d. Leveraged buyout

52. In business or economics a _____ is a combination of two companies into one larger company. Such actions are commonly voluntary and involve stock swap or cash payment to the target. Stock swap is often used as it allows the shareholders of the two companies to share the risk involved in the deal. A _____ can resemble a takeover but result in a new company name (often combining the names of the original companies) and in new branding; in some cases, terming the combination a '_____' rather than an acquisition is done purely for political or marketing reasons.

a. BMC Software, Inc.
b. 3M Company
c. Merger
d. BNSF Railway

53. The phrase _____ refers to the aspect of corporate strategy, corporate finance and management dealing with the buying, selling and combining of different companies that can aid, finance, or help a growing company in a given industry grow rapidly without having to create another business entity.

a. BMC Software, Inc.
b. BNSF Railway
c. 3M Company
d. Mergers and acquisitions

Chapter 11. Financial Statement Analysis

54. In economics, a _____ is a general slowdown in economic activity in a country over a sustained period of time, or a business cycle contraction. During _____s, many macroeconomic indicators vary in a similar way. Production as measured by Gross Domestic Product (GDP), employment, investment spending, capacity utilization, household incomes and business profits all fall during _____s.
    a. Perfect competition
    b. Recession
    c. Market Failure
    d. Market

55. An _____ is the buying of one company by another. An _____ may be friendly or hostile. In the former case, the companies cooperate in negotiations; in the latter case, the takeover target is unwilling to be bought or the target's board has no prior knowledge of the offer. _____ usually refers to a purchase of a smaller firm by a larger one. Sometimes, however, a smaller firm will acquire management control of a larger or longer established company and keep its name for the combined entity. This is known as a reverse takeover.
    a. ABC Television Network
    b. AMEX
    c. AIG
    d. Acquisition

56. _____ is a term used to describe the value of an entity's assets less the value of its liabilities. The term is commonly used in relation to collective investment schemes. It may also be used as a synonym for the book value of a firm.

    For collective investment schemes (such as US mutual funds and hedge funds), the _____ is the total value of the fund's portfolio less its liabilities. Its liabilities may be money owed to lending banks or fees owed to investment managers, for example.

    a. BNSF Railway
    b. BMC Software, Inc.
    c. 3M Company
    d. Net asset value

57. A _____ is any one of a variety of different systems, institutions, procedures, social relations and infrastructures whereby persons trade, and goods and services are exchanged, forming part of the economy. It is an arrangement that allows buyers and sellers to exchange things. _____s vary in size, range, geographic scale, location, types and variety of human communities, as well as the types of goods and services traded.
    a. Recession
    b. Market Failure
    c. Perfect competition
    d. Market

58. _____ is an economic concept with commonplace familiarity. It is the price that a good or service is offered at, or will fetch, in the marketplace. It is of interest mainly in the study of microeconomics.
    a. Spot rate
    b. Financial instruments
    c. Transfer agent
    d. Market price

59. _____ is a mathematical science pertaining to the collection, analysis, interpretation or explanation, and presentation of data. It also provides tools for prediction and forecasting based on data. It is applicable to a wide variety of academic disciplines, from the natural and social sciences to the humanities, government and business.
    a. Probability distribution
    b. Time series
    c. Variance
    d. Statistics

Chapter 11. Financial Statement Analysis

60. The _____ of 2002 (Pub.L. 107-204, 116 Stat. 745, enacted July 30, 2002), also known as the Public Company Accounting Reform and Investor Protection Act of 2002, is a United States federal law enacted on July 30, 2002 in response to a number of major corporate and accounting scandals including those affecting Enron, Tyco International, Adelphia, Peregrine Systems and WorldCom. The legislation establishes new or enhanced standards for all U.S. public company boards, management, and public accounting firms. It does not apply to privately held companies.

a. FCPA
b. Lease
c. Fair Labor Standards Act
d. Sarbanes-Oxley Act

61. The zeroth item is the initial item of a _____ sequence (that is, a sequence which is numbered beginning from zero rather than one), such as the non-negative integers

This kind of numbering is common in array references in computer systems, so hackers, computer scientists, and computer professionals often use zeroth where others might use first, and so forth. Although there is logical reasoning for this in programming and mathematics (as explained below), it is sometimes used in other areas as well.

a. BMC Software, Inc.
b. Zero-based
c. BNSF Railway
d. 3M Company

62. _____ is an American publishing and financial information firm.

The company was founded in 1882 by three reporters: Charles Dow, Edward Jones, and Charles Bergstresser. Like The New York Times and the Washington Post, the company was in recent years publicly traded but privately controlled.

a. MicroStrategy
b. Multinational corporation
c. Professional association
d. Dow Jones ' Company

63. _____ is the planning process used to determine whether a firm's long term investments such as new machinery, replacement machinery, new plants, new products, and research development projects are worth pursuing. It is budget for major capital, or investment, expenditures.

Many formal methods are used in _____, including the techniques such as

- Net present value
- Profitability index
- Internal rate of return
- Modified Internal Rate of Return
- Equivalent annuity

These methods use the incremental cash flows from each potential investment, or project. Techniques based on accounting earnings and accounting rules are sometimes used - though economists consider this to be improper - such as the accounting rate of return, and 'return on investment.' Simplified and hybrid methods are used as well, such as payback period and discounted payback period.

a. Cash flow
b. Capital budgeting
c. Preferred stock
d. Gross profit

Chapter 12. Managerial Accounting and Cost-Volume-Profit Relationships

1. _____, in managerial economics is a form of cost accounting. It is a simplified model, useful for elementary instruction and for short-run decisions.

Cost-volume-profit (CVP) analysis expands the use of information provided by breakeven analysis.

- a. Cost of quality
- b. Cost accounting
- c. Fixed costs
- d. Cost-volume-profit analysis

2. _____ is concerned with the provisions and use of accounting information to managers within organizations, to provide them with the basis to make informed business decisions that will allow them to be better equipped in their management and control functions.

In contrast to financial accountancy information, _____ information is:

- usually confidential and used by management, instead of publicly reported;
- forward-looking, instead of historical;
- pragmatically computed using extensive management information systems and internal controls, instead of complying with accounting standards.

This is because of the different emphasis: _____ information is used within an organization, typically for decision-making.

- a. Nonassurance services
- b. Governmental accounting
- c. Grenzplankostenrechnung
- d. Management accounting

3. In economics ' business, specifically cost accounting, the _____ is the point at which cost or expenses and revenue are equal: there is no net loss or gain, and one has 'broken even'. A profit or a loss has not been made, although opportunity costs have been paid, and capital has received the risk-adjusted, expected return.

For example, if the business sells less than 200 tables each month, it will make a loss, if it sells more, it will be a profit.

- a. Defined benefit pension plan
- b. Break-even point
- c. BMC Software, Inc.
- d. 3M Company

4. _____ is a process of planning and controlling the performance or execution of any type of activity, such as:

- a project (project _____) or
- a process (process _____, sometimes referred to as the process performance measurement and management system.)

Organization's senior management is responsible for carrying out its _____.

- a. Management process
- b. 3M Company
- c. BMC Software, Inc.
- d. BNSF Railway

Chapter 12. Managerial Accounting and Cost-Volume-Profit Relationships   151

5. _____ can be regarded as an outcome of mental processes (cognitive process) leading to the selection of a course of action among several alternatives. Every _____ process produces a final choice. The output can be an action or an opinion of choice.

    a. BMC Software, Inc.   b. BNSF Railway
    c. 3M Company   d. Decision making

6. _____ describes the situation when output from (or information about the result of) an event or phenomenon in the past will influence the same event/phenomenon in the present or future. When an event is part of a chain of cause-and-effect that forms a circuit or loop, then the event is said to 'feed back' into itself.

_____ is also a synonym for:

- _____ Signal; the information about the initial event that is the basis for subsequent modification of the event.
- _____ Loop; the causal path that leads from the initial generation of the _____ signal to the subsequent modification of the event.

_____ is a mechanism, process or signal that is looped back to control a system within itself. Such a loop is called a _____ loop.

    a. Controllable   b. BMC Software, Inc.
    c. 3M Company   d. Feedback

7. An _____ is a practitioner of accountancy, which is the measurement, disclosure or provision of assurance about financial information that helps managers, investors, tax authorities and other decision makers make resource allocation decisions.

The word '_____' is derived from the French 'Compter' which took its origin from the Latin 'Computare'. The word was formerly written in English as 'Accomptant', but in process of time the word, which was always pronounced by dropping the 'p', became gradually changed both in pronunciation and in orthography to its present form.

    a. AIG   b. AMEX
    c. ABC Television Network   d. Accountant

8. In economics, business, retail, and accounting, a _____ is the value of money that has been used up to produce something, and hence is not available for use anymore. In economics, a _____ is an alternative that is given up as a result of a decision. In business, the _____ may be one of acquisition, in which case the amount of money expended to acquire it is counted as _____.

    a. Cost   b. Prime cost
    c. Cost allocation   d. Cost of quality

9. In economics, _____ are business expenses that are not dependent on the activities of the business They tend to be time-related, such as salaries or rents being paid per month. This is in contrast to variable costs, which are volume-related (and are paid per quantity.)

Chapter 12. Managerial Accounting and Cost-Volume-Profit Relationships

In management accounting, _____ are defined as expenses that do not change in proportion to the activity of a business, within the relevant period or scale of production.

- a. Cost accounting
- b. Fixed costs
- c. Marginal cost
- d. Cost of quality

10. In economics, and cost accounting, _____ describes the total economic cost of production and is made up of variable costs, which vary according to the quantity of a good produced and include inputs such as labor and raw materials, plus fixed costs, which are independent of the quantity of a good produced and include inputs (capital) that cannot be varied in the short term, such as buildings and machinery. _____ in economics includes the total opportunity cost of each factor of production in addition to fixed and variable costs.

The rate at which _____ changes as the amount produced changes is called marginal cost.

- a. Total cost
- b. 3M Company
- c. BNSF Railway
- d. BMC Software, Inc.

11. _____s are expenses that change in proportion to the activity of a business. In other words, _____ is the sum of marginal costs. It can also be considered normal costs.
- a. Fixed costs
- b. Variable cost
- c. Cost accounting
- d. Quality costs

12. _____ is a term used in accounting, economics and finance to spread the cost of an asset over the span of several years.

In simple words we can say that _____ is the reduction in the value of an asset due to usage, passage of time, wear and tear, technological outdating or obsolescence, depletion, inadequacy, rot, rust, decay or other such factors.

In accounting, _____ is a term used to describe any method of attributing the historical or purchase cost of an asset across its useful life, roughly corresponding to normal wear and tear.

- a. General ledger
- b. Net profit
- c. Current asset
- d. Depreciation

13. In accounting, _____ has a very specific meaning. It is an outflow of cash or other valuable assets from a person or company to another person or company. This outflow of cash is generally one side of a trade for products or services that have equal or better current or future value to the buyer than to the seller.
- a. ABC Television Network
- b. AIG
- c. AMEX
- d. Expense

14. In cost-volume-profit analysis, a form of management accounting, _____ is the marginal profit per unit sale. It is a useful quantity in carrying out various calculations, and can be used as a measure of operating leverage.

Chapter 12. Managerial Accounting and Cost-Volume-Profit Relationships

The Total _____ is Total Revenue (TR, or Sales) minus Total Variable Cost (TVC):

Tcontribution margin = TR − TVC

The Unit _____ (C) is Unit Revenue (Price, P) minus Unit Variable Cost (V):

C = P − V

The _____ Ratio is the percentage of Contribution over Total Revenue, which can be calculated from the unit contribution over unit price or total contribution over Total Revenue:

$$\frac{C}{P} = \frac{P-V}{P} = \frac{\text{Unit Contribution Margin}}{\text{Price}} = \frac{\text{Total Contribution Margin}}{\text{Total Revenue}}$$

For instance, if the price is $10 and the unit variable cost is $2, then the unit _____ is $8, and the _____ ratio is $8/$10 = 80%.

- a. Factory overhead
- b. Profit center
- c. Contribution margin
- d. Cost management

15. _____ is the calculated approximation of a result which is usable even if input data may be incomplete or uncertain.

In statistics, see _____ theory, estimator.

In mathematics, approximation or _____ typically means finding upper or lower bounds of a quantity that cannot readily be computed precisely and is also an educated guess .

- a. AIG
- b. ABC Television Network
- c. AMEX
- d. Estimation

16. _____ is a company's financial statement that indicates how the revenue is transformed into the net income The purpose of the _____ is to show managers and investors whether the company made or lost money during the period being reported.

The important thing to remember about an _____ is that it represents a period of time.

- a. AMEX
- b. AIG
- c. ABC Television Network
- d. Income statement

17. _____ is the difference between operating revenues and operating expenses, but it is also sometimes used as a synonym for EBIT and operating profit. This is true if the firm has no non-_____.

A professional investor contemplating a change to the capital structure of a firm first evaluates a firm's fundamental earnings potential (reflected by Earnings Before Interest, Taxes, Depreciation and Amortization EBITDA and EBIT), and then determines the optimal use of debt vs. equity.

a. AMEX
b. Operating income
c. ABC Television Network
d. AIG

18. A _____ is the pinnacle activity involved in selling products or services in return for money or other compensation. It is an act of completion of a commercial activity.

A _____ is completed by the seller, the owner of the goods.

a. Tertiary sector of economy
b. High yield stock
c. Maturity
d. Sale

19. The _____ is a measure of how revenue growth translates into growth in operating income. It is a measure of leverage, and of how risky (volatile) a company's operating income is.

There are various measures of _____, which can be interpreted analogously to financial leverage.

a. AlphaIC
b. Upside potential ratio
c. Operating leverage
d. Information ratio

20. _____ and converging technologies are terms used to cover various cutting-edge developments in the emergence and convergence of technology.

_____ are those which represent new and significant developments within a field; converging techologies represent previously distinct fields which are in some way moving towards stronger inter-connection and similar goals.

Over time, new methods and topics are developed and opened up.

a. International Accounting Standards Board
b. American Payroll Association
c. East Asia Economic Caucus
d. Emerging technologies

Chapter 13. Cost Accounting and Reporting Systems

1. In economics, business, retail, and accounting, a _____ is the value of money that has been used up to produce something, and hence is not available for use anymore. In economics, a _____ is an alternative that is given up as a result of a decision. In business, the _____ may be one of acquisition, in which case the amount of money expended to acquire it is counted as _____.
    a. Cost allocation
    b. Cost of quality
    c. Cost
    d. Prime cost

2. In management accounting, _____ establishes budget and actual cost of operations, processes, departments or product and the analysis of variances, profitability or social use of funds. Managers use _____ to support decision-making to cut a company's costs and improve profitability. As a form of management accounting, _____ need not follow standards such as GAAP, because its primary use is for internal managers, rather than outside users, and what to compute is instead decided pragmatically.
    a. Cost-volume-profit analysis
    b. Marginal cost
    c. Prime cost
    d. Cost accounting

3. _____ is concerned with the provisions and use of accounting information to managers within organizations, to provide them with the basis to make informed business decisions that will allow them to be better equipped in their management and control functions.

In contrast to financial accountancy information, _____ information is:

- usually confidential and used by management, instead of publicly reported;
- forward-looking, instead of historical;
- pragmatically computed using extensive management information systems and internal controls, instead of complying with accounting standards.

This is because of the different emphasis: _____ information is used within an organization, typically for decision-making.

    a. Management accounting
    b. Governmental accounting
    c. Nonassurance services
    d. Grenzplankostenrechnung

4. _____ is the process whereby companies use cost accounting to report or control the various costs of doing business.

The term _____ is widely used in business today. Unfortunately _____ has no uniform definition.

    a. Cost management
    b. Contribution margin analysis
    c. Contribution margin
    d. Process costing

5. _____ can be regarded as an outcome of mental processes (cognitive process) leading to the selection of a course of action among several alternatives. Every _____ process produces a final choice. The output can be an action or an opinion of choice.
    a. 3M Company
    b. BMC Software, Inc.
    c. Decision making
    d. BNSF Railway

Chapter 13. Cost Accounting and Reporting Systems

6. The _____ is a concept from business management that was first described and popularized by Michael Porter in his 1985 best-seller, Competitive Advantage: Creating and Sustaining Superior Performance.

A _____ is a chain of activities. Products pass through all activities of the chain in order and at each activity the product gains some value.

   a. Market segmentation
   b. Value chain
   c. Customer relationship management
   d. Product differentiation

7. A _____ is a tangible input for a product manufactured/Service provided, like labor or material. For example a cloth manufacturing firm requires some amount of predetermined labor and predetermined raw material for any amount of cloth being manufactured. The cost of employing labor can be directly fixed as 'per man per hour' or 'per man per day', so the labor is a _____ as you can directly associate cost with it.
   a. Round-tripping
   b. Cost object
   c. 3M Company
   d. Residual value

8. Total _____ is a method of Accounting cost which entails the full cost of manufacturing or providing a service. This includes not just the costs of materials and labour, but also of all manufacturing overheads (whether e;fixede; or e;variablee;.) One of the main reasons for absorbing overheads into the cost of units is for inventory valuation purposes.
   a. AMEX
   b. AIG
   c. ABC Television Network
   d. Absorption costing

9. _____s are expenses that change in proportion to the activity of a business. In other words, _____ is the sum of marginal costs. It can also be considered normal costs.
   a. Cost accounting
   b. Variable cost
   c. Fixed costs
   d. Quality costs

10. _____ are costs that are not directly accountable to a particular function or product. _____ may be either fixed or variable. _____ include taxes, administration, personnel and security costs, and are also known as overhead.
    a. Activity-based costing
    b. Activity-based management
    c. ABC Television Network
    d. Indirect costs

11. In business, _____, Overhead cost or _____ expense refers to an ongoing expense of operating a business. The term _____ is usually used to group expenses that are necessary to the continued functioning of the business, but do not directly generate profits.

_____ expenses are all costs on the income statement except for direct labor and direct materials.

   a. Intangible assets
   b. Overhead
   c. ABC Television Network
   d. AIG

12. A _____ is something that is acted upon or used by or by human labour or industry, for use as a building material to create some product or structure. Often the term is used to denote material that came from nature and is in an unprocessed or minimally processed state. Iron ore, logs, and crude oil, would be examples.

a. BMC Software, Inc.	b. BNSF Railway
c. Raw material	d. 3M Company

13. In economics, the _____, (or _____) measures the payments that flow between any individual country and all other countries. It is used to summarize all international economic transactions for that country during a specific time period, usually a year. The _____ is determined by the country's exports and imports of goods, services, and financial capital, as well as financial transfers.

a. Yield to maturity	b. Moving average
c. Balance of payments	d. Stock split

14. _____s are goods that have completed the manufacturing process but have not yet been sold or distributed to the end user.

Manufacturing has three classes of inventory:

1. Raw material
2. Work in process
3. _____s

A good purchased as a 'raw material' goes into the manufacture of a product. A good only partially completed during the manufacturing process is called 'work in process'. When the good is completed as to manufacturing but not yet sold or distributed to the end-user is called a '_____'.

a. Finished good	b. Reorder point
c. 3M Company	d. FIFO and LIFO accounting

15. _____ or in-process inventory includes the set at large of unfinished items for products in a production process. These items are not yet completed but either just being fabricated or waiting in a queue for further processing or in a buffer storage. The term is used in production and supply chain management.

a. BMC Software, Inc.	b. 3M Company
c. BNSF Railway	d. Work in process

16. _____ refers to the methods, practices and operations conducted to promote and sustain certain categories of commercial activity. The term is understood to have different specific meanings depending on the context. Merchandise is a sale goods at a store

In marketing, one of the definitions of _____ is the practice in which the brand or image from one product or service is used to sell another.

a. BMC Software, Inc.	b. Merchandise
c. 3M Company	d. Merchandising

17. _____ is an umbrella term which refers to the various accounting systems used by various public sector entities. In the United States, for instance, there are two levels of government which follow different accounting standards set forth by independent, private sector boards. At the federal level, the Federal Accounting Standards Advisory Board (FASAB) sets forth the accounting standards to follow.

a. Nonassurance services
c. Product control
b. Governmental accounting
d. Management accounting

18. In financial accounting, _____ or cost of sales includes the direct costs attributable to the production of the goods sold by a company. This amount includes the materials cost used in creating the goods along with the direct labor costs used to produce the good. It excludes indirect expenses such as distribution costs and sales force costs.
   a. Cost of goods sold
   b. FIFO and LIFO accounting
   c. Reorder point
   d. 3M Company

19. The _____ is one of the basic financial statements as per Generally Accepted Accounting Principles, and it explains the changes in a company's retained earnings over the reporting period. It breaks down changes affecting the account, such as profits or losses from operations, dividends paid, and any other items charged or credited to retained earnings. A retained earnings statement is required by Generally Accepted Accounting Principles whenever comparative balance sheets and income statements are presented.
   a. Notes to the financial statements
   b. Statement of retained earnings
   c. 3M Company
   d. Financial statements

20. A _____ is an internal document extensively used by projects-based, manufacturing, building and fabrication businesses. A _____ may be for products and/or services. In a manufacturing environment, a _____ is used to signal the start of a manufacturing process and will most probably be linked to a bill of material.
   a. Job order
   b. Six Sigma
   c. Lean manufacturing
   d. Make to order

21. _____ is an accounting methodology that traces and accumulates direct costs, and allocates indirect costs of a manufacturing process. Costs are assigned to products, usually in a large batch, which might include an entire month's production. Eventually, costs have to be allocated to individual units of product.
   a. Profit center
   b. Cost driver
   c. Cost management
   d. Process costing

22. _____ measures the rate of return on the ownership interest (shareholders' equity) of the common stock owners. It measures a firm's efficiency at generating profits from every dollar of shareholders' equity (also known as net assets or assets minus liabilities.) It shows how well a company uses investment dollars to generate earnings growth.
   a. Like for like
   b. Sortino ratio
   c. Return on equity
   d. Return on capital employed

23. _____ of something is, in finance, the adding together of interest or different investments over a period of time such as atoms (1 - the act or process of accruing; 2 - the amount that accrues.) It holds specific meanings in accounting and payroll.

_____, in accounting, describes the accounting method known as _____ basis, whereby revenues and expenses are recognized when they are accrued, i.e. accumulated (earned or incurred), regardless when the actual cash is received or paid out.

Chapter 13. Cost Accounting and Reporting Systems

a. Accrual

c. Assets

b. Earnings before interest, taxes, depreciation and amortization

d. Accounts receivable

24. An _____ is a tax levied on the financial income of people, corporations, or other legal entities. Various _____ systems exist, with varying degrees of tax incidence. Income taxation can be progressive, proportional, or regressive.

a. Implied level of government service

c. Individual Retirement Arrangement

b. Ordinary income

d. Income tax

25. In business and accounting, _____ are everything of value that is owned by a person or company. It is a claim on the property your income of a borrower. The balance sheet of a firm records the monetary value of the _____ owned by the firm.

a. Assets

c. Accrual basis accounting

b. Earnings before interest, taxes, depreciation and amortization

d. Accounts receivable

26. _____, in accrual accounting, is any account where the asset or liability is not realized until a future date (accounting period), e.g. annuities, charges, taxes, income, etc. The _____ item may be carried, dependent on type of deferral, as either an asset or liability.

a. Deferred

c. Cash basis accounting

b. Pro forma

d. Payroll

27. A '_____' is the unit of an activity that causes the change of an activity cost. A _____ is any activity that causes a cost to be incurred. The Activity Based Costing (ABC) approach relates indirect cost to the activities that drive them to be incurred.

a. Cost driver

c. Factory overhead

b. Contribution margin analysis

d. Profit center

28. _____ is a costing model that identifies activities in an organization and assigns the cost of each activity resource to all products and services according to the actual consumption by each: it assigns more indirect costs (overhead) into direct costs.

In this way an organization can establish the true cost of its individual products and services for the purposes of identifying and eliminating those which are unprofitable and lowering the prices of those which are overpriced.

In a business organization, the ABC methodology assigns an organization's resource costs through activities to the products and services provided to its customers.

a. ABC Television Network

c. Indirect costs

b. Activity-based costing

d. Activity-based management

29. _____ is a method of identifying and evaluating activities that a business performs using activity-based costing to carry out a value chain analysis or a re-engineering initiative to improve strategic and operational decisions in an organization. Activity-based costing establishes relationships between overhead costs and activities so that overhead costs can be more precisely allocated to products, services, or customer segments. _____ focuses on managing activities to reduce costs and improve customer value.

a. Activity-based costing
b. Activity-based management
c. ABC Television Network
d. Indirect costs

Chapter 14. Cost Analysis for Planning

1. In economics, _____ or _____ goods or real _____ refers to factors of production used to create goods or services that are not themselves significantly consumed (though they may depreciate) in the production process. _____ goods may be acquired with money or financial _____. In finance and accounting, _____ generally refers to financial wealth, especially that used to start or maintain a business.
   - a. Disclosure
   - b. Capital
   - c. Screening
   - d. Vyborg Appeal

2. _____ is the planning process used to determine whether a firm's long term investments such as new machinery, replacement machinery, new plants, new products, and research development projects are worth pursuing. It is budget for major capital, or investment, expenditures.

   Many formal methods are used in _____, including the techniques such as

   - Net present value
   - Profitability index
   - Internal rate of return
   - Modified Internal Rate of Return
   - Equivalent annuity

   These methods use the incremental cash flows from each potential investment, or project. Techniques based on accounting earnings and accounting rules are sometimes used - though economists consider this to be improper - such as the accounting rate of return, and 'return on investment.' Simplified and hybrid methods are used as well, such as payback period and discounted payback period.
   - a. Gross profit
   - b. Cash flow
   - c. Preferred stock
   - d. Capital budgeting

3. _____ can be regarded as an outcome of mental processes (cognitive process) leading to the selection of a course of action among several alternatives. Every _____ process produces a final choice. The output can be an action or an opinion of choice.
   - a. BNSF Railway
   - b. 3M Company
   - c. BMC Software, Inc.
   - d. Decision making

4. Project _____: The project _____ is a prediction of the costs associated with a particular company project. These costs include labor, materials, and other related expenses. The project _____ is often broken down into specific tasks, with task _____s assigned to each.
   - a. 3M Company
   - b. BNSF Railway
   - c. BMC Software, Inc.
   - d. Budget

5. The _____ of 2002 (Pub.L. 107-204, 116 Stat. 745, enacted July 30, 2002), also known as the Public Company Accounting Reform and Investor Protection Act of 2002, is a United States federal law enacted on July 30, 2002 in response to a number of major corporate and accounting scandals including those affecting Enron, Tyco International, Adelphia, Peregrine Systems and WorldCom. The legislation establishes new or enhanced standards for all U.S. public company boards, management, and public accounting firms. It does not apply to privately held companies.
   - a. FCPA
   - b. Lease
   - c. Fair Labor Standards Act
   - d. Sarbanes-Oxley Act

6. In economics, and cost accounting, _____ describes the total economic cost of production and is made up of variable costs, which vary according to the quantity of a good produced and include inputs such as labor and raw materials, plus fixed costs, which are independent of the quantity of a good produced and include inputs (capital) that cannot be varied in the short term, such as buildings and machinery. _____ in economics includes the total opportunity cost of each factor of production in addition to fixed and variable costs.

The rate at which _____ changes as the amount produced changes is called marginal cost.

a. BNSF Railway
b. BMC Software, Inc.
c. 3M Company
d. Total cost

7. _____s are expenses that change in proportion to the activity of a business. In other words, _____ is the sum of marginal costs. It can also be considered normal costs.
a. Cost accounting
b. Variable cost
c. Quality costs
d. Fixed costs

8. In economics, business, retail, and accounting, a _____ is the value of money that has been used up to produce something, and hence is not available for use anymore. In economics, a _____ is an alternative that is given up as a result of a decision. In business, the _____ may be one of acquisition, in which case the amount of money expended to acquire it is counted as _____.
a. Cost of quality
b. Prime cost
c. Cost allocation
d. Cost

9. In economics, _____ are business expenses that are not dependent on the activities of the business They tend to be time-related, such as salaries or rents being paid per month. This is in contrast to variable costs, which are volume-related (and are paid per quantity.)

In management accounting, _____ are defined as expenses that do not change in proportion to the activity of a business, within the relevant period or scale of production.

a. Marginal cost
b. Cost of quality
c. Cost accounting
d. Fixed costs

10. In financial accounting, a _____ or statement of financial position is a summary of a person's or organization's balances. Assets, liabilities and ownership equity are listed as of a specific date, such as the end of its financial year. A _____ is often described as a snapshot of a company's financial condition.
a. Statement of retained earnings
b. 3M Company
c. Balance sheet
d. Financial statements

11. _____ and bottom-up are strategies of information processing and knowledge ordering, mostly involving software, but also other humanistic and scientific theories In practice, they can be seen as a style of thinking and teaching. In many cases _____ is used as a synonym of analysis or decomposition, and bottom-up of synthesis.
a. BNSF Railway
b. 3M Company
c. Top-down
d. BMC Software, Inc.

Chapter 14. Cost Analysis for Planning

12. The zeroth item is the initial item of a _____ sequence (that is, a sequence which is numbered beginning from zero rather than one), such as the non-negative integers

This kind of numbering is common in array references in computer systems, so hackers, computer scientists, and computer professionals often use zeroth where others might use first, and so forth. Although there is logical reasoning for this in programming and mathematics (as explained below), it is sometimes used in other areas as well.

    a. Zero-based   b. BMC Software, Inc.
    c. 3M Company   d. BNSF Railway

13. _____ is a technique of planning and decision-making which reverses the working process of traditional budgeting. In traditional incremental budgeting, departmental managers justify only increases over the previous year budget and what has been already spent is automatically sanctioned. No reference is made to the previous level of expenditure.

    a. BNSF Railway   b. 3M Company
    c. Zero-based budgeting   d. BMC Software, Inc.

14. _____ is a method of identifying and evaluating activities that a business performs using activity-based costing to carry out a value chain analysis or a re-engineering initiative to improve strategic and operational decisions in an organization. Activity-based costing establishes relationships between overhead costs and activities so that overhead costs can be more precisely allocated to products, services, or customer segments. _____ focuses on managing activities to reduce costs and improve customer value.

    a. ABC Television Network   b. Indirect costs
    c. Activity-based costing   d. Activity-based management

15. An _____ is the annual budget of an activity stated in terms of Budget Classification Code, functional/subfunctional categories and cost accounts. It contains estimates of the total value of resources required for the performance of the operation including reimbursable work or services for others. It also includes estimates of workload in terms of total work units identified by cost accounts.

    a. Inventory turnover ratio   b. Internality
    c. Authorised capital   d. Operating budget

16. A _____ is the pinnacle activity involved in selling products or services in return for money or other compensation. It is an act of completion of a commercial activity.

A _____ is completed by the seller, the owner of the goods.

    a. Tertiary sector of economy   b. High yield stock
    c. Maturity   d. Sale

17. A _____ refers to the process by which governments create and approve a budget. Â· The Financial Service Department prepares worksheets to assist the department head in preparation of department budget estimates Â· The Administrator calls a meeting of managers and they present and discuss plans for the following yeare;s projected level of activity. Â· The managers can work with the Financial Services, or work alone to prepare an estimate for the departments coming year.

Chapter 14. Cost Analysis for Planning

a. Budget process
c. BNSF Railway
b. 3M Company
d. BMC Software, Inc.

18. In financial accounting, _____ or cost of sales includes the direct costs attributable to the production of the goods sold by a company. This amount includes the materials cost used in creating the goods along with the direct labor costs used to produce the good. It excludes indirect expenses such as distribution costs and sales force costs.
a. 3M Company
c. Reorder point
b. Cost of goods sold
d. FIFO and LIFO accounting

19. A _____ is the period of time between the initiation of any process of production and the completion of that process. Thus the _____ for ordering a new car from a manufacturer may be anywhere from 2 weeks to 6 months. In industry, _____ reduction is an important part of lean manufacturing.
a. 3M Company
c. BMC Software, Inc.
b. BNSF Railway
d. Lead time

20. A _____ is something that is acted upon or used by or by human labour or industry, for use as a building material to create some product or structure. Often the term is used to denote material that came from nature and is in an unprocessed or minimally processed state. Iron ore, logs, and crude oil, would be examples.
a. Raw material
c. BNSF Railway
b. BMC Software, Inc.
d. 3M Company

21. Total _____ is a method of Accounting cost which entails the full cost of manufacturing or providing a service. This includes not just the costs of materials and labour, but also of all manufacturing overheads (whether e;fixede; or e;variablee;.) One of the main reasons for absorbing overheads into the cost of units is for inventory valuation purposes.
a. ABC Television Network
c. AIG
b. AMEX
d. Absorption costing

22. An _____, operating expenditure, operational expense, operational expenditure or OPEX is an on-going cost for running a product, business, or system. Its counterpart, a capital expenditure (CAPEX), is the cost of developing or providing non-consumable parts for the product or system. For example, the purchase of a photocopier is the CAPEX, and the annual paper and toner cost is the OPEX.
a. AMEX
c. ABC Television Network
b. AIG
d. Operating expense

23. In accounting, _____ has a very specific meaning. It is an outflow of cash or other valuable assets from a person or company to another person or company. This outflow of cash is generally one side of a trade for products or services that have equal or better current or future value to the buyer than to the seller.
a. AMEX
c. ABC Television Network
b. AIG
d. Expense

24. _____ is a company's financial statement that indicates how the revenue is transformed into the net income The purpose of the _____ is to show managers and investors whether the company made or lost money during the period being reported.

The important thing to remember about an _____ is that it represents a period of time.

Chapter 14. Cost Analysis for Planning

a. ABC Television Network
c. AIG
b. AMEX
d. Income statement

25. In business, _____, Overhead cost or _____ expense refers to an ongoing expense of operating a business. The term _____ is usually used to group expenses that are necessary to the continued functioning of the business, but do not directly generate profits.

_____ expenses are all costs on the income statement except for direct labor and direct materials.

a. AIG
c. Overhead
b. ABC Television Network
d. Intangible assets

26. In economics, the _____ is the theory that the price of an object or condition is determined by the sum of the cost of the resources that went into making it. The cost can compose any of the factors of production (including labour, capital, or land) and taxation.

The theory makes the most sense under assumptions of constant returns to scale and the existence of just one non-produced factor of production.

a. BMC Software, Inc.
c. Cost-of-production theory of value
b. BNSF Railway
d. 3M Company

27. _____ Process Deming saw it as part of the 'system' whereby feedback from the process and customer were evaluated against organisational goals.
a. Sole proprietorship
c. Sensitivity analysis
b. Continuous improvement
d. Procurement

28. In engineering and manufacturing, _____ and quality engineering are used in developing systems to ensure products or services are designed and produced to meet or exceed customer requirements. Refer to the definition by Merriam-Webster for further information . These systems are often developed in conjunction with other business and engineering disciplines using a cross-functional approach.
a. Quality control
c. BNSF Railway
b. BMC Software, Inc.
d. 3M Company

29. A _____, also client, buyer or purchaser is the buyer or user of the paid products of an individual or organization, mostly called the supplier or seller. This is typically through purchasing or renting goods or services.
a. 3M Company
c. BNSF Railway
b. BMC Software, Inc.
d. Customer

30. In probability theory and statistics, the _____ of a random variable, probability distribution averaging the squared distance of its possible values from the expected value (mean.) Whereas the mean is a way to describe the location of a distribution, the _____ is a way to capture its scale or degree of being spread out. The unit of _____ is the square of the unit of the original variable.
a. Monte Carlo methods
c. Variance
b. Statistics
d. Time series

Chapter 14. Cost Analysis for Planning

31. In statistics, _____ (ANOVA) is a collection of statistical models, and their associated procedures, in which the observed variance is partitioned into components due to different explanatory variables. In its simplest form ANOVA gives a statistical test of whether the means of several groups are all equal, and therefore generalizes Student's two-sample t-test to more than two groups.

There are three conceptual classes of such models:

1. Fixed-effects models assumes that the data came from normal populations which may differ only in their means. (Model 1)
2. Random effects models assume that the data describe a hierarchy of different populations whose differences are constrained by the hierarchy. (Model 2)
3. Mixed-effect models describe situations where both fixed and random effects are present. (Model 3)

In practice, there are several types of ANOVA depending on the number of treatments and the way they are applied to the subjects in the experiment:

- One-way ANOVA is used to test for differences among two or more independent groups. Typically, however, the one-way ANOVA is used to test for differences among at least three groups, since the two-group case can be covered by a T-test (Gossett, 1908.)

a. Open database connectivity
b. Intergenerational equity
c. Analysis of variance
d. IMF

32. A _____ is a legal document that is often passed by the legislature, and approved by the chief executive-or president. For example, only certain types of revenue may be imposed and collected. Property tax is frequently the basis for municipal and county revenues, while sales tax and/or income tax are the basis for state revenues, and income tax and corporate tax are the basis for national revenues.

a. 3M Company
b. BMC Software, Inc.
c. Value capture
d. Government budget

Chapter 15. Cost Analysis for Control

1. In economics, business, retail, and accounting, a _____ is the value of money that has been used up to produce something, and hence is not available for use anymore. In economics, a _____ is an alternative that is given up as a result of a decision. In business, the _____ may be one of acquisition, in which case the amount of money expended to acquire it is counted as _____.
   a. Cost of quality
   b. Cost
   c. Cost allocation
   d. Prime cost

2. _____ can be regarded as an outcome of mental processes (cognitive process) leading to the selection of a course of action among several alternatives. Every _____ process produces a final choice. The output can be an action or an opinion of choice.
   a. BNSF Railway
   b. BMC Software, Inc.
   c. 3M Company
   d. Decision making

3. In economics, _____ are business expenses that are not dependent on the activities of the business They tend to be time-related, such as salaries or rents being paid per month. This is in contrast to variable costs, which are volume-related (and are paid per quantity.)

   In management accounting, _____ are defined as expenses that do not change in proportion to the activity of a business, within the relevant period or scale of production.

   a. Cost accounting
   b. Cost of quality
   c. Marginal cost
   d. Fixed costs

4. _____s are expenses that change in proportion to the activity of a business. In other words, _____ is the sum of marginal costs. It can also be considered normal costs.
   a. Cost accounting
   b. Fixed costs
   c. Variable cost
   d. Quality costs

5. In probability theory and statistics, the _____ of a random variable, probability distribution averaging the squared distance of its possible values from the expected value (mean.) Whereas the mean is a way to describe the location of a distribution, the _____ is a way to capture its scale or degree of being spread out. The unit of _____ is the square of the unit of the original variable.
   a. Statistics
   b. Time series
   c. Variance
   d. Monte Carlo methods

6. In statistics, _____ (ANOVA) is a collection of statistical models, and their associated procedures, in which the observed variance is partitioned into components due to different explanatory variables. In its simplest form ANOVA gives a statistical test of whether the means of several groups are all equal, and therefore generalizes Student's two-sample t-test to more than two groups.

There are three conceptual classes of such models:

1. Fixed-effects models assumes that the data came from normal populations which may differ only in their means. (Model 1)
2. Random effects models assume that the data describe a hierarchy of different populations whose differences are constrained by the hierarchy. (Model 2)
3. Mixed-effect models describe situations where both fixed and random effects are present. (Model 3)

In practice, there are several types of ANOVA depending on the number of treatments and the way they are applied to the subjects in the experiment:

- One-way ANOVA is used to test for differences among two or more independent groups. Typically, however, the one-way ANOVA is used to test for differences among at least three groups, since the two-group case can be covered by a T-test (Gossett, 1908.)

a. IMF
b. Analysis of variance
c. Open database connectivity
d. Intergenerational equity

7. In financial accounting, a _____ or statement of financial position is a summary of a person's or organization's balances. Assets, liabilities and ownership equity are listed as of a specific date, such as the end of its financial year. A _____ is often described as a snapshot of a company's financial condition.

a. Statement of retained earnings
b. Financial statements
c. 3M Company
d. Balance sheet

8. In economics, and cost accounting, _____ describes the total economic cost of production and is made up of variable costs, which vary according to the quantity of a good produced and include inputs such as labor and raw materials, plus fixed costs, which are independent of the quantity of a good produced and include inputs (capital) that cannot be varied in the short term, such as buildings and machinery. _____ in economics includes the total opportunity cost of each factor of production in addition to fixed and variable costs.

The rate at which _____ changes as the amount produced changes is called marginal cost.

a. 3M Company
b. Total cost
c. BNSF Railway
d. BMC Software, Inc.

9. _____ is a 'policy by which management devotes its time to investigating only those situations in which actual results differ significantly from planned results. The idea is that management should spend its valuable time concentrating on the more important items (such as shaping the company's future strategic course.) Attention is given only to material deviations requiring investigation.'

It is not entirely synonymous with the concept of exception management in that it describes a policy where absolute focus is on exception management, in contrast to moderate application of exception management.

Chapter 15. Cost Analysis for Control

a. Management by exception
c. Performance measurement
b. Best practice
d. Cash cow

10. The _____ of 2002 (Pub.L. 107-204, 116 Stat. 745, enacted July 30, 2002), also known as the Public Company Accounting Reform and Investor Protection Act of 2002, is a United States federal law enacted on July 30, 2002 in response to a number of major corporate and accounting scandals including those affecting Enron, Tyco International, Adelphia, Peregrine Systems and WorldCom. The legislation establishes new or enhanced standards for all U.S. public company boards, management, and public accounting firms. It does not apply to privately held companies.

a. FCPA
c. Lease
b. Sarbanes-Oxley Act
d. Fair Labor Standards Act

11. Government _____ are designed to show nonfinancial aspects of government operations. For example, a government financial report might include the number of arrests, number of convictions by crime category as well as the change (i.e., increase or decrease) in crime rate. Government _____ usually provide data on environmental conditions, education and conditions of streets and roads.

a. BNSF Railway
c. BMC Software, Inc.
b. 3M Company
d. Performance reports

12. In economics, _____ or _____ goods or real _____ refers to factors of production used to create goods or services that are not themselves significantly consumed (though they may depreciate) in the production process. _____ goods may be acquired with money or financial _____. In finance and accounting, _____ generally refers to financial wealth, especially that used to start or maintain a business.

a. Screening
c. Disclosure
b. Capital
d. Vyborg Appeal

13. _____ is the planning process used to determine whether a firm's long term investments such as new machinery, replacement machinery, new plants, new products, and research development projects are worth pursuing. It is budget for major capital, or investment, expenditures.

Many formal methods are used in _____, including the techniques such as

- Net present value
- Profitability index
- Internal rate of return
- Modified Internal Rate of Return
- Equivalent annuity

These methods use the incremental cash flows from each potential investment, or project. Techniques based on accounting earnings and accounting rules are sometimes used - though economists consider this to be improper - such as the accounting rate of return, and 'return on investment.' Simplified and hybrid methods are used as well, such as payback period and discounted payback period.

a. Preferred stock
c. Gross profit
b. Cash flow
d. Capital budgeting

14. Total _____ is a method of Accounting cost which entails the full cost of manufacturing or providing a service. This includes not just the costs of materials and labour, but also of all manufacturing overheads (whether e;fixede; or e;variablee;.) One of the main reasons for absorbing overheads into the cost of units is for inventory valuation purposes.
   a. AMEX
   b. ABC Television Network
   c. AIG
   d. Absorption costing

15. Project _____: The project _____ is a prediction of the costs associated with a particular company project. These costs include labor, materials, and other related expenses. The project _____ is often broken down into specific tasks, with task _____s assigned to each.
   a. BMC Software, Inc.
   b. BNSF Railway
   c. 3M Company
   d. Budget

16. A _____ is something that is acted upon or used by or by human labour or industry, for use as a building material to create some product or structure. Often the term is used to denote material that came from nature and is in an unprocessed or minimally processed state. Iron ore, logs, and crude oil, would be examples.
   a. BMC Software, Inc.
   b. 3M Company
   c. BNSF Railway
   d. Raw material

17. In business, _____, Overhead cost or _____ expense refers to an ongoing expense of operating a business. The term _____ is usually used to group expenses that are necessary to the continued functioning of the business, but do not directly generate profits.

_____ expenses are all costs on the income statement except for direct labor and direct materials.

   a. AIG
   b. ABC Television Network
   c. Intangible assets
   d. Overhead

18. _____ in economics and business is the result of an exchange and from that trade we assign a numerical monetary value to a good, service or asset. If Alice trades Bob 4 apples for an orange, the _____ of an orange is 4 apples. Inversely, the _____ of an apple is 1/4 oranges.
   a. Discounts and allowances
   b. Price discrimination
   c. Transactional Net Margin Method
   d. Price

19. The materials _____ is computed as follows:

   Vmp = (Actual Unit Cost - Standard Unit Cost) * Actual Quantity Purchased

or

   Vmp = (Actual Quantity Purchased * Actual Unit Cost) - (Actual Quantity Purchased * Standard Unit Cost.)

When the Actual Materials Price is higher than the Standard Materials Price, the variance is said to be unfavorable, since the Actual price paid on materials purchased is greater than the allowed standard. The variance is said to be favorable when the Standard materials Price is higher than the Actual Materials Price, since less money was spent in purchasing the materials than the allowed standard.

Chapter 15. Cost Analysis for Control

a. Liquidating dividend
c. Fund accounting
b. Consolidated financial statements
d. Price variance

20. _____ is a common concept in economics, and gives rise to derived concepts such as consumer debt. Generally _____ is defined by opposition to production. But the precise definition can vary because different schools of economists define production quite differently.
   a. Starving the beast
   c. Mitigating Control
   b. Consumption
   d. Yield

21. _____ of something is, in finance, the adding together of interest or different investments over a period of time such as atoms (1 - the act or process of accruing; 2 - the amount that accrues.) It holds specific meanings in accounting and payroll.

   _____, in accounting, describes the accounting method known as _____ basis, whereby revenues and expenses are recognized when they are accrued, i.e. accumulated (earned or incurred), regardless when the actual cash is received or paid out.

   a. Accrual
   c. Accounts receivable
   b. Earnings before interest, taxes, depreciation and amortization
   d. Assets

22. _____ is the process of comparing the cost, cycle time, productivity, or quality of a specific process or method to another that is widely considered to be an industry standard or best practice. Essentially, _____ provides a snapshot of the performance of your business and helps you understand where you are in relation to a particular standard. The result is often a business case for making changes in order to make improvements.
   a. Strategic business unit
   c. BMC Software, Inc.
   b. 3M Company
   d. Benchmarking

23. _____ is a nonprofit, scientific, technical, and educational organization which promotes the technological advancement of the printing industry worldwide.

   The Foundation fulfills its missions through its five divisions: research, training, consulting, quality controls, and publications.

   Its headquarters in Sewickley, Pennsylvania, a suburb of Pittsburgh, includes state-of-the-art prepress, pressrooms, testing laboratories, libraries, and classrooms that provide a platform for sheetfed and web printing research.

   a. 3M Company
   c. BMC Software, Inc.
   b. BNSF Railway
   d. Graphic Arts Technical Foundation

24. _____ in economics refers to metrics and measures of output from production processes, per unit of input. Labor _____, for example, is typically measured as a ratio of output per labor-hour, an input. _____ may be conceived of as a metrics of the technical or engineering efficiency of production.

a. Productivity
b. Deming Prize
c. Cellular manufacturing
d. Value engineering

25. _____ is systematic determination of merit, worth, and significance of something or someone using criteria against a set of standards. _____ often is used to characterize and appraise subjects of interest in a wide range of human enterprises, including the arts, criminal justice, foundations and non-profit organizations, government, health care, and other human services.

Depending on the topic of interest, there are professional groups which look to the quality and rigor of the _____ process.

a. AMEX
b. AIG
c. ABC Television Network
d. Evaluation

26. An _____, operating expenditure, operational expense, operational expenditure or OPEX is an on-going cost for running a product, business, or system. Its counterpart, a capital expenditure (CAPEX), is the cost of developing or providing non-consumable parts for the product or system. For example, the purchase of a photocopier is the CAPEX, and the annual paper and toner cost is the OPEX.

a. AMEX
b. Operating expense
c. ABC Television Network
d. AIG

27. In accounting, _____ has a very specific meaning. It is an outflow of cash or other valuable assets from a person or company to another person or company. This outflow of cash is generally one side of a trade for products or services that have equal or better current or future value to the buyer than to the seller.

a. AMEX
b. Expense
c. AIG
d. ABC Television Network

28. _____ is a company's financial statement that indicates how the revenue is transformed into the net income The purpose of the _____ is to show managers and investors whether the company made or lost money during the period being reported.

The important thing to remember about an _____ is that it represents a period of time.

a. AIG
b. ABC Television Network
c. AMEX
d. Income statement

29. An _____ is a classification used for business units within an enterprise. The essential element of an _____ is that it is treated as a unit which is measured against its use of capital, as opposed to a cost or profit center, which are measured against raw costs or profits.

The advantage of this form of measurement is that it tends to be more encompassing, since it accounts for all uses of capital.

a. ABC Television Network
b. AMEX
c. AIG
d. Investment center

30. _____s are parts of a corporation that directly add to its profit.

A _____ manager is held accountable for both revenues, and costs (expenses), and therefore, profits. What this means in terms of managerial responsibilities is that the manager has to drive the sales revenue generating activities which leads to cash inflows and at the same time control the cost (cash outflows) causing activities.

a. Cost management
b. Cost driver
c. Profit center
d. Contribution margin

31. _____ is a concept that denotes the precise probability of specific eventualities. Technically, the notion of _____ is independent from the notion of value and, as such, eventualities may have both beneficial and adverse consequences. However, in general usage the convention is to focus only on potential negative impact to some characteristic of value that may arise from a future event.

a. Discounting
b. Risk adjusted return on capital
c. Discount factor
d. Risk

32. The _____ is a performance management tool which began as a concept for measuring whether the smaller-scale operational activities of a company are aligned with its larger-scale objectives in terms of vision and strategy.

By focusing not only on financial outcomes but also on the operational, marketing and developmental inputs to these, the _____ helps provide a more comprehensive view of a business, which in turn helps organizations act in their best long-term interests. This tool is also being used to address business response to climate change and greenhouse gas emissions.

a. Best practice
b. Management by objectives
c. Trustee
d. Balanced scorecard

Chapter 16. Cost Analysis for Decision Making

1. In economics, _____ or _____ goods or real _____ refers to factors of production used to create goods or services that are not themselves significantly consumed (though they may depreciate) in the production process. _____ goods may be acquired with money or financial _____. In finance and accounting, _____ generally refers to financial wealth, especially that used to start or maintain a business.
   - a. Screening
   - b. Capital
   - c. Vyborg Appeal
   - d. Disclosure

2. _____ is the planning process used to determine whether a firm's long term investments such as new machinery, replacement machinery, new plants, new products, and research development projects are worth pursuing. It is budget for major capital, or investment, expenditures.

   Many formal methods are used in _____, including the techniques such as

   - Net present value
   - Profitability index
   - Internal rate of return
   - Modified Internal Rate of Return
   - Equivalent annuity

   These methods use the incremental cash flows from each potential investment, or project. Techniques based on accounting earnings and accounting rules are sometimes used - though economists consider this to be improper - such as the accounting rate of return, and 'return on investment.' Simplified and hybrid methods are used as well, such as payback period and discounted payback period.

   - a. Capital budgeting
   - b. Gross profit
   - c. Cash flow
   - d. Preferred stock

3. _____ can be regarded as an outcome of mental processes (cognitive process) leading to the selection of a course of action among several alternatives. Every _____ process produces a final choice. The output can be an action or an opinion of choice.
   - a. Decision making
   - b. 3M Company
   - c. BNSF Railway
   - d. BMC Software, Inc.

4. In economics, business, retail, and accounting, a _____ is the value of money that has been used up to produce something, and hence is not available for use anymore. In economics, a _____ is an alternative that is given up as a result of a decision. In business, the _____ may be one of acquisition, in which case the amount of money expended to acquire it is counted as _____.
   - a. Cost of quality
   - b. Cost allocation
   - c. Prime cost
   - d. Cost

5. _____ or economic opportunity loss is the value of the next best alternative foregone as the result of making a decision. _____ analysis is an important part of a company's decision-making processes but is not treated as an actual cost in any financial statement. The next best thing that a person can engage in is referred to as the _____ of doing the best thing and ignoring the next best thing to be done.
   - a. Inflation
   - b. Opportunity cost
   - c. AIG
   - d. ABC Television Network

Chapter 16. Cost Analysis for Decision Making

6. _____ is used to assign the available resources in an economic way. It is part of resource management.

In strategic planning,is a plan for using available resources, for example human resources, especially in the near term, to achieve goals for the future.

   a. BMC Software, Inc.
   b. BNSF Railway
   c. 3M Company
   d. Resource allocation

7. The _____ of 2002 (Pub.L. 107-204, 116 Stat. 745, enacted July 30, 2002), also known as the Public Company Accounting Reform and Investor Protection Act of 2002, is a United States federal law enacted on July 30, 2002 in response to a number of major corporate and accounting scandals including those affecting Enron, Tyco International, Adelphia, Peregrine Systems and WorldCom. The legislation establishes new or enhanced standards for all U.S. public company boards, management, and public accounting firms. It does not apply to privately held companies.
   a. Lease
   b. FCPA
   c. Fair Labor Standards Act
   d. Sarbanes-Oxley Act

8. In economics, the concept of the _____ refers to the decision-making time frame of a firm in which at least one factor of production is fixed. Costs which are fixed in the _____ have no impact on a firms decisions. For example a firm can raise output by increasing the amount of labour through overtime.
   a. Short-run
   b. 3M Company
   c. BMC Software, Inc.
   d. Long-run

9. _____ is the process whereby companies use cost accounting to report or control the various costs of doing business.

The term _____ is widely used in business today. Unfortunately _____ has no uniform definition.

   a. Contribution margin
   b. Process costing
   c. Contribution margin analysis
   d. Cost management

10. _____ is one of the four Ps of the marketing mix. The other three aspects are product, promotion, and place. It is also a key variable in microeconomic price allocation theory.
    a. Price
    b. Target costing
    c. Pricing
    d. Cost-plus pricing

11. _____ is a pricing method used by firms. It is defined as 'a cost management tool for reducing the overall cost of a product over its entire life-cycle with the help of production, engineering, research and design'. A target cost is the maximum amount of cost that can be incurred on a product and with it the firm can still earn the required profit margin from that product at a particular selling price.
    a. Discounts and allowances
    b. Penetration pricing
    c. Pricing
    d. Target costing

Chapter 16. Cost Analysis for Decision Making

12. _____, known in the United States as antitrust law, has three main elements:

- prohibiting agreements or practices that restrict free trading and competition between business entities. This includes in particular the repression of cartels.
- banning abusive behaviour by a firm dominating a market, or anti-competitive practices that tend to lead to such a dominant position. Practices controlled in this way may include predatory pricing, tying, price gouging, refusal to deal, and many others.
- supervising the mergers and acquisitions of large corporations, including some joint ventures. Transactions that are considered to threaten the competitive process can be prohibited altogether, or approved subject to 'remedies' such as an obligation to divest part of the merged business or to offer licences or access to facilities to enable other businesses to continue competing.

The substance and practice of _____ varies from jurisdiction to jurisdiction. Protecting the interests of consumers (consumer welfare) and ensuring that entrepreneurs have an opportunity to compete in the market economy are often treated as important objectives. _____ is closely connected with law on deregulation of access to markets, state aids and subsidies, the privatisation of state owned assets and the establishment of independent sector regulators. In recent decades, _____ has been viewed as a way to provide better public services.

a. Hospital Survey and Construction Act
b. Malpractice
c. Lease
d. Competition law

13. _____ are designed to ensure fair competition and the free flow of truthful information in the marketplace. The laws are designed to prevent businesses that engage in fraud or specified unfair practices from gaining an advantage over competitors and may provide additional protection for the weak and unable to take care of themselves. _____ are a form of government regulation which protects the interests of consumers.

a. Trust Indenture Act of 1939
b. Staple right
c. Due diligence
d. Consumer protection laws

14. The _____ is an independent agency of the United States government, established in 1914 by the _____ Act. Its principal mission is the promotion of 'consumer protection' and the elimination and prevention of what regulators perceive to be harmfully 'anti-competitive' business practices, such as coercive monopoly.

The _____ Act was one of President Wilson's major acts against trusts.

a. BMC Software, Inc.
b. BNSF Railway
c. 3M Company
d. Federal Trade Commission

15. The _____ of 1936 (or Anti-Price Discrimination Act, 15 U.S.C. § 13) is a United States federal law that prohibits what were considered, at the time of passage, to be anticompetitive practices by producers, specifically price discrimination. It grew out of practices in which chain stores were allowed to purchase goods at lower prices than other retailers.

a. Lien
b. Robinson-Patman Act
c. Limited liability
d. Consumer protection laws

16. The _____ is a concept from business management that was first described and popularized by Michael Porter in his 1985 best-seller, Competitive Advantage: Creating and Sustaining Superior Performance.

Chapter 16. Cost Analysis for Decision Making

A _____ is a chain of activities. Products pass through all activities of the chain in order and at each activity the product gains some value.

a. Product differentiation
b. Market segmentation
c. Customer relationship management
d. Value chain

17. _____ is subcontracting a process, such as product design or manufacturing, to a third-party company. The decision to outsource is often made in the interest of lowering cost or making better use of time and energy costs, redirecting or conserving energy directed at the competencies of a particular business, or to make more efficient use of land, labor, capital, (information) technology and resources. _____ became part of the business lexicon during the 1980s.

a. Economic Growth and Tax Relief Reconciliation Act of 2001
b. US Airways, Inc.
c. USA Today
d. Outsourcing

18. Project _____: The project _____ is a prediction of the costs associated with a particular company project. These costs include labor, materials, and other related expenses. The project _____ is often broken down into specific tasks, with task _____s assigned to each.

a. BNSF Railway
b. BMC Software, Inc.
c. 3M Company
d. Budget

19. An _____ is the annual budget of an activity stated in terms of Budget Classification Code, functional/subfunctional categories and cost accounts. It contains estimates of the total value of resources required for the performance of the operation including reimbursable work or services for others. It also includes estimates of workload in terms of total work units identified by cost accounts.

a. Authorised capital
b. Operating budget
c. Inventory turnover ratio
d. Internality

20. A _____ is a body of elected or appointed members who jointly oversee the activities of a company or organization. The body sometimes has a different name, such as board of trustees, board of governors, board of managers, or executive board. It is often simply referred to as 'the board.'

A board's activities are determined by the powers, duties, and responsibilities delegated to it or conferred on it by an authority outside itself.

a. Chief Financial Officers Act of 1990
b. Hospital Survey and Construction Act
c. Board of directors
d. Consumer protection laws

21. A _____ is an expenditure creating future benefits. A _____ is incurred when a business spends money either to buy fixed assets or to add to the value of an existing fixed asset with a useful life that extends beyond the taxable year. Capex are used by a company to acquire or upgrade physical assets such as equipment, property, or industrial buildings.

a. BMC Software, Inc.
b. 3M Company
c. Cost of capital
d. Capital expenditure

Chapter 16. Cost Analysis for Decision Making

22. In economic models, the _____ time frame assumes no fixed factors of production. Firms can enter or leave the marketplace, and the cost (and availability) of land, labor, raw materials, and capital goods can be assumed to vary. In contrast, in the short-run time frame, certain factors are assumed to be fixed, because there is not sufficient time for them to change.
    a. Short-run
    b. BMC Software, Inc.
    c. 3M Company
    d. Long-run

23. In finance, _____ also known as return on investment, rate of profit or sometimes just return, is the ratio of money gained or lost on an investment relative to the amount of money invested. The amount of money gained or lost may be referred to as interest, profit/loss, gain/loss, or net income/loss. The money invested may be referred to as the asset, capital, principal, or the cost basis of the investment.
    a. Debt to capital ratio
    b. Capital employed
    c. Theoretical ex-rights price
    d. Rate of return

24. In financial accounting, a _____ or statement of financial position is a summary of a person's or organization's balances. Assets, liabilities and ownership equity are listed as of a specific date, such as the end of its financial year. A _____ is often described as a snapshot of a company's financial condition.
    a. Balance sheet
    b. Statement of retained earnings
    c. 3M Company
    d. Financial statements

25. _____ are made by investors and investment managers.

Investors commonly perform investment analysis by making use of fundamental analysis, technical analysis and gut feel.

_____ are often supported by decision tools.

    a. ABC Television Network
    b. Incremental capital-output ratio
    c. Investment decisions
    d. AIG

26. _____ is a demonstration of a process -- such as a variable, term, or object -- relative in terms of the specific process or set of validation tests used to determine its presence and quantity. Properties described in this manner must be sufficiently accessible, so that persons other than the definer may independently measure or test for them at will. An _____ is generally designed to model a conceptual definition.
    a. AMEX
    b. AIG
    c. ABC Television Network
    d. Operational definition

Chapter 16. Cost Analysis for Decision Making

27. _____ is the balance of the amounts of cash being received and paid by a business during a defined period of time, sometimes tied to a specific project. Measurement of _____ can be used

- to evaluate the state or performance of a business or project.
- to determine problems with liquidity. Being profitable does not necessarily mean being liquid. A company can fail because of a shortage of cash, even while profitable.
- to project rate of returns. The time of _____s into and out of projects are used as inputs to financial models such as internal rate of return, and net present value.
- to examine income or growth of a business when it is believed that accrual accounting concepts do not represent economic realities. Alternately, _____ can be used to 'validate' the net income generated by accrual accounting.

_____ as a generic term may be used differently depending on context, and certain _____ definitions may be adapted by analysts and users for their own uses. Common terms include operating _____ and free _____.

a. Controlling interest
b. Commercial paper
c. Flow-through entity
d. Cash flow

28. The _____ is an expected return that the provider of capital plans to earn on their investment.

Capital (money) used for funding a business should earn returns for the capital providers who risk their capital. For an investment to be worthwhile, the expected return on capital must be greater than the _____.

a. 3M Company
b. BMC Software, Inc.
c. Capital flight
d. Cost of capital

29. Discounting is a financial mechanism in which a debtor obtains the right to delay payments to a creditor, for a defined period of time, in exchange for a charge or fee. Essentially, the party that owes money in the present purchases the right to delay the payment until some future date. The _____, or charge, is simply the difference between the original amount owed in the present and the amount that has to be paid in the future to settle the debt.

a. Discounting
b. Risk aversion
c. Discount
d. Discount factor

30. The _____ is an interest rate a central bank charges depository institutions that borrow reserves from it.

The term _____ has two meanings:

- the same as interest rate; the term 'discount' does not refer to the meaning of the word, but to the purpose of using the quantity, such as computations of present value, e.g. net present value or discounted cash flow

- the annual effective _____, which is the annual interest divided by the capital including that interest; this rate is lower than the interest rate; it corresponds to using the value after a year as the nominal value, and seeing the initial value as the nominal value minus a discount; it is used for Treasury Bills and similar financial instruments

The annual effective _____ is the annual interest divided by the capital including that interest, which is the interest rate divided by 100% plus the interest rate. It is the annual discount factor to be applied to the future cash flow, to find the discount, subtracted from a future value to find the value one year earlier.

For example, suppose there is a government bond that sells for $95 and pays $100 in a year's time.

a. Convertible bond
c. Process time
b. Municipal bond
d. Discount rate

31. _____ is the value on a given date of a future payment or series of future payments, discounted to reflect the time value of money and other factors such as investment risk. _____ calculations are widely used in business and economics to provide a means to compare cash flows at different times on a meaningful 'like to like' basis.

The most commonly applied model of the time value of money is compound interest.

a. Present value
c. 3M Company
b. Future value
d. Net present value

32. _____ measures the rate of return on the ownership interest (shareholders' equity) of the common stock owners. It measures a firm's efficiency at generating profits from every dollar of shareholders' equity (also known as net assets or assets minus liabilities.) It shows how well a company uses investment dollars to generate earnings growth.

a. Like for like
c. Return on capital employed
b. Sortino ratio
d. Return on equity

33. Simply put, _____ is the value of money figuring in a given amount of interest for a given amount of time. For example 100 dollars of todays money held for a year at 5 percent interest is worth 105 dollars, therefore 100 dollars paid now or 105 dollars paid exactly one year from now is the same amount of payment of money with that given intersest at that given amount of time. This notion dates at least to Martín de Azpilcueta of the School of Salamanca.

a. Time value of money
c. Competition law
b. Collusion
d. Merck ' Co., Inc.

34. _____ is a term used in accounting, economics and finance to spread the cost of an asset over the span of several years.

In simple words we can say that _____ is the reduction in the value of an asset due to usage, passage of time, wear and tear, technological outdating or obsolescence, depletion, inadequacy, rot, rust, decay or other such factors.

In accounting, _____ is a term used to describe any method of attributing the historical or purchase cost of an asset across its useful life, roughly corresponding to normal wear and tear.

a. Current asset
c. General ledger
b. Net profit
d. Depreciation

Chapter 16. Cost Analysis for Decision Making

35. _____ or net present worth (NPW) is defined as the total present value (PV) of a time series of cash flows. It is a standard method for using the time value of money to appraise long-term projects. Used for capital budgeting, and widely throughout economics, it measures the excess or shortfall of cash flows, in present value terms, once financing charges are met.
    a. Present value
    b. 3M Company
    c. Future value
    d. Net present value

36. _____ identifies the relationship of investment to payoff of a proposed project. The ratio is calculated as follows:

$$\text{Profitability index} = \frac{\text{PV of future cash flows}}{\text{PV of initial investment}}$$

_____ is also known as Profit Investment Ratio, abbreviated to P.I. and Value Investment Ratio (V.I.R.). _____ is a good tool for ranking projects because it allows you to clearly identify the amount of value created per unit of investment, thus if you are capital constrained you wish to invest in those projects which create value most efficiently first.

Nota Bene; Statements below this paragraph assume the cash flow calculated does not include the investment made in the project.

   a. Debt ratio
   b. 3M Company
   c. Profitability index
   d. Finance lease

37. In accounting, _____ has a very specific meaning. It is an outflow of cash or other valuable assets from a person or company to another person or company. This outflow of cash is generally one side of a trade for products or services that have equal or better current or future value to the buyer than to the seller.
    a. AIG
    b. ABC Television Network
    c. AMEX
    d. Expense

38. An _____ is a term used in behavioral economics to describe those types of behaviors that impose costs on a person in the long-run that are not taken into account when making decisions in the present. Classical Economics discourages government from creating legislation that targets internalities, because it is assumed that the consumer takes these personal costs into account when paying for the good that causes the _____. For example, cigarettes should be taxed because of the negative consumption externalities that they impose, such as second-hand smoke, not because the smoker harms him or herself by smoking.
    a. Internality
    b. Authorised capital
    c. Inventory turnover ratio
    d. Operating budget

39. The _____ is a capital budgeting metric used by firms to decide whether they should make investments. It is also called discounted cash flow rate of return (DCFROR) or rate of return (ROR.) It is an indicator of the efficiency or quality of an investment, as opposed to net present value (NPV), which indicates value or magnitude.
    a. AMEX
    b. Internal rate of return
    c. ABC Television Network
    d. AIG

40. In the mathematical subfield of numerical analysis, _____ is a method of constructing new data points within the range of a discrete set of known data points.

Chapter 16. Cost Analysis for Decision Making

In engineering and science one often has a number of data points, as obtained by sampling or experimentation, and tries to construct a function which closely fits those data points. This is called curve fitting or regression analysis.

a. AMEX
b. Interpolation
c. ABC Television Network
d. AIG

41. The term _____ is used in finance theory to refer to any terminating stream of fixed payments over a specified period of time. This usage is most commonly seen in academic discussions of finance, usually in connection with the valuation of the stream of payments, taking into account time value of money concepts such as interest rate and future value.

Examples of these are regular deposits to a savings account, monthly home mortgage payments and monthly insurance payments.

a. Annuity
b. Intangible
c. Appropriation
d. Improvement

42. An _____ is a tax levied on the financial income of people, corporations, or other legal entities. Various _____ systems exist, with varying degrees of tax incidence. Income taxation can be progressive, proportional, or regressive.

a. Ordinary income
b. Individual Retirement Arrangement
c. Implied level of government service
d. Income tax

43. _____ is a financial metric which represents operating liquidity available to a business. Along with fixed assets such as plant and equipment, _____ is considered a part of operating capital. It is calculated as current assets minus current liabilities.

a. Working capital
b. BMC Software, Inc.
c. Working capital management
d. 3M Company

44. In mathematics _____s are numbers or other things that get multiplied. In particular, see:

- Factorization, the decomposition of an object into a product of other objects
- Integer factorization, the process of breaking down a composite number into smaller non-trivial divisors
- A coefficient
- A divisor of a particular number, or of an element of a monoid
- A von Neumann algebra with a trivial center

In statistics

- _____ analysis is the study of how _____s or certain variables affect variables.

Chapter 16. Cost Analysis for Decision Making

In technology:

- Human _____s, a profession that focuses on how people interact with products, tools, or procedures
- 'Functionality, Application domain, Conditions, Technology, Objects and Responsibility;', In object-oriented programming

In computer science and information technology:

- Authentication _____, a piece of information used to verify a person's identity for security purposes
- _____, a Unix command for numbers factorization
- _____ (programming language), an experimental Forth-like programming language

In television:

- The O'Reilly _____, an American talk show hosted by Bill O'Reilly on Fox News.
- The Krypton _____, a British game show hosted by Gordon Burns, formally on ITV. Also had an American version.

.
a. Merck ' Co., Inc.
b. Factor
c. Valuation
d. The Goodyear Tire ' Rubber Company

45. In finance, the _____ approach describes a method of valuing a project, company, or asset using the concepts of the time value of money. All future cash flows are estimated and discounted to give their present values. The discount rate used is generally the appropriate WACC, that reflects the risk of the cashflows.
a. 3M Company
b. Future value
c. Net present value
d. Discounted cash flow

46. _____ in business and economics refers to the period of time required for the return on an investment to 'repay' the sum of the original investment. For example, a $1000 investment which returned $500 per year would have a two year _____. It intuitively measures how long something takes to 'pay for itself.' Shorter _____s are obviously preferable to longer _____s (all else being equal.)
a. Segregated portfolio company
b. Payback period
c. Net worth
d. Fair market value

47. In finance, _____ is the process of estimating the potential market value of a financial asset or liability. They can be done on assets (for example, investments in marketable securities such as stocks, options, business enterprises, or intangible assets such as patents and trademarks) or on liabilities (e.g., Bonds issued by a company.) A _____ is required in many contexts including investment analysis, capital budgeting, merger and acquisition transactions, financial reporting, taxable events to determine the proper tax liability, and in litigation.
a. Vyborg Appeal
b. Valuation
c. Daybook
d. Disclosure

Chapter 16. Cost Analysis for Decision Making

48. _____ LLP, based in Chicago, was once one of the 'Big Five' accounting firms among PricewaterhouseCoopers, Deloitte Touche Tohmatsu, Ernst ' Young and KPMG, providing auditing, tax, and consulting services to large corporations. In 2002, the firm voluntarily surrendered its licenses to practice as Certified Public Accountants in the United States after being found guilty of criminal charges relating to the firm's handling of the auditing of Enron, the energy corporation, resulting in the loss of 85,000 jobs. Although the verdict was subsequently overturned by the Supreme Court of the United States, it has not returned as a viable business.

   a. AMEX
   b. ABC Television Network
   c. AIG
   d. Arthur Andersen

49. _____ is the statutory title of qualified accountants in the United States who have passed the Uniform _____ Examination and have met additional state education and experience requirements for certification as a _____. Individuals who have passed the Exam but have not either accomplished the required on-the-job experience or have previously met it but in the meantime have lapsed their continuing professional education are, in many states, permitted the designation '_____ Inactive' or an equivalent phrase. In most U.S. states, only _____s who are licensed are able to provide to the public attestation (including auditing) opinions on financial statements.

   a. Chartered Accountant
   b. Certified public accountant
   c. Certified General Accountant
   d. Chartered Certified Accountant

50. _____ is concerned with the provisions and use of accounting information to managers within organizations, to provide them with the basis to make informed business decisions that will allow them to be better equipped in their management and control functions.

In contrast to financial accountancy information, _____ information is:

- usually confidential and used by management, instead of publicly reported;
- forward-looking, instead of historical;
- pragmatically computed using extensive management information systems and internal controls, instead of complying with accounting standards.

This is because of the different emphasis: _____ information is used within an organization, typically for decision-making.

   a. Governmental accounting
   b. Nonassurance services
   c. Management Accounting
   d. Grenzplankostenrechnung

51. An _____ is a practitioner of accountancy, which is the measurement, disclosure or provision of assurance about financial information that helps managers, investors, tax authorities and other decision makers make resource allocation decisions.

The word '_____' is derived from the French 'Compter' which took its origin from the Latin 'Computare'. The word was formerly written in English as 'Accomptant', but in process of time the word, which was always pronounced by dropping the 'p', became gradually changed both in pronunciation and in orthography to its present form.

a. AIG
b. ABC Television Network
c. AMEX
d. Accountant

52. Core competency is something that a firm can do well and that meets the following three conditions:

1. It provides consumer benefits
2. It is not easy for competitors to imitate
3. It can be leveraged widely to many products and markets.

A core competency can take various forms, including technical/subject matter know how, a reliable process, and/or close relationships with customers and suppliers (Mascarenhas et al. 1998.) It may also include product development or culture, such as employee dedication.

_____ are particular strengths relative to other organizations in the industry which provide the fundamental basis for the provision of added value.

a. BNSF Railway
b. Core competencies
c. BMC Software, Inc.
d. 3M Company

53. The _____ founded on April 1, 2001 is the successor of the International Accounting Standards Committee (IASC) founded in June 1973 in London. It is responsible for developing the International Financial Reporting Standards (new name for the International Accounting Standards issued after 2001), and promoting the use and application of these standards.

The _____ is an independent, privately-funded accounting standard-setter based in London, UK.

a. Information Systems Audit and Control Association
b. Emerging technologies
c. Institute of Management Accountants
d. International Accounting Standards Board

54. _____ was founded in June 1973 in London and replaced by the International Accounting Standards Board on April 1, 2001. It was responsible for developing the International Accounting Standards and promoting the use and application of these standards.

186   *Chapter 16. Cost Analysis for Decision Making*

The _____ was founded as a result of an agreement between accountancy bodies in the following countries:

- Australia (Institute of Chartered Accountants in Australia (ICAA) and the CPA Australia (formerly known as Australian Society of Certified Practising Accountants (ASCPA))

- Canada (Canadian Institute of Chartered Accountants (CICA))

- France (Ordre des Experts Comptable et des Comptables Agrees (Order of Accounting Experts and Qualified Accountants))

- Germany and the Wirtschaftsprüferkammer (WPK) (Chamber of Auditors))

- Japan Nihon Kouninkaikeishi Kyoukai)

- Mexico (Instituto Mexicano de Contadores Publicos (IMCP) (Mexican Institute of Public Accountants)) (removed from the board in 1987 due to non-payment of dues; resumed in 1995.)

- the Netherlands (Nederlands Instituut van Registeraccountants (NIVRA)

(Netherlands Institute of Registered Auditors))

- the United Kingdom and Ireland (counted as one) (Institute of Chartered Accountants in England and Wales (ICAEW), Institute of Chartered Accountants of Scotland (ICAS), Institute of Chartered Accountants in Ireland (ICAI), Association of Certified Accountants, Institute of Cost and Management Accountants, and the Institute of Municipal Treasurers and Accountants)

- the United States of America (American Institute of Certified Public Accountants (AICPA))

The Institute of Chartered Accountants of Nigeria became an associate member in 1976 and a member of the board from 1978 to 1987.

The National Council of Chartered Accountants (South Africa) became an associate member in 1974 and joined the board in 1978.

a. International Accounting Standards Board
b. American Payroll Association
c. International Accounting Standards Committee
d. American Accounting Association

55. In management accounting, _____ establishes budget and actual cost of operations, processes, departments or product and the analysis of variances, profitability or social use of funds. Managers use _____ to support decision-making to cut a company's costs and improve profitability. As a form of management accounting, _____ need not follow standards such as GAAP, because its primary use is for internal managers, rather than outside users, and what to compute is instead decided pragmatically.

Chapter 16. Cost Analysis for Decision Making

a. Marginal cost
c. Cost accounting
b. Prime cost
d. Cost-volume-profit analysis

56. _____ is the recording of the value of assets, liabilities, income, and expenses in the daybooks, journals, and ledgers, in which debit and credit entries are chronologically posted to record changes in value. _____ is often mistaken for accounting, which is the system of recording, verifying, and reporting such information. Practitioners of accounting are called accountants.
    a. Controlling account
    c. Debit and credit
    b. Bookkeeping
    d. Double-entry bookkeeping

57. A _____ is used in research to outline possible courses of action or to present a preferred approach to an idea or thought. For example, the philosopher Isaiah Berlin used the 'hedgehogs' versus 'foxes' approach; a 'hedgehog' might approach the world in terms of a single organizing principle; a 'fox' might pursue multiple conflicting goals simultaneously. Alternatively, an empiricist might approach a subject by direct examination, whereas an intuitionist might simply intuit what's next.
    a. BMC Software, Inc.
    c. Conceptual Framework
    b. BNSF Railway
    d. 3M Company

58. A _____ is a fungible, negotiable instrument representing financial value. they are broadly categorized into debt securities (such as banknotes, bonds and debentures), and equity securities; e.g., common stocks. The company or other entity issuing the _____ is called the issuer.
    a. Security
    c. Tracking stock
    b. 3M Company
    d. BMC Software, Inc.

59. The U.S. _____ is an independent agency of the United States government which holds primary responsibility for enforcing the federal securities laws and regulating the securities industry, the nation's stock and options exchanges, and other electronic securities markets. The SEC was created by section 4 of the Securities Exchange Act of 1934 (now codified as 15 U.S.C. §Â§ 78d and commonly referred to as the 1934 Act.)
    a. BNSF Railway
    c. Securities and Exchange Commission
    b. 3M Company
    d. BMC Software, Inc.

60. _____ of something is, in finance, the adding together of interest or different investments over a period of time such as atoms (1 - the act or process of accruing; 2 - the amount that accrues.) It holds specific meanings in accounting and payroll.

    _____, in accounting, describes the accounting method known as _____ basis, whereby revenues and expenses are recognized when they are accrued, i.e. accumulated (earned or incurred), regardless when the actual cash is received or paid out.

    a. Assets
    c. Earnings before interest, taxes, depreciation and amortization
    b. Accrual
    d. Accounts receivable

Chapter 16. Cost Analysis for Decision Making

61. _____ is the process of extracting hidden patterns from data. As more data is gathered, with the amount of data doubling every three years, _____ is becoming an increasingly important tool to transform this data into information. It is commonly used in a wide range of profiling practices, such as marketing, surveillance, fraud detection and scientific discovery.
   a. BNSF Railway
   b. Data mining
   c. 3M Company
   d. BMC Software, Inc.

62. _____ is a repository of an organization's electronically stored data. _____s are designed to facilitate reporting and analysis.

This definition of the _____ focuses on data storage.

   a. BNSF Railway
   b. 3M Company
   c. BMC Software, Inc.
   d. Data warehouse

63. A _____ is computer software that manages databases. DBMSes may use any of a variety of database models, such as the network model or relational model. In large systems, a DBMS allows users and other software to store and retrieve data in a structured way.
   a. Dow Jones ' Company
   b. Restricted stock
   c. Database management system
   d. Notes receivable

64. A _____ is a commercial building for storage of goods. _____s are used by manufacturers, importers, exporters, wholesalers, transport businesses, customs, etc. They are usually large plain buildings in industrial areas of cities and towns.
   a. BNSF Railway
   b. BMC Software, Inc.
   c. 3M Company
   d. Warehouse

65. _____ is an open standard which supports information modeling and the expression of semantic meaning commonly required in business reporting. _____ is XML-based. It uses the XML syntax and related XML technologies such as XML Schema, XLink, XPath, and Namespaces to articulate this semantic meaning. One use of _____ is to define and exchange financial information, such as a financial statement.
   a. XBRL
   b. BMC Software, Inc.
   c. BNSF Railway
   d. 3M Company

66. In computing, _____ provides a standard software API method for using database management systems (DBMS.) The designers of ODBC aimed to make it independent of programming languages, database systems, and operating systems.

ODBC uses as its basis the various Call Level Interface (CLI) specifications from the SQL Access Group, X/Open (now part of The Open Group), and the ISO/IEC.

   a. Office of Management and Budget
   b. Open database connectivity
   c. Empowerment
   d. Analysis of variance

Chapter 16. Cost Analysis for Decision Making

67. An _____ is a comprehensive report on a company's activities throughout the preceding year. _____s are intended to give shareholders and other interested persons information about the company's activities and financial performance. Most jurisdictions require companies to prepare and disclose _____s, and many require the _____ to be filed at the company's registry.

   a. AMEX
   b. AIG
   c. ABC Television Network
   d. Annual report

Chapter 1

1. d	2. a	3. d	4. d	5. b	6. c	7. d	8. d	9. d	10. d
11. d	12. d	13. a	14. b	15. c	16. c	17. c	18. a	19. a	20. a
21. b	22. d	23. d	24. d	25. b	26. d	27. b	28. c	29. d	30. b
31. a	32. d	33. c	34. d	35. d	36. b	37. d	38. a	39. b	40. d
41. d	42. a	43. d	44. d	45. a	46. c	47. d	48. d	49. b	50. c
51. a	52. d	53. b	54. a	55. a	56. a	57. d	58. d	59. b	60. d
61. c	62. b	63. d	64. d	65. d	66. d	67. d	68. a	69. d	70. d

Chapter 2

1. d	2. c	3. d	4. d	5. d	6. d	7. a	8. d	9. d	10. c
11. d	12. b	13. d	14. d	15. a	16. d	17. d	18. c	19. a	20. d
21. a	22. b	23. a	24. c	25. b	26. d	27. d	28. b	29. b	30. d
31. d	32. a	33. d	34. c	35. c	36. a	37. d	38. c	39. b	40. c
41. d	42. a	43. d	44. b	45. d	46. d	47. d	48. d	49. d	50. a
51. d	52. d	53. a	54. d	55. d	56. d	57. a	58. b	59. d	60. d
61. a	62. d	63. b	64. d	65. a	66. d	67. d	68. a	69. b	70. d
71. b	72. a	73. d	74. b	75. a	76. b	77. d	78. a	79. d	80. d
81. b	82. d								

Chapter 3

1. d	2. a	3. b	4. a	5. d	6. b	7. d	8. a	9. a	10. d
11. d	12. c	13. d	14. d	15. c	16. b	17. c	18. d	19. d	20. d
21. a	22. d	23. d	24. d	25. b	26. d	27. d	28. c	29. c	30. c
31. c	32. a	33. a	34. d	35. b					

Chapter 4

1. d	2. a	3. c	4. b	5. d	6. a	7. b	8. d	9. c	10. d
11. b	12. d	13. c	14. d	15. d	16. d	17. d	18. d	19. d	20. b
21. b	22. d	23. c	24. a	25. a	26. b	27. d	28. c	29. d	30. c
31. c	32. a	33. d	34. d						

Chapter 5

1. c	2. d	3. d	4. d	5. d	6. d	7. a	8. d	9. d	10. d
11. d	12. d	13. d	14. d	15. b	16. b	17. b	18. d	19. b	20. b
21. d	22. c	23. d	24. d	25. a	26. d	27. d	28. c	29. d	30. d
31. d	32. d	33. a	34. d	35. a	36. b	37. c	38. a	39. b	40. c
41. d	42. d	43. b	44. d	45. a	46. d	47. d	48. c	49. d	50. b
51. d	52. c	53. a	54. d	55. c	56. d	57. d	58. d	59. c	60. d
61. d	62. d	63. a	64. c	65. d	66. a	67. b	68. d	69. a	70. d
71. d	72. d	73. d	74. d	75. d					

ANSWER KEY

Chapter 6

1. c	2. b	3. d	4. d	5. c	6. d	7. a	8. d	9. c	10. c
11. d	12. a	13. b	14. d	15. b	16. d	17. d	18. d	19. a	20. d
21. b	22. d	23. d	24. d	25. b	26. c	27. d	28. d	29. a	30. c
31. c	32. d	33. d	34. d	35. a	36. a	37. a	38. a	39. a	40. c
41. b	42. b	43. b	44. a	45. b	46. c	47. d	48. a	49. d	50. d
51. d	52. c	53. d	54. d	55. d	56. a	57. d	58. a	59. a	60. d

Chapter 7

1. d	2. c	3. d	4. b	5. a	6. b	7. d	8. c	9. d	10. d
11. d	12. d	13. a	14. a	15. b	16. c	17. a	18. d	19. c	20. d
21. d	22. d	23. a	24. d	25. c	26. c	27. d	28. d	29. d	30. d
31. d	32. a	33. b	34. d	35. b	36. d	37. b	38. d	39. d	40. a
41. c	42. d	43. a	44. a	45. c	46. c	47. a	48. b	49. d	50. d
51. a	52. d	53. d	54. d	55. d	56. a	57. c	58. a	59. a	60. a
61. a	62. d	63. d	64. d	65. a	66. a	67. c	68. d	69. d	70. a
71. d	72. b	73. d	74. d	75. d	76. d	77. c	78. b	79. a	80. d
81. a	82. d	83. d	84. c	85. b	86. d	87. b	88. b	89. d	90. d

Chapter 8

1. c	2. a	3. b	4. c	5. c	6. d	7. d	8. d	9. b	10. d
11. d	12. b	13. b	14. c	15. d	16. d	17. d	18. c	19. c	20. c
21. d	22. c	23. c	24. b	25. d	26. c	27. b	28. d	29. d	30. d
31. b	32. d	33. d	34. d	35. c	36. a	37. d	38. d	39. b	40. d
41. c	42. d	43. d	44. d	45. d	46. d	47. d	48. d	49. b	50. d
51. c	52. b	53. d	54. c	55. d	56. d	57. a	58. d	59. d	60. d

Chapter 9

1. d	2. d	3. d	4. b	5. b	6. b	7. b	8. d	9. d	10. c
11. d	12. c	13. d	14. d	15. b	16. d	17. d	18. c	19. d	20. d
21. b	22. a	23. b	24. d	25. c	26. c	27. d	28. b	29. a	30. a
31. c	32. d	33. d	34. d	35. c	36. b	37. a	38. b	39. d	40. b
41. b	42. d	43. d	44. a	45. d	46. d	47. d	48. d	49. d	50. d
51. d	52. a	53. d	54. c	55. a	56. d	57. d			

Chapter 10

1. d	2. d	3. d	4. b	5. d	6. a	7. d	8. c	9. d	10. c
11. c	12. a	13. d	14. b	15. d	16. a	17. c	18. d	19. d	20. a
21. d	22. d	23. c	24. d	25. d	26. a	27. b	28. d	29. c	30. b
31. d	32. d	33. d	34. d	35. a	36. b	37. d	38. a	39. b	40. c
41. b	42. a	43. b	44. d	45. d	46. d	47. d	48. d	49. b	50. d
51. d	52. a	53. d	54. d	55. c	56. a	57. a	58. d	59. d	60. d
61. a	62. d	63. b	64. d	65. d	66. d	67. d	68. c	69. a	70. c
71. d	72. b	73. c	74. d	75. d	76. d	77. c	78. d		

Chapter 11

1. d	2. d	3. d	4. d	5. a	6. d	7. d	8. d	9. d	10. d
11. a	12. d	13. d	14. d	15. d	16. b	17. d	18. d	19. d	20. d
21. d	22. c	23. d	24. c	25. b	26. d	27. d	28. d	29. d	30. b
31. a	32. d	33. a	34. d	35. d	36. a	37. c	38. b	39. d	40. d
41. d	42. d	43. b	44. d	45. c	46. d	47. d	48. d	49. b	50. d
51. d	52. c	53. d	54. b	55. d	56. d	57. d	58. d	59. d	60. d
61. b	62. d	63. b							

Chapter 12

1. d	2. d	3. b	4. a	5. d	6. d	7. d	8. a	9. b	10. a
11. b	12. d	13. d	14. c	15. d	16. d	17. b	18. d	19. c	20. d

Chapter 13

1. c	2. d	3. a	4. a	5. c	6. b	7. b	8. d	9. b	10. d
11. b	12. c	13. c	14. a	15. d	16. d	17. b	18. a	19. b	20. a
21. d	22. c	23. a	24. d	25. a	26. a	27. a	28. b	29. b	

Chapter 14

1. b	2. d	3. d	4. d	5. d	6. d	7. b	8. d	9. d	10. c
11. c	12. a	13. c	14. d	15. d	16. d	17. a	18. b	19. d	20. a
21. d	22. d	23. d	24. d	25. c	26. c	27. b	28. a	29. d	30. c
31. c	32. d								

Chapter 15

1. b	2. d	3. d	4. c	5. c	6. b	7. d	8. b	9. a	10. b
11. d	12. b	13. d	14. d	15. d	16. d	17. d	18. d	19. d	20. b
21. a	22. d	23. d	24. a	25. d	26. b	27. b	28. d	29. d	30. c
31. d	32. d								

Chapter 16

1. b	2. a	3. a	4. d	5. b	6. d	7. d	8. a	9. d	10. c
11. d	12. d	13. d	14. d	15. b	16. d	17. d	18. d	19. b	20. c
21. d	22. d	23. d	24. a	25. c	26. d	27. d	28. d	29. c	30. d
31. a	32. d	33. a	34. d	35. d	36. c	37. d	38. a	39. b	40. b
41. a	42. d	43. a	44. b	45. d	46. b	47. b	48. d	49. b	50. c
51. d	52. b	53. d	54. c	55. c	56. b	57. c	58. a	59. c	60. b
61. b	62. d	63. c	64. d	65. a	66. b	67. d			

www.ingramcontent.com/pod-product-compliance
Lightning Source LLC
Chambersburg PA
CBHW081353230426
43667CB00017B/2816